REBEL YOUTH

GEBL-BK
$ 34.60

Ian Milligan

REBEL YOUTH

1960s Labour Unrest,
Young Workers, and New Leftists
in English Canada

UBCPress · Vancouver · Toronto

22 21 20 19 18 17 16 15 14   5 4 3 2 1

Printed in Canada on FSC-certified ancient-forest-free paper
(100% post-consumer recycled) that is processed chlorine- and acid-free.

Library and Archives Canada Cataloguing in Publication

Milligan, Ian, 1983-, author
    Rebel youth : 1960s labour unrest, young workers, and new leftists in English Canada /
Ian Milligan.

Includes bibliographical references and index.
Issued in print and electronic formats.
ISBN 978-0-7748-2687-7 (bound). – ISBN 978-0-7748-2688-4 (pbk.). –
ISBN 978-0-7748-2689-1 (pdf). – ISBN 978-0-7748-2690-7 (epub)

    1. Young adults – Employment – Canada – History – 20th century. 2. Young adults – Canada – Social conditions – 20th century. 3. Young adults – Political activity – Canada – History – 20th century. 4. Labor movement – Canada – History – 20th century. 5. Canada – Social conditions – 1945-1971. I. Title.

HD6276.C3M54 2014	331.3'4097109046	C2014-900718-3
		C2014-900719-1

Canadä

UBC Press gratefully acknowledges the financial support for our publishing program of the Government of Canada (through the Canada Book Fund), the Canada Council for the Arts, and the British Columbia Arts Council.

Printed and bound in Canada by Friesens
Set in Kozuka Gothic and Minion by Artegraphica Design Co. Ltd.
Copy editor: Judy Phillips
Proofreader: Jillian Shoichet Gunn

UBC Press
The University of British Columbia
2029 West Mall
Vancouver, BC V6T 1Z2
www.ubcpress.ca

Contents

Acknowledgments

Many thanks are necessary to the many people who made the publication of *Rebel Youth* possible. This book had its origins in York University's Graduate Program in History. There, Craig Heron was an exceptionally supportive, knowledgeable, and rigorous supervisor. He's the model of an academic: generous with his time and insights, and he makes the PhD at York the wonderful program that it is. Special thanks are also due to Marlene Shore, Paul Axelrod, and Marcel Martel. David Frank, Ian McKay, Doug Owram, Mark Thomas, and Bryan Palmer provided suggestions and comments that helped flesh out the project. Significant thanks are due to those who shared their thoughts and experiences with me. I profoundly appreciate their generosity and willingness to take time out of their busy lives to meet with me for an hour or two (or more, in some cases). Without them, this project would not be what it is.

From reading chapters to providing much-needed time away from it, colleagues and peers helped shape and improve the book. Special thanks are due to those from my graduate school days: Alban Bargain, Katharine Bausch, Ben Bryce, Dan Bullard, Jim Clifford, Valerie Deacon, Bruce Douville, Brittany Luby, Brian MacDowell, Christine McLaughlin, Ian Mosby, Thomas Peace, Angela Rooke, Andrew Watson, and Jay Young. Also, my new home at the University of Waterloo is a wonderful one, and I'm grateful to have such an engaging and inspiring place to work today. My new colleagues in the History Department are amazing, and I feel like I've won the jackpot every day I come in to work.

Financial support for this book was forthcoming from the Ontario Government's Sir John A. Macdonald Graduate Fellowship in Canadian History, the Avie Bennett Historica Dominion Institute Dissertation Scholarship in Canadian History, and the Social Sciences and Humanities Research Council, as well as from assorted funds from York University and the University of Waterloo.

UBC Press has been a perfect publishing house. This manuscript was significantly strengthened at every stage, and Darcy Cullen was a wonderful editor as she stewarded this book through the process. Sincere thanks, Darcy, for making this book possible! Special thanks also to Ann Macklem, who adroitly moved the book through the production stages, and to Judy Phillips for her phenomenal copyediting. This book is far stronger thanks to all of their help, although any errors remain my responsibility. Elsewhere in the publishing world, my thanks to scholarly journals that allowed some of the early dissemination of this work and subsequently gave permission for the works to appear here. An abridged treatment of Chapter 6 appeared as "'The Force of All Our Numbers': New Leftists, Labour, and the 1973 Artistic Woodwork Strike," *Labour/Le Travail* 66 (Fall 2010), and a portion of Chapter 4, concerning itself with Simon Fraser University, appeared as "Coming off the Mountain: Forging an Outward-Looking New Left at Simon Fraser University," *BC Studies* 171 (Autumn 2011).

At the end of the day, my family deserves the biggest thanks of all. My parents Cecile, John, Peter, and Terry have been an important part of my life – there for advice, dinners, lunches, and even more than a few reads of this manuscript. Finally, my sincerest and heartfelt thanks go to Jennifer. Your support is always unwavering, whether over trips to archives or late nights writing, and for that reason, this book is for you.

Abbreviations

CBRT	Canadian Brotherhood of Railway, Transport and General Workers Union
CCF	Co-operative Commonwealth Federation
CCU	Council of Canadian Unions
CDP	Canadian Driver Pool
CERC	Community Education and Research Centre
CFAWU	Canadian Food and Allied Workers Union
CLC	Canadian Labour Congress
CN	Canadian National Railway
CP	Canadian Pacific Railway
CPC(ML)	Communist Party of Canada (Marxist-Leninist)
CTCU	Canadian Textile and Chemical Union
CUCND	Combined Universities Campaign for Nuclear Disarmament
CUP `	Canadian University Press
CUPE	Canadian Union of Public Employees
CUS	Canadian Union of Students
CYC	Company of Young Canadians
ECSM	East Coast Socialist Movement
KCP	Kingston Community Project
Inco	International Nickel Company

NDP	New Democratic Party
NDY	New Democratic Youth
NFU	National Farmers Union
NLC	New Left Caucus
NLC	New Left Committee
NSFL	Nova Scotia Federation of Labour
OFL	Ontario Federation of Labour
OUS	Ontario Union of Students
PSA	Political Science, Sociology, and Anthropology Department (SFU)
SDU	Students for a Democratic University
SFL	Saskatchewan Federation of Labour
SFU	Simon Fraser University
SORWUC	Service, Office and Retail Workers Union of Canada
Stelco	Steel Company of Canada
SUPA	Student Union for Peace Action
TSM	Toronto Student Movement
UAW	United Automobile Workers
UE	United Electrical Workers
UFAWU	United Fishermen and Allied Workers Union
USWA	United Steelworkers of America
VWC	Vancouver Women's Caucus
WSA	Worker-Student Alliance

REBEL YOUTH

Introduction

Canada's 1960s were profoundly shaped by labour. Skyrocketing labour unrest captivated young people, their elders, the media, and governments alike. Young workers, who made up the majority of the baby boom generation, brought an anti-authoritarian sentiment to their workplaces, a critical story underlying much of the decade. New Leftists, too, were sundered by their failure to find any agreement on the labour question, would the working class play a significant role in strategies of fundamental social change, or had economic and cultural changes moved the praxis toward a nebulous "dispossessed"? After a brief flirtation with a new path forward, New Leftists returned to ideas of organizing among a working class, and with unions – but on new terrain. There would be a hesitant *rapprochement* with labour, an emphasis on social justice and non-material gains, and an idea of direct engagement with working people rather than through union organs. This new terrain was a significant legacy of the sixties.

Three powerful social, cultural, and political currents converged during the decade. Young people in growing numbers embraced a new culture of defiant anti-authoritarianism and self-expression. Young activists combined this new youth culture with a new brand of radicalism, which became known as the New Left, and aimed to build alliances with marginalized groups. At the same time, young workers defied their aging union leaders in a wave of renewed militancy, including wildcat strikes. We need to understand these three currents as aspects of a single youth phenomenon.

The Canadian sixties can also further be understood around the central question of the working class and labour unrest. This perspective presents a significant lens through which to view the major intellectual developments, debates, and events that transformed Canada from the mid-1960s to the early 1970s. Labour formed the backdrop for most young Canadians at the time – nearly 90 percent of youth moved directly into the paid labour market instead of post-secondary institutions after high school. Here, they brought elements of the same culture and spirit that animated New Leftists, with very different results. Although labour is not the only lens through which to view the sixties – it was also a decade of significant upheaval in the realm of women's rights, human rights, and self-expression – the pages that follow stress its centrality to our understanding of the period. As much as any other current, this was labour's decade.

Some illustrative vignettes convey the breadth and depth of this youthful phenomenon. Through the summer of 1966, youth unrest swept across large English Canadian industrial cities. This was very different from the type of unrest commonly seen in Canadian universities. In Sudbury, 2,200 feet (670 metres) below ground level, young workers gathered at mine cages, banging their lunch pails and shouting at their foreman, demanding a return to the customary right of having their lunch before a work shift. These young men had listened to the old hands and were now on the cusp of shutting down the Sudbury mining operations of the International Nickel Company of Canada for more than three weeks, leading almost sixteen thousand fellow workers out onto the picket lines. A month later, young workers – hired into clustered low-seniority jobs at the massively expanding Hilton Works of the Steel Company of Canada – led their colleagues out onto the streets, lashing out at management and their United Steelworkers local alike. Sitting on the warm pavement of Hamilton's Burlington Avenue as police officers arrested several of their colleagues, these youth formed a critical yet insufficiently understood part of postwar English Canadian youth culture.

Throughout Canada's 1960s, largely middle-class New Leftists also grappled with how they could transform a society that many increasingly saw as fundamentally unjust and unequal. Would they look to the "dispossessed" – Aboriginals, blacks, the working poor – to animate fundamental social change? Or could the working class be redeemed, returned to its traditional Marxist position as *the* agent of social change? I use the term "New Leftist" purposely throughout, as opposed to a more homogenizing "New Left." Both were part of a shared social movement, to be sure, but their disagreements and debates lie at the heart of much of this book. Indeed, as we will see, debates on social change became key to the very foundation of English Canadian New Leftists, and their inability to grapple with this question led to the dissolution of the largest group, the Student Union for Peace Action.

Whereas in 1965 many New Leftists would have written off the working class as co-opted or marginalized, even undeserving of a special place in theories of social transformation, by 1968, and certainly by 1969, a widespread turn toward Marxism and the working class had dramatically transformed the landscape. At places as widely disparate as Cape Breton; the University of Saskatchewan's Regina campus; Simon Fraser University, on Burnaby Mountain; and Peterborough, Kitchener-Waterloo, and Brantford, with their union struggles, New Leftists moved outward to the working class in a variety of ways. New Leftist activity was motivated by this fundamental desire to reach out into the surrounding community, to affect change, and to be an outward-looking rather than inward-looking group. When New Leftists declared "The university is for people," they did so in a context that recognized the social role of the institution but also its classed nature.

By late 1973, when a few dozen immigrant picture-frame makers in Toronto went on strike at Artistic Woodwork, hundreds of young men and women would wake before dawn, take buses out to a cold picket line in a desolate suburban industrial park, and stand together in solidarity. As the 1970s progressed, the two currents of New Leftists and labour ultimately began to come together. The latter started to look for a new generation of staff representatives and members who could help them make sense of the youthful upsurge of the 1960s, while many in the former were beginning to look for work and ways to continue their activism. It turned out that the gulf between New Leftists and the labour movement was, after all, not as big as it may have seemed to many onlookers in the late 1960s.

The decade was one of dramatic change and unrest, not simply on the campus or in the coffee houses of places like Toronto's bohemian Yorkville. In the wake of the Second World War, a massive demographic and economic change reshaped Canada. As I explore in Chapter 1, the baby boom generation emerged out of a postwar craze in children and child rearing, leading to almost 4 million births between 1946 and 1955. With the lessons of Nazi Germany fresh in the minds of elites and parents alike, these children grew up in an environment where permissiveness and democracy were upheld as ideals (if not a reality). As the discussion that follows reveals, however, the degree to which these ideals were implemented depended in large part on parents' class backgrounds. The backdrop of the longest sustained economic boom in Canadian history animated this generation. In this context of so many children and youth, in an economic boom time, more and more completed high school, more went to university than before, and a common youth culture apart from mainstream culture emerged. Out of this youth culture came a sense of youth apart that sparked much of what would follow.

As Canadian universities came alive with cries for a new world, or a fairer world, or a more equitable world – in many cases, all of the above – picket lines sprang up across the country, many led by young workers demanding that society live up to its professed ideals. Our popular and scholarly understanding of the baby boom generation has been informed by a particular set of parameters, largely middle-class, on-campus actors; this book demonstrates that the story of young workers developed along similar lines. Working- and middle-class youth alike developed a shared sense of difference, which found divergent expression, first in youth subcultures (the working-class motorcycle gang versus the middle-class sock hop) and then in "work" environments (the working-class factory versus the middle-class university). Chapter 1 deals with the emergence of this common culture, and Chapter 2 continues by focusing on the lesser-known story of working-class youth during the 1960s and 1970s.

Class was a key structural component, which had profound impact on the period's youth, alongside discussions of gender and ethnicity. Although there was a degree of social mobility during the period, structural categories and forces shaped individual experiences and outcomes. To that end, this book explores several questions. How were identities formed during the postwar period? To what degree can we speak of a common youth culture that spanned social classes or, conversely, how divided was it? Can we see elements of class or generational consciousness in upheavals during the period? Chapter 3 explores some of the points of division that emerged, tracing the parallel and ultimately divergent path taken by university-destined youth during the upheavals driven by working-class youth.

Canadian youth realized that they were not alone in their alienating perception of being somehow apart from society. Globally, youth began to revolt. In the United States, this occurred at university campuses such as Berkeley and Columbia and in the streets outside the Democratic National Convention in Chicago during the summer of 1968. Beyond Canada and the United States, youth seethed in Paris during the famous uprisings of 1968; in Poland, where Eastern European youth rose up against Communism; and in Mexico City, Prague, London, and beyond.[1] Events such as the Vietnam War, the civil rights movement, and community organizing movements gave a sense of urgency and inspiration to young Canadian youths. As this book shows, even a young person in a place as seemingly remote as rural Manitoba would begin to feel connected to this broader movement.

Global trends would see unique expression across English Canada, which is the framework for this book. This story played out at a national level, between the individual experiences of campuses, workplaces, and cities and the overarching youthquake that shook the Western world. Local studies do not do the story justice, since they are too restrictive. Focus on only Vancouver or Toronto would occlude a national story. The local does matter, as is evidenced by the recent scholarly attention given to the Canadian student movement at such active campuses as Simon Fraser University and the University of Saskatchewan's Regina campus.[2] A common theme of these studies is that radical campus leaderships, often dominated by New Leftists, frequently outstretched the humbler aims of students, who were instead focused on more immediate issues affecting their everyday lives. My interest here is in the related off-campus activities: the building of community support, activities with trade unions, and the enduring legacies that ensued.

The various experiences of young workers and New Leftists interacting with regional traditions and histories were borne out by the diverse stories and sources I gathered, from Metropolitan Vancouver's Burnaby Mountain to the communities by Cape Breton's Strait of Canso, from small-city Sudbury to Metropolitan Toronto. As I argue in Chapters 4, 5, and 6, these places all saw distinctive realizations of New Leftist, labour, and worker cooperation emerge. Yet this story is bigger than the sum of its separate geographical parts. A national study allows me to stitch together these disparate local contexts; a similar intellectual culture motivated comparable yet divergent reactions throughout English Canada. The most substantial contribution to our pan-Canadian understanding is Bryan Palmer's impressive *Canada's 1960s: The Ironies of Identity in a Rebellious Era,* which provides a thematic overview of major issues that dominated the decade. He maintains that the decade destabilized Canadians' self-conception as a British society, fragmenting identity so that it could not be distilled to a single narrative. Significantly, Palmer's book has extensive sections on young workers and on the early Canadian New Left, providing substantial narratives and discussions of both.[3]

I aim in this book to add to this picture by focusing on three critical currents – New Leftists, young workers, and youth culture generally – and argue that the narrative of labour and class lies at the centre of this story. The influences playing on students and activists in Vancouver were, in many ways, similar to what was playing out across Canada in Halifax. Yet, because of Canada's history and development, this story – while connected to the global – developed along its own lines. As I note in Chapter 3, English Canadians began to engage with the same thinkers, and read the same publications, forming an intellectual network that motivated their actions.

French Canada stands apart, however. The Quiet Revolution fundamentally transformed many aspects of Québécois and francophone society, leading to radically distinctive experiences in the two poles of English and French Canada. Certainly, both were shaped by common global events, and there was some intellectual engagement between these two groups – primarily through print media such as *Our Generation,* published in Montreal and distributed across the continent – but this was ultimately rather limited. Repeated evidence emerged from interviews and archives concerning political developments that created distinctively different intellectual, political, and cultural spheres for Franco- and Anglo-Canadians. There is little doubt that this sphere created a very rich and active oppositional movement in Montreal, borne out in contemporary politics. However, this world looked more to the Third World – not only to francophone nations but also beacons of liberation such as Cuba – for intellectual inspiration than to the North American English experience.[4] In this regard, Sean Mills's *The Empire Within* is of immeasurable significance and importance, especially for understanding the francophone experience.[5] It is important, of course, to not draw too much of a dividing line between these two aspects of Canada in the 1960s. As the pages that follow reveal, English Canadians did look to French Canadians for inspiration, especially those in Montreal; the two histories are intimately connected.

As a work of engaged scholarship, *Rebel Youth* builds on, complements, and challenges the growing literature on the Canadian sixties. Before the relatively recent explosion of historical interest in this period, the sixties were generally under-studied in Canada. The reason for this has been traced in part to the general reluctance of New Leftists to write of their experiences and memories, a notable difference between Canadian and American participants.[6] A triptych of works dominated the field until recently: Cyril Levitt's (1984) *Children of Privilege,* Doug Owram's (1996) *Born at the Right Time,* and Myrna Kostash's substantial and evocative semi-autobiographical (1980) *Long Way from Home.* Each provides valuable insight into its subjects, although Levitt's thesis that the student New Left in Canada can be understood as a revolt of "privilege against privilege" is insufficient and overly reductionist. Students were disproportionately privileged as compared with their non-student peers (a critical point established by the exhaustive travails of the Canadian Union of Students itself), but this universalizing model ignores opportunities for social mobility: working-class youngsters *were* attending universities in smaller numbers, which gave the movement a particular flavour absent in previous periods of student unrest.[7] I further believe that we see New Leftists in that period moving out into the community, onto picket lines, and into working-class settings in an attempt to effect fundamental social change, a revision of Levitt's argument concerning a post-1967 New Left retreat to campus.[8]

For this book, I selected two bookends to the "long sixties" as defined here. The year 1964 is a useful starting point, as it saw the transformation of Canada's Combined Universities Campaign for Nuclear Disarmament into the overtly political and extra-parliamentary Student Union for Peace Action. By the following year, both the English Canadian New Left and the youth wildcat strike wave were emerging. Until a few years ago, the story of the wildcat wave was known primarily through survey treatments by Craig Heron and Bryan Palmer.[9] More recent work by Palmer in *Canada's 1960s,* as well as a chapter by Peter McInnis on the subject, have solidly established the broad contours of events.[10] Through in-depth treatments of particular case studies using oral interviews and archival research, this book seeks to move beyond the wildcat wave, noting the importance of this time period as a statistical period but arguing that many seeds were sown and processes begun that would not culminate until the late 1960s or even the early 1970s.

For that reason, if late 1964 is a useful starting point, 1973 is a compelling end point for political, economic, and cultural reasons. The economy, which had been faltering since the late 1960s, was brought to a crisis point in October of that year with the oil embargo crisis, leading to precipitous impacts on the labour markets, as well as on the post-secondary sector. From that point onward, labour would be on defensive territory, and fears of post-secondary under-employment as well as on-campus reforms would quell on-campus dissent. Yet the 1970s would also see the eventual coming together of New Leftists and labour unions.

Minutes were rarely taken and reports rarely written by both workers and New Leftists. Consequently, oral histories provide one of the few inroads to the questions asked in this book, especially when establishing people's intellectual viewpoints. Indeed, many of the important discussions key to shaping the intellectual world of the English Canadian New Left took place over drinks – in pubs, sitting on lawns at meetings, and at innumerable kitchen tables in communal homes. Some of this was written down in *Our Generation,* an important New Left periodical, or other sites of discussion, such as *Canadian Dimension* and the *SUPA Newsletter* (published by the Student Union for Peace Action), but most was not. To hear these stories, I crossed Canada, travelling from the Atlantic coast to the Pacific coast, from Springhill, Nova Scotia (and an interview in the Springhill Miners Hall), to Vancouver, British Columbia. I found interviewees through archival sources, as well as Internet searches and Canada 411 online, and through tapping into peer networks. My methodology was to start with a few rote, scripted questions (background, path toward political activity, particular events, and so on) and to then let the interview evolve into a conversation. In my interviews, I sought to ensure that questions involved the interviewees' thoughts on labour unions and class as a category of analysis, but I did not want them to be overly prescriptive. As a result, I tried to keep my initial questions as general as possible so that the interview could evolve to include areas I may not have thought of. Interviews often ended with a list of more people to contact. My initial goal of finding thirty interviewees quickly revealed itself as too limited; by the project's end, I had met over seventy.

Oral history is invaluable for our understanding of these individuals and social movements but, of course, it does not provide a perfect representative snapshot of the period or these movements. More men were interviewed than woman, with only nineteen of the latter having their voices recorded for this book. This is partly because of historical circumstances: the unionized workplaces discussed in Chapter 2 were overwhelmingly male during the period under question, and as I note there, penetrating these social networks was difficult. Women were involved in the strikes discussed, especially as family members, but newspapers and archives did not record individual names, and I was unable to learn them. Similarly, the early New Left was particularly male-dominated. Many of the intellectual debates contained within this book involved men arguing with other men. Indeed, some women eventually tired of the neglect and endemic sexism, forming women's caucuses and women's liberation groups; by 1967, they had begun meeting separately.[11] In some questions of New Leftists and labour, however, more women found themselves involved and here these voices come out more: in Vancouver, with the pro-labour activities of the Vancouver Women's Caucus, and especially in Toronto, with the critical organizing roles played by vital young women at the Artistic Woodwork strike of 1973. Yet, on the whole, the male-dominated nature of the interview pool does need to be kept in mind, as the men interviewed reflect a particular current within the movement. Further work remains to be done in order for us to have a more comprehensive picture of the gendered understandings and roles within these social movements.

Since recollections are tempered through the intervening decades – often more than forty years – and subsequent life events and political developments skew one's remembrance of the past, such sources must be interpreted with critical care. Oral histories are intriguing not simply because of the window they offer onto events that may otherwise be beyond the reach of the historian but also because of their very forms, their status as singular constructed entities of the meeting of an interviewer and an interviewee, and the social context of these meetings.[12]

Many of the people interviewed saw these events as important waypoints on the route toward future activism, from involvement with political parties to trade union activism, social justice, the environmental movement, or continuing engagement within academia. I am taking snippets from a particular period in their life, and in the book's Conclusion I trace their onward trajectories. Throughout the book, I have made clear when I am drawing on recollections rather than documents produced at the time.[13] There is also the potential for the participant to consciously or unconsciously self-select, to privilege or repress certain memories. It is the historian's duty to sift through and compare testimonies with archives and each other, and to advance a case for a particular narrative. Competing authorities are at work: the authority of the historian, rooted in professional training and breadth of inquiry, and the authority of the participant, by virtue of his or her lived experiences.[14] Even if these two factors cannot always be balanced, we need to be aware of them.

In the six chapters that follow, I demonstrate the salience of labour and how this significantly affected the direction of radical and not-so-radical political and cultural movements through the long sixties. We move forward from an introduction of youth culture and its classed dimensions to the realization of an outward-looking New Left, in the final three chapters. Profound transformations took place in the way many young Canadians interpreted labour by the end of the period. The early sixties ideas of C. Wright Mills, arguing for the obsolescence of the traditional working class as an agent of change, gave way to widespread Marxism, both within and outside the universities, as hundreds of youngsters took to the streets – from Vancouver to Cape Breton – in support of a working class. Yet their understanding had been profoundly shaped and altered by a combination of intellectual debates and practical experiences. The labour movement would similarly become unsettled by the end of the sixties; formerly quiescent and seemingly docile, it would now have to increasingly engage with youth issues as the Canadian economic context shifted under its feet. Although the period is commonly seen as one of profound change, labour histories need to view the period as a significant site for their own narratives. As much as for any other group, the 1960s were labour's decade in Canada.

1

The Challenge of Rebel Youth

Evelyn Dumas, the prominent Québécois journalist and writer, observed that, in 1968, more than half of Canadians were under the age of twenty-five. "These young people have new needs and aspirations," she wrote in the *Montreal Star;* "The cry of youth for involvement which can be heard in universities could also be heard in the plant and in the union if we cared to listen."[1] The sixties were more than just privileged middle-class students rebelling against alienation and liberalism. Middle- and working-class youth faced differing material realities as well as political consciousnesses, but their experiences need to be positioned within broader patterns of youth experience. They formed constituent parts of a broad youth culture, developing out of a shared sense of difference from the 1950s. We, of course, need to keep in mind that these youth often had different experiences based on their class backgrounds (complementing and complicating gender and ethnic identities) or on whether they went to the workplace or to school. Although far from universalizing, this postwar youth culture needs to be understood both as a classed phenomenon and as something that encompassed all youth.

During the sixties, a minority of youth actively sought to challenge the structural constraints of postwar capitalism and transform the world. Youth had developed a sense of difference through the 1950s; the 1960s saw some adopt radical or simply anti-authoritarian politics, or join the counterculture and become "weird." This chapter discusses the story of largely middle-class New Left and university-based student movements, and that of challenges mounted from within the decidedly working-class world of unionized industry. Indeed, this latter challenge is especially significant, as 87 percent of the baby boom generational cohort did not attend post-secondary institutions, instead entering the workforce for largely waged labour.[2] University admission was a classed phenomenon as well as a gendered and racialized one; white men were the majority of university attendees.

This youth challenge stemmed from several socio-economic or cultural forces that offered a lens through which to understand their material circumstances. In some cases, this might have been as straightforward as a young woman or man coming to understand their experiences through the prism of socio-economic class. Yet, in many more cases, various cultural lenses enabled young people to develop a more radical critique of postwar society. By having the gap between their lived experiences and explicit promises of postwar prosperity and democracy processed in a particular way, some New Leftists and militant workers alike saw their social, economic, and political circumstances in a new, radical manner. Recognizing this helps us understand the rise of rebellious youth in the 1960s.

What Is "Youth"?

There is no universal definition of "youth," the nebulous period of a person's life between childhood and full adulthood. After much debate, in 1971, Canada's federal Committee on Youth defined youth as simply those aged fourteen to twenty-five, an inclusionary approach justified on the then-prevailing literature.[3] Although this does capture the generational politics implicit in the oft-quoted sixties mantra "Don't trust anybody over thirty," a strictly numbers-based understanding of youth is unsatisfactory. Peter Braunstein, writing on American youth, has suggested that the very concept of youth needs to be understood beyond numbers; it is an attitude or mindset toward life that could be accessible to all.[4] Stuart Henderson, in his study of Toronto's Yorkville neighbourhood in the sixties, agrees, saying that youth needs to be understood more as an "ethic, an act, not so much about age as ... about spirit."[5] In 1969, the president of the Ontario Federation of Labour – whose constituent members were grappling with their own youth problems – advanced a similar definition: "Dialogue in many cases has broken down because of the 'generation gap.' The generation gap is not always a matter of differences in chronological age, but a difference of attitudes that represent a completely different outlook on life."[6] These cultural definitions are the most fruitful. Above all, it is important to keep in mind that youth was and is an inherently unstable category of analysis.

Not all youth discussed here were baby boomers. A first wave of youth born during the Second World War provided leadership among New Leftists and young workers. These "wartime babies" also experienced a sense of youth apart in the 1950s, though they would largely miss the cultural intensification that became felt during the 1960s with the sheer demographic size of the baby boom generation; this intensity led to distinctive expression in the counterculture. Yet, like baby boomers, wartime babies had a divergent experience from their parents, as they were the first to encounter the intensive postwar commercialization of youth culture, remained in school much longer, and had easier access to automobiles (and their attendant symbolic and real freedom) and youth-oriented clothing. For wartime babies and baby boomers, everything began with a sense of difference.

The 1950s: Youth Apart

To make sense of youth culture, we need to understand the process through which youth came to see themselves as increasingly apart from their elders. What were the shared experiences of many young English Canadians, be they from working- or middle-class households? Just as importantly, however, what were their divergent experiences? A shared youth culture did emerge to some extent, but it was fragmented along the lines of the material reality of class. Much of what follows pertains to Canadian-born, white youth. Many Aboriginal youth experienced a very different situation, as did new Canadians who were faced with the challenges of acculturating to a new society.[7] We will return to this point shortly.

After the Second World War, a distinct demographic event began to transform Canadian society. Returning soldiers and their partners began to have kids – a lot of them. Babies being born led to pressures on other potential parents to have babies too, as society was swept by a craze in children and child rearing. Peer pressure, experts, and state policy all combined to create a favourable structural climate for child rearing. Between 1946 and 1955, about 3.9 million babies were born in Canada, a significant number for a country that had only 14 million people at the time of the 1951 census. Parenting experts, such as Dr. Benjamin Spock, preached a parental style of permissiveness. Democracy was something fragile, something that could be easily lost, as the experience of Weimar Germany had shown Canadians. Spock thus maintained that democracy had to become a part of everyday domestic life. If democratic rights were suppressed in the home, experts believed, then children were likely to rebel.[8]

The longest sustained economic boom in Canadian history accompanied this demographic explosion. Despite government planners' fears that the wartime economic boom would falter with the return to peacetime, this did not happen, thanks to interventionist Keynesian policies. Instead, consumer spending dramatically increased – reflecting its suppression during the Depression and Second World War – and investment numbers spurred expansion of major industries, including that of resource extraction.[9] The booming economy was a structural backdrop for youngsters throughout the period. Indeed, activism is seen to wane as a result of the faltering postwar boom beginning around 1968, a trend made crystal clear with the 1973 OPEC crisis.[10] The causes of this are far more complicated than simply the economy, but it is a useful starting point in understanding youth radicalism and revolt during the sixties.

With the economic boom came fuller and more consistent employment, a consequence of government intervention that sought, through Keynesian economics, to mitigate the business cycle. The private sector grew, responding to high aggregate demand that did not falter despite fears of observers, and creating steady and long-term employment. This sustained economic boom allowed working-class families to enjoy a measure of economic security, the ability to purchase mortgages in growing new suburbs, and, in a minority of cases, to secure post-secondary education for the children. The period also saw an explosion of unionism, and many working people fortunate enough to be in a union had increased security of income and position. Unionization reached new peaks: between January 1965 and early 1966, union numbers grew 9.3 percent, to reach a record 1,736,000 members or 24.5 percent of the total labour force.[11]

Families themselves were being actively constructed during this period, as psychologists attempted to impose an acceptable "normal" family. Based on the ideal of a middle-class family, this model was promulgated by psychologists and distributed through mass media.[12] This would form a cultural backdrop for young Canadians. Although it is hard to determine whether families accepted these discourses, they did provide a cultural ideal. These processes would continue into elementary and high schools, where growing numbers of young people attended longer than ever before. There, youth formed a captive market to further homogenizing, normalizing forces. More youth were attending high school: in 1951, the majority of youth aged fourteen to seventeen were not attending high school; by 1960, only one-third were not.[13] They were staying longer, too. The 1950s saw high school become an increasingly common experience for youth, and the statistics bear this out: 50 percent were reaching Grade 12 on time.[14]

Approved curriculums stressed democracy, encouraging questioning and stressing a child-centred perspective – though these curriculums were implemented to a mixed degree.[15] Rather than developing through teachers a sense of anti-authoritarianism, as a cursory reading of the curriculums might suggest, young men and women may have learned these ideas from each other – they were now spending far more time in the exclusive company of other youth. A proviso is necessary, however. Streaming in secondary schools would see many working-class youth separated out to the technical wing of a composite school or even a separate building. These youth faced a very different experience, with harsher discipline and a greater emphasis on applied workplace skills, and limited post-secondary opportunities.

Now is a good point to pause and discuss how I define class as a category of analysis. Is class a static category, linked to parental occupations? Or is it linked to income, as many commentators at the time believed? Others have an understanding of class as a simple representation of consumer purchasing power, which resonates today with the "middle class" of contemporary Canadian and American politics. This is unsatisfactory. An example by Michael Zweig demonstrates the problems of equating class to purchasing power. His example is that of a union bus driver, a university professor, and a business owner, each of whom make $50,000 a year. A consumerist understanding of class would see them as equal, as they all enjoy comparable purchasing power in the market.[16] Yet the business owner, the university professor, and the bus driver face unequal experiences: they face different opportunities and access to power and autonomy in their workplaces, and they live very different lives.

Workers, in the sense used in this book, are alienated from the product of their labour. They generally work for often-unstable wages and enjoy little autonomy within their work environments. Class does not simply happen, however; it is culturally constructed. As E.P. Thompson advanced in his still-seminal *Making of the English Working Class,* class is a historical relationship, predicated not only on understanding the commonalities of one's own identity but also as against others. "Class happens when some men, as a result of common experiences[,] feel and articulate the identity of their interests as between themselves, and as against other men whose interests are different from (and usually opposed to) theirs," Thompson argued, further noting that the "class experience is largely determined by the productive relations into which men are born – or enter voluntarily." Class consciousness, then, is the cultural incorporation and embodiment of this into "traditions, value-systems, ideas, and institutional forms."[17] This definition was put into action as young men and women became acutely aware that their class interests diverged from those of others.

Far from being abstractions, these class differences could be seen in school, at home, and in cultural life. Not all youth had an upbringing that stressed the permissive Dr. Spock. Many youth, especially girls, grew up with strict parents, and different cultures and ethnicities had different child-rearing approaches. Although the classed dimensions of Spock remain murky, a study of letters to Spock demonstrated a middle-class bias; at least some working-class mothers felt that he was for "rich kids."[18] Permissiveness appears to have been less pronounced in some working-class households. One 1971 study of a downtown neighbourhood in east Toronto found that working-class children had more autonomy and freedom, though they were not treated as "good friends," as middle-class parents tended to treat their children. When discipline came, however, it was "direct and immediate": shouts or slaps, impulsive rather than drawn-out.[19]

There were further differences in how working- and middle-class youth experienced this shared youth culture. In Ontario, for example, working-class students were more likely to leave high school at seventeen or eighteen, rather than remaining for grade 13 in that province's five-year system. Having less money also left them out of certain commercialized aspects of this mass culture. We can see evidence of this in the ways youth culture was manifested. A potent example of working-class youth culture is the motorcycle gang. Celebrated in movies such as 1954's *The Wild One,* this was a working-class response to broader youth trends.[20] Astride this would be the distinctively middle-class sock hop, a dance so named for the practice of removing one's shoes in order to not scuff the school cafeteria or gymnasium floor. One study of postwar students claims that sock hops served to separate young, middle-class female students from "the most threatening" parts of the new youth culture: males, working class, often black.[21] With these differences in mind, however, we can speak of a common sense of separation defining these youth.

With so many young people now gathered in single, centralized locations, albeit segregated along academic tracks, and for much longer than in the past, a new youth culture of difference was developing. The fact that students increasingly remained in school until the age of eighteen led to a period of prolonged adolescence. This in turn led many advertisers to focus on youth as a market. A "cult of the teenager" emerged, centred on growing schools, and the marketing of distinctive clothing, music, and other items that further contributed to a sense of youth apart.[22]

Music was important. Teenagers exercised their tastes, which drove an industry led by icons such as Elvis Presley. They thus further generated a shared youth culture that was created from below, by youth tastes, but increasingly marketed to and shaped from above.[23] The growing gulf between this youth culture and the older generation was demonstrated in the 1954 film *Blackboard*

Jungle, a hit in Canada and a film essential to understanding how teen culture developed. In one scene, a "square" teacher tries to reach out to his students by introducing them to his dated jazz collection.[24] The students respond by violently smashing the records, making clear to popular audiences and commentators that youth were a force to be reckoned with.[25] Indeed, in stark contrast, *Blackboard Jungle* elevated Bill Haley & His Comets' "Rock Around the Clock" to the status of a rock anthem; as Paul Friedlander puts it, it was an "anthem of rebellion."[26] These mass phenomena contributed to the formation of a broader youth culture.

By the mid-1950s, a mass youth culture had emerged and increasingly was holding itself – and was being held – apart from the mainstream. The world of youth was spreading. Yet the trend in secondary education of mass schooling – reaching a significant majority of young Canadians – did not continue after secondary school. Here we see youth – who had been encountering a common pattern of mass schooling and the discursive construction of youth – take differing paths based on their material and class realities.

The 1960s: Can We Speak of a Cross-Class Youth Culture?

Universities were expanding. More students had the opportunity to attend university, and participation rates slowly crept up. In the 1955/56 academic year, 6 percent of youth aged eighteen to twenty-four were enrolled in post-secondary institutions and 5 percent in university. Ten years later, the numbers had increased to 13 and 11 percent, respectively.[27] The remaining cohort participated and worked in the labour market.

Some working-class children did reach the post-secondary realm, but not many. There is some truth to the basic narrative that places emphasis on relatively affluent, privileged university students. The Canadian Union of Students (CUS) carried out an extensive Student Means Survey, commissioned in 1964 and published in February 1966, to get an indication of students' financial resources and opportunities. It contracted Robert Rabinovitch, a former CUS executive member and then doctoral candidate in finance at the University of Pennsylvania – not to mention a future president of the Canadian Broadcasting Corporation (1999 to 2007) – to carry out the survey. All English-language universities were surveyed, with 10,221 questionnaires distributed and 7,611 responses.[28] The survey was originally undertaken to back up the claim that students were financially destitute, but the findings surprised CUS: one of its widely distributed brochures noted that "on the whole Canadian students *aren't* broke. The students who manage to get into university, that is."[29]

The survey had made it clear to leaders that "only a chosen few who happened to have affluent parents were getting an education."[30] Household income played a large role in who was able to attend university. Nine percent of students came from households with incomes of less than $3,000, as opposed to 22.1 percent of Canadians more generally; only 6.1 percent of Canadian households earned more than $10,000, yet 25 percent of students came from those households.[31] However, as noted, income alone does not determine one's class. Rabinovitch also showed that 48 percent of students came from managerial or professional backgrounds, as opposed to 23.3 percent of Canadians more generally; similarly, only 35 percent of students came from working-class families, as opposed to the 64.1 percent of the broader population.[32] We can fairly definitively then hold that middle-class students were overrepresented in English Canadian universities.

But these surveys can be interpreted in another light. Twenty-five percent of the university population nationally came from homes making less than $5,000 a year, a minority of the university body as a whole. Whereas most university students came from middle-class households, a considerable number did come from working-class or at least lower-income families. Some class mobility was permitted thanks to university expansion, and to credentials that offered further career and job opportunities. We can also see some of the myopia regarding gender and ethnicity that permeated the student movement. As Pat Armstrong pointed out to me in an interview, the survey did not even ask questions about gender.[33]

Working-class students found university an avenue to class mobility, with many securing good-paying jobs after their studies, though they would experience differences while at school. The insecurity of family economies led substantial numbers of working-class students, such as those at Hamilton's McMaster University, to quit their studies to work when large industrial employers were hiring.[34] Don Mitchell, future vice-president of the Canadian Union of Students, had to take a term off to work in order to finance his studies at the University of Saskatchewan.[35] University students were continually influenced and shaped by their family backgrounds. Many working-class youth felt a class difference between them and their more affluent counterparts. At Simon Fraser University (SFU), an example we return to later in this chapter, Sharon Yandle acutely noticed this; she pursued her degree year-round and felt that some New Leftist leaders did not recognize the sacrifice working-class students had to make to attend school.[36]

What of the students who did not pursue post-secondary education and instead went directly into the workforce? Although unemployment rates were about two percentage points higher for youth aged twenty to twenty-four, most were able to find consistent employment.[37] Following a brief economic recession between 1957 and 1961, Canada entered a sustained period of economic growth from 1962 to 1973. Youth enjoyed a good bargaining position in the labour market as universities and heavy industry expanded during the period.

With 87 percent of Canadian youth in 1965/66 in the workforce and the remainder in the world of post-secondary education, can we still speak of the youth culture that I wrote of earlier with reference to secondary education? To some degree we can, although we see here the divergent material realities creating different lived experiences. While working and university-bound youth took different paths, there were many similarities that speak of a shared youth consciousness and occasional subsequent revolt.

The Rise of Rebel Youth

Emerging from prolonged schooling, mass marketing, and a sense of economic success, baby boomers built an anti-authoritarian youth culture. Some became involved in the counterculture, which blossomed with 1967's Summer of Love. Most did not, instead remaining within mainstream youth culture. A minority moved into radicalism. Depending on which fork in the road youth found themselves on, their shared sense of difference – inculcated in the 1950s – saw different expression as they became the rebel youth of the 1960s. A difference emerged between the wartime babies and the baby boomers, as the latter's formative years took place in an intense cultural milieu, leading to an anti-authoritarian, libertarian edge.

In the universities, the story of student alienation is well known. Promised the world, yet arriving at campuses dominated by impersonal modernist or brutalist architecture, punch-card computers, swelling student numbers, queues, and large lecture halls, students found their expectations unmet, and reaction came quick. Facing moral regulation, control over course selection, and even a host of mundane regulations governing, to various degrees, tobacco, alcohol, language, and sex, students chafed at the *in loco parentis* (in place of the parent) role administrators played.[38]

The shared desire for control and democracy could be seen among youth who went into the workplace. In this we can see evidence of a shared cross-class youth culture. Certainly, many labour leaders drew connections between youth challenges throughout society. Dennis McDermott, Canadian director of the United Auto Workers, held in his 1968 Labour Day speech that strike waves showed that workers – just like much of the rest of Canadian society – were dissatisfied with the status quo.[39] The Ontario Federation of Labour president echoed this.[40] Other commentators, such as John Crispo and Harry Arthurs, noted the lack of seriousness among young workers – and bemoaned that they "look[ed] upon the possibility of a strike as something of a lark."[41]

Youth from all classes were demanding more control over their lives. Rank-and-file unionists and young workers confronted issues similar to those faced by university students, especially that of how to engage with a world that did not allow them to reach their potential and enjoy the autonomy they so desired and culturally expected. In the newspaper of the Canadian Brotherhood of Railway, Transport and General Workers Union, one author suggested that, despite the class differences between students and workers, "differences would soon fade if there was a coalition of conscience between student and worker. After all, they are both questioning the status quo and both feel the alienation of large bureaucratic settings of factory or university."[42]

Indeed, some of the best examples of cooperation between youth in universities and in workplaces – or at least the desire to see it realized – could be seen here. *Our Generation* produced a literature kit on workers' control, distributed at a labour conference on industrial democracy.[43] In 1972, the journal would dedicate a whole issue to this subject.[44] In Moose Jaw, New Left leader John Conway – a student radical at the nearby University of Saskatchewan's Regina campus – realized that there was a common spirit animating young workers there who he came to know through his work with the Moose Jaw and District Labour Council, as he later recalled: "The youth rebellion, the estrangement between the old and younger generation, cut across class lines. It took different forms in the working class ... but it was as real as the estrangement ... that the middle class felt."[45]

Stan Gray, a Student Union for Peace Action leader and McGill University contract professor, went to work at a large Westinghouse factory in Hamilton in a conscious attempt to break away from his Montreal New Leftist celebrity. Gray recalls that a newspaper article had been written about him, and was discovered by co-workers. They were supportive:

> When I first started working there in '73, every young guy in the plant,
> almost 99 percent, were on dope and had long hair – and had all the sort of
> cultural revolution attitudes, you know? They listened to the same music,
> Led Zeppelin, so here I'm thinking ... these guys look exactly the same,
> same music.[46]

On the factory floor, Gray had discovered a mass youth culture that broached class boundaries. Although in the workplace this was a male-generated and -dominated culture, reflecting the broader demographic makeup of the unionized manufacturing workforce, it does shed light on how we need to understand 1960s youth culture more broadly.

These younger men brought cultural changes to union life through the period, both on and off the job. Drugs were mentioned in several interviews as a key indicator of this anti-authoritarian shift within workplaces. David Patterson remembers the changes that took place when he first arrived at the International Nickel Company (Inco) in late 1968 to work at the Stobie Mine. Over the next few years, young men streamed into the union, leading to longer hair, changing music, and a general shift toward marijuana and away from alcohol.[47] This happened elsewhere, too. In 1969, Mike Hersh began working at a factory of the home-appliance manufacturer Inglis in downtown Toronto. It was a young workplace, at one point hiring up to a hundred people who queued outside. As Hersh recollects, "I wasn't doing dope anymore, but the young guys at Inglis were. And they used to do it just outside the automatic lines, or the paint line too, upstairs. So there was, I mean, that's part of the counterculture." Jim Brophy went to work at Chrysler in Windsor in the early 1970s. There had been a big hiring in 1968, he says, and "the whole engine line, where all these young workers were, they were completely stoned. In fact, it was so open ... a lot of drinking, a lot of smoking pot, a lot of partying." In Winnipeg, Dave Hall remembers a considerable amount of marijuana being smoked by young workers, not "unusual among young blue collar workers at that point – [they did not have] a lot of sophistication but kind of a strong anti-authoritarian streak."[48]

With an upbringing that stressed personal freedom, individual expression, and democracy above all else, youth chafed at the traditionally authoritarian structures of the university and of the workplace. They began to grow their hair longer, experiment with recreational drugs, eschew social restrictions on extra-marital sex, and create a "counterculture" to the dominant social paradigms. Rather than reading too much into Dr. Spock, I instead argue that this was the cultural construction of an idealized upbringing and the message promulgated by experts, the media, and popular culture. This was not *the* counterculture per se, but one with a more generalized and elusive sense of personal liberty and anti-authoritarianism centred on an overarching desire for democracy that was shared by students and workers alike.

Although there were similarities within this large youth culture, from a desire for anti-authoritarianism and democracy to musical tastes, there were also important classed, racialized, and gendered differences that must not be underemphasized. Working-class and middle-class youth drew differently from this shared culture. In their study of Yorkville, Reginald Smart and David Jackson determined various types that made up the village's milieu. Hippies, they said, came largely from middle-class homes, whereas those part of a separate greaser subculture came from the ranks of the working class. (There were also two other important types, weekends and motorcycle gang members, alongside the "minor" types – tourists, bohemians, rounders, police, and diggers.) Unlike hippies, who typically renounced material and economic success, greasers strived to succeed. As one explained to Smart and Jackson, justifying this, "Rich people can afford to be bums. Poor people have no choice."[49] Despite the common memory of Yorkville that conflates the village with hippies – also a view that was popularly held during the period – Smart and Jackson determined that there were 1,163 greasers, compared with 377 hippies.[50] Gendered differences also materialized among these youth groups. They were most pronounced in the workplace, where women were generally barred by employer policies and collective agreements, but also seen in middle-class culture. These differences proved troublesome in the late 1960s as fissures within the New Left and student movements came to a head (discussed further in Chapter 3).

Beyond class, youth culture needs to be understood as having serious racial cleavages. As young community organizers discovered as they went into Aboriginal communities, First Nations truly lived a life apart. Material wealth was unevenly distributed in postwar Canada, but no more so than for Aboriginals, who did not even gain full citizenship until 1960.[51] Red Power, a youth-driven struggle for Aboriginal self-determination and governance, began to gain momentum by the end of the decade, laying the groundwork for an energetic response to the 1969 White Paper. Although inspired by movements like Black Power and by the American experience, and drawing on trans-border links, Red Power and the New Left came out of different traditions. Similarly, black Canadians in the 1960s, particularly in Nova Scotia but also elsewhere, had faced generations of overt and covert stigma and racism. Young black men and women shared in some aspects of youth culture, finding themselves, for instance, in organizations such as the Black United Front, but their experiences were filtered through the realities of their race.[52] Black activism was part of this youth explosion, especially in cities like Halifax, Toronto, and Montreal. Both because it was an important issue and as a way to distinguish themselves from Americans, Canadian New Leftists began – by the mid-1960s – to engage fruitfully with questions of race and social change.

Class, too, was a considerable obstacle for young people working together, despite their shared age group. Examples of attempts to bridge this gap between working class and student youth are illustrative. As the discussion stretched on into the night at one Student Union for Peace Action meeting where both workers and community members were in attendance, Harvey Shepherd remembers member André Beckerman denouncing his New Leftist colleagues: "Look, you people don't understand that a lot of these people have to get up in the morning and go to work."[53] This sentiment was echoed elsewhere. Halifax-based New Leftist Ken Clare recalled his realization that the "working class gets up early in the morning" and that a realm of work began before the sun came up.[54] These are not trivial distinctions but important ones that speak to the different lifestyles of young people. A new world may have been dawning, but it was certainly dawning earlier for some than for others.

Coming out of a common youth culture forged in high schools, music billboards, and families, young men and women faced divergent material experiences, depending on whether they pursued post-secondary education or directly entered the workforce. Common patterns of mass schooling led to a common youth culture, which was culturally constructed as a mass phenomenon and perceived as such. Yet, while there was this common experience, there were also divergent lived experiences that inhibited cooperation within this broader culture, and that would inhibit New Leftist attempts to reach out to the working class in the mid- to late 1960s.

"The Same Sociological Bag": Observing Youth Revolt

With the broad angles of English Canadian youth culture established, let's turn now to how it was understood. By the mid- to late sixties, many observers envisioned youth unrest as a much broader phenomenon than just the student movement and New Left within universities. This was partly because of the 1965/66 wildcat wave (discussed in the next chapter) but also because of various activity that vexed labour leaders, university administrators, and academics. Youth unrest was a much broader – and pan-class – issue than historians often assume.

By 1968, labour leaders were grappling with youth unrest. On Labour Day 1968, participants in a United Auto Workers parade gathered in Windsor to hear Dennis McDermott speak. That year, McDermott declared, "[would] be recorded in recent history as the year of the strike ... Why? Because of an enlightened aggressive leadership? An aroused rank and file? A frustrated membership? Partly yes on all counts." Yet labour unrest alone could not account for what made 1968 unique:

If I were a sociologist, I would take the wave of strikes in 1968 – the black revolution to the south of us – student demonstrations here and elsewhere – the apparent consumer unrest – the so-called quiet revolution in Quebec – the hippy [sic] movement – and I would place them all in the same sociological bag. Because all of them in one way or another, are a manifestation of obvious dissatisfaction with the status quo.[55]

McDermott was making a claim for labour's place within the historical experience of 1968. He was conceptualizing a broad youth culture that, while possibly seeing material differences on the basis of class, was somehow united by virtue of a shared consciousness.

McDermott was not alone in seeing youth unrest during the 1960s in this manner. Speaking to the thirteenth annual convention of the Ontario Federation of Labour, federation president David Archer looked back on 1969 as the most exciting year of his life. He declared in his annual address that all institutions, including trade unions, were being questioned by youth.[56] Despite being a middle-aged Textile Workers Union of America representative who had been president since 1958, Archer was a strong proponent of the place of young workers within the broader milieu of sixties unrest. "This has been a year of unrest," wrote Archer in his 1969 Labour Day message. "Not only unions but students, tenants, social workers, have all been questioning today's values."[57]

Others echoed these concerns, especially when it came to industrial democracy: Steelworkers representative Chris Trower connected labour unrest to a "general expression of dissent" throughout society, for example, and some academics connected trade union unrest to university unrest.[58] Ed Finn, a leading labour columnist with the *Toronto Star* and research director of the Canadian Brotherhood of Railway, Transport and General Workers Union, argued throughout the decade that young workers needed to be conceptualized as a "New Left of Labour," to be explicitly viewed as facets of a shared youth revolt.[59] In *Canadian Forum*, Louis Greenspan wrote, "Just as the bureaucratized universities have created the militant student and faculty so have the bureaucratized plants created the new generation of union militants."[60] Commissioned to write a history of Canadian industrial relations for the 1968 Woods Task Force on Industrial Relations, Stuart Jamieson maintained that labour unrest needed to be seen in the same context as university unrest: "It is to be expected that this widespread revolt against traditional authority – in the home, and in governments at all levels – should carry over into the industrial relations scene."[61] John Crispo, director of the University of Toronto's Centre for Industrial Relations, and Harry Arthurs of Osgoode Hall Law School noted that these young trade unionists, "like so many in our society, seem less disposed today to accept the status quo."[62] A 1972 article in the *Globe and Mail* claimed that youth "in the trade union movement represents a new militancy within organized labor. The younger members are more impatient, less docile and question the union leadership more than their elders."[63] Labour leaders, commentators, and individuals were all realizing how widespread youth unrest really was.

From Youth Apart to Youth in Revolt

This book largely focuses on youth who sought to be active agents of change by challenging existing conditions and structures. Thanks to the cultural sense of difference in the fifties and the growing cultural tropes of anti-authoritarian and libertarianism in the sixties as the baby boom moved into workplaces and post-secondary institutions, we can speak of a common lived experience for many youth. A minority became radicalized. They did so thanks to various discourses in different political, cultural, and economic contexts that gave them lenses through which to view their material reality and adopt a new questioning attitude. These forces enabled them to process their experience in a new and radical manner.

Three contextual issues intensified during the sixties and led several toward adopting a radical perspective on current events: Vietnam, civil rights, and the economy. The twin issues of the Vietnam War and the African American civil rights movement were culturally significant. Vietnam provided a constant undercurrent for all activities, even though young Canadians were not subject to conscription. These two events were almost inescapable during the period: seen on television, discussed in newspapers and in classrooms, pubs, houses, and the streets. With the war, onlookers saw the American Empire in action, lending credence to a world view that either singled out American imperialism or condemned all Western imperialism. Furthermore, they were inspired by those – such as the Viet Cong – who resisted the American Empire. Many New Leftists, students, and radical youth also saw Canada as complicit, even though the country did not provide direct military support. Jim Brophy, an American studying at the University of Windsor, says that his radicalism came from practice rather than theory: the Windsor student council was voting on whether to support war resisters, and his fellow Americans were so virulent that Brophy instinctively found himself drawn to the radicals.[64] The Vietnam War could be felt throughout the country. In a small industrial city such as Sarnia, Ontario, Canadians lived in the shadow of chemical conglomerates, including napalm-producing Dow Chemical. The officially distributed reason that it was to "defeat the world communist conspiracy" had little resonance in the ears of young, politically active youth.[65]

The Vietnam War and the civil rights movement must be emphasized as important factors in shaping the period's political scene and driving youth to action. These issues filled the pages of student and New Left papers, providing a shared experience and lesson of resistance. Some of the largest rallies occurred in front of American consulates in Montreal and Toronto, bringing together people who may have disagreed on minute questions of political change. Steve Hart recalls the effects of these formative experiences on undergraduates at the University of King's College, a constituent college on the Dalhousie University campus. Hart, who would be a prominent member in both the Nova Scotia New Democratic Youth and the subsequent East Coast Socialist Movement, says that the civil rights struggle created "a context into which one felt you could join something that was bigger than King's, and bigger than Halifax." Even if the issue was initially simply obtaining something as basic as co-ed dining halls, the struggle could be recast into this broader context of rights: "It's so basic to why a lot of people at that point in history felt somewhat comfortable moving forward into a struggle. They just saw it as almost natural in some ways."[66] Other activists echo Hart's sentiments, attributing their political development to the impact and influence of civil rights and the Vietnam War.[67]

Hugh Armstrong, CUS president in 1967/68, observed how the war could be used as a catalyst to radicalize fights over university governance and conditions. It served as an important bridge between New Leftists and the broader student or community milieu. Students initially voiced concern with university governance, democracy, and representation, as well as with rising tuition and residence fees. Armstrong explains the approach CUS took regarding a prominent mid-1960s student issue: "So how come residence fees are going up? Well, they're building new residences and the mortgage rates are very high, it's very expensive to borrow money." The tendrils connecting the Vietnam War to the university could then be exposed: the Vietnam War was causing inflation, and thus "you start from the cost of going to university and you end up denouncing American imperialism."[68] This argument became the backbone of many students' radicalization, regardless of their background. The Vietnam War and the civil rights movement certainly facilitated wide-ranging contacts between various left groups and individuals. For young Canadians across the country, civil rights violations and the Vietnam War represented much of what was wrong with the vision of the world sold to them.

In the United States, the Vietnam War served as one of the key dividing issues between mainstream labour and the student and New Left movements. For radical young workers, this must have accentuated the earlier sense of separateness inculcated in the 1950s. George Meany, then president of the American Federation of Labor and Congress of Industrial Organizations, publicly backed the Vietnam War. Support for the war became one of the most important dividing points between student New Leftists and the organized working class. The best example of this is the oft-cited story of New York City construction workers physically assaulting anti-war student demonstrators while expounding slogans such as "Love It or Leave It" and "Don't Worry, They Don't Draft Faggots."[69] This was far from a universal stance within the American labour movement, with large unions such as the United Automobile Workers distancing themselves from it, as did substantial numbers of unionists who were concerned with this direction.[70] Regardless, labour's perceived and actual support for the war was a substantial barrier to cooperation between labour and the left in the United States.

This obstacle was less apparent in Canada. The Vancouver and District Labour Council, for example, explicitly passed a motion – following a confrontation between longshoremen and unemployed youth – calling on their membership to not "become involved in so-called 'hard hat' demonstrations against the youth of the country."[71] The Canadian Labour Congress and other major labour federations opposed the war, though many workers saw large international unions as complicit with the broader American imperialist project.[72] As early as 1965, the Ontario Federation of Labour passed a resolution against the war, condemning all parties to the conflict, declaring that they were all complicit in escalating the war and threatening global peace. Several labour delegates pressed for even stricter wording.[73] There was not complete agreement, of course, and fights continued to break out at conventions over this issue.

There was also the material reality created by the booming economy, which certainly helped shape English Canadian youth culture, and formed the backdrop and structure for radical youth. Fuller employment for youth enabled many to take risks that they would not have been able to take had the spectre of unemployment been an ever-present danger. As Crispo and Arthurs note, workers had "nothing to lose and everything to gain" by striking.[74] When young workers led a seemingly sudden wildcat strike of 11,037 workers at Hamilton's Steel Company of Canada in August 1966, the works had just hit their all-time employment level; they had grown by 4,504 jobs since 1960.[75] Indeed, as we will see, this very expansion gave opportunities to the young workers who would urge their colleagues to walk out.

Economic conditions also made it possible for ever-increasing numbers of middle-class youth, as well as a much smaller number from the working class, to attend rapidly growing universities. There was truth behind the general narrative of post-secondary privilege. Material reasons alone, however, cannot explain why so many youth actively challenged the societal and political status quo. Instead, we must look toward cultural forces that gave many a radical lens through which to understand their circumstances.

Many of the leaders and members of various New Left groups were "red-diaper babies" or "pink-diaper babies," the sons and daughters of Communists and social democrats, respectively. This provided an obvious radical lens for these youth, though not always straightforwardly, as parents hesitated as they saw their children taking such views.[76] Many student leaders came out of this tradition, including Stan Gray at McGill University, John Conway at Simon Fraser and Regina, and James Laxer, the Student Union for Peace Action theorist and eventual leader of the left-wing, nationalist New Democratic Party faction known as the Waffle.[77] Canada's political context, with its established mainstream social democratic party, may have allowed a more organic continuity between older and newer leftists, especially in provinces where these traditions were deeply ingrained.

This connection had a tremendous impact on these youth, some of whom, like Laxer, took an active role in the political world of their parents. Other red-diaper and pink-diaper babies, however, associated radical politics with fear and repression, because their parents may have turned their back on the Communist Party out of fear during the post–Second World War Red Scare. As Judith Pocock says, recalling her own upbringing, some parents may have tried to shelter and protect their children so they would not have to keep secrets as youngsters in an anti-Communist climate.[78] The impact of the 1956 invasion of Hungary and the revelations of Stalin's crimes also may have tempered some parents' earlier enthusiasm. For example, Anthony Hyde, who grew up in a red family and later became a New Leftist leader with Student Union for Peace Action, upset his parents by adopting radical political views; they felt he was putting himself in danger.[79] Such origins also helped radical movements establish their identity as distinct from the earlier Old Left.

Ethnic and religious lefts played a role in engaging young people with radical politics as well. They provided a lens through which young people could view their youthful experiences, and led to a distinctive radicalizing process. One example is Camp Kinderland, in Brampton, Ontario. Part of Camp Naivelt (meaning "new world"), it is one of several Jewish summer camps in Ontario, Quebec, and New York State. It had been a formative experience for many on the Canadian left since its 1925 founding (the children's camp closed in 1972, but the adult camp continues to this day).[80] These camps, coupled with parents who also provided a leftist upbringing, were important routes toward radical politics. At camp, Jewish children developed an understanding of class politics, intermixing politics and play. James Laxer recalls his formative experiences at Camp Naivelt, in particular a concert Pete Seeger put on for the campers that led him to believe "we were a vessel bound for a better world."[81] At places like Naivelt, a new generation of Jewish leftists was inculcated with strong progressive traditions.

Christianity also played an important role in bringing individuals toward a radical interpretation of social and economic realities. This was a critical route, undertaken with organizations such as the Student Christian Movement or because of personal conviction.[82] The roots of the Canadian New Left can be found partially in liberal Christianity, which forms an implicit part of its discourse; the Student Christian Movement in part played the role of midwife (as the group put it) to the Student Union for Peace Action.[83]

Many prominent Christians were involved in New Left groups. Seminaries were hotbeds of political activity, contributing to the radicalization of individuals. Doug Ward and Peter Warrian, both CUS presidents who directed the student movement toward a more activist position, were seminarians. John Lang, who became involved in radical unionism through the Council of Canadian Unions, recalls formative experiences at a Catholic seminary; the Second Vatican Council had engendered tremendous debates within the seminary. For Lang, the Catholic seminary created a path to radicalism by encouraging active questioning of the status quo. Doug Ward remembers the influence of J.S. Woodsworth and the Social Gospel while at Trinity College. Indeed, in writing a paper on Woodsworth, he learned that the preacher had declared himself to be "more concerned with people's lives after birth than their lives after death." This was an epiphany for Ward, the moment when he realized he was "in it for the Social Gospel things, and that really I [c]ould probably pursue that happier outside"; he subsequently went into student politics.[84]

Although a significant minority of activists did come from households with a left tradition or were exposed to religious lenses through which to develop a radical consciousness, many more had no such background. These young people developed a radical lens through their experiences in daily life. However, specific issues that conflicted with a general liberal sensibility could galvanize them to action. Simon Fraser University, the site of the most radical student upheavals in Canada, was situated in the burgeoning postwar suburb of Burnaby, British

30   Chapter 1

Columbia. The university drew many of its students from this and surrounding suburbs. These were politically solidly social democratic ridings, many consistently voting for the New Democratic Party throughout the 1960s. The on-campus events, however, such as the immediate dismissal of five teaching assistants for their political activities or the overturning of established tenure and promotion procedures by a ham-fisted administration, would lead many students with mainstream political inclinations into a radical milieu. Liberal precepts, dating from John Stuart Mill (quoted in the student newspaper, the *Peak*), led some to action as they noted the gap between the rhetoric of liberalism and reality. Rob McAninch, who had been a young Liberal through junior high and throughout the radical period of Simon Fraser University politics, recalls how this idealism was transformed. He was an "idealistic" fan of Lester Pearson, and McAninch speculates that this made him open to activism: "I was hugely committed to Pearson and his vision ... You didn't have to be a radical to agree that it [the firing of five teaching assistants for protesting] was an injustice. And that did start the process of greater radicalism."[85] Administrators miscalculated the degree to which youth would chafe at *in loco parentis* – "an archaic notion for the university to hold towards students in their late teens or early twenties," says Simon Fraser student Gordon Hardy – thereby contributing to campus radicalism through its overreaction.[86]

Students fought the *in loco parentis* role of universities. Some historians have seen this as an important avenue toward student political activity, though the dismantling of this system also opened up additional space for student autonomy and thus activism.[87] Control over one's world, over one's life, was seen as an important part of fighting a world perceived to be authoritarian and impersonal. Sociologist Kenneth Westhues has posited that the institutional deficiency, the gap between expectations and reality, was a primary reason for social unrest during the period.[88] The example he uses is the difference between happy suburbia and the universities, but this could certainly be extended to the stark reality of the assembly line.

The students' youthful counterparts in the workplace and industry also took issue with control. Many labour leaders and older rank-and-file members shared this cry for industrial democracy, the democratic sharing of control in the workplace, albeit to differing degrees. There has been a long history of the labour movement's call for industrial democracy, most notably during the Workers' Revolt of 1917-25.[89] Industrial democracy had long been a stated goal of unions, but labour leaders increasingly abandoned it in the wake of the postwar settlement. The passage of order-in-council PC 1003 in 1944 and the subsequent enshrinement of these wartime regulations in the 1948 Industrial Disputes Investigation Act enshrined unions as "junior partners" and gave them codified legal status, but required them to assume responsibility for controlling unruly members.[90] Strikes would be permitted only on the expiration of a collective agreement; workers who struck in violation of this could receive punitive individual and union fines. Crucially, these changes also reduced the ability of labour to bargain in areas outside strict economic provisions. Members could not legally contest changes imposed on the workplace during the length of the collective agreement. The automatic dues check-off guaranteed by the Rand formula increased union security at the expense of regular daily rank-and-file contact with union officials.[91]

At the 1970 Canadian Labour Congress convention, "youthful" workers urged for bargaining to be extended to issues of technological change and workplace control.[92] Several labour leaders opposed this demand on practical grounds. Canadian Labour Congress leader Donald MacDonald dismissed calls for workers' control in a rare candid comment to other union leaders at a Canadian Union of Postal Workers conference on workers' control in 1972 in Edmonton: "Advocates of workers' control want to use union workers as shock troops to establish the dictatorship of the proletariat in Canada. What that really means is that a few intellectuals would rule by telling workers what is good for them."[93] Other leaders echoed this at the conference, emphasizing that they needed to focus on the economic gains they had achieved and to attempt to hold onto them. Young workers' demands, while certainly distinctive and representing a labour perspective, reflected a broader youth culture.

However, there was not much of a generalized radical critique that emerged from the demands of young workers in the sixties, and many of these battles were waged as separate ones. There was site-by-site struggle by young workers, but no cohesive movement emerged. Labour structures, such as the provincial federations of labour or the Canadian Labour Congress, actively worked against illegal labour actions. But unlike the workplaces, universities gave birth to a pan-Canadian expression of discontent separate from official structures: the New Left.

Faculty and ideology were key in reconceptualizing individual events of control and freedom into a broader critique with traction. At SFU, for example, governance struggles were processed through a particular frame of political and social consciousness, inculcated by student activists and radical faculty members. They attempted to demonstrate that seemingly isolated events – the firing of five teaching assistants, for example – could be seen in a broader context of capitalist society. Who did the university represent, and who was on its Board of Governors? There were many young, idealist faculty members at SFU, thanks to the university's establishment in 1965, and several radical professors staffed the Political Science, Sociology and Anthropology Department.[94] Gordon Hardy, who was involved with on-campus newspaper the *Peak* and Students for a Democratic University at SFU, observed the interplay between these radical ideas, faculty, and repressive events, and how Marxism connected with impressionistic, excited high school students.[95] In hindsight, Hardy feels embittered by what he now sees as "indoctrination" by professors who betrayed their mission of liberal education, but at the time it moved him toward a more radical politic.[96] Others, however, were attracted to SFU because of the very message of the faculty, or soon gravitated toward the radical energy of the department.[97] Many of the graduate student leaders at SFU – John Conway, Jim Harding, John Cleveland, and Martin Loney – came to the campus because of the supervisory potential and activism of professors such as the Marxist Tom Bottomore. The analyses advanced by radical faculty helped develop a particular political frame through which to view events.

The growing move toward a class or Marxist analysis among New Leftists helped allow others from working-class backgrounds to process their material circumstances in a manner that led to a radical consciousness. Socio-economic class rarely leads schematically to political radicalism, but a particular lens could spur action. Sharon Yandle, for example, was from a leftist unionist family background. At SFU she encountered radical faculty who introduced to her "a much broader theoretical perspective on the world" and challenged her "implicit belief in some idea of progress." In her case, radical faculty built on an earlier working-class socialist consciousness.[98] A 1973 survey carried out at the University of Toronto's St. George campus attempted to determine the class origin of politically engaged students through their parents' occupations, and posited that an inverse correlation appeared between the father's education and leftism.[99] New Left veteran Jim Harding has speculated that, contrary to the privilege thesis, privileged students (based on his personal experiences at the University of Regina, Simon Fraser University, and the University of Waterloo) were more likely to support the status quo.[100]

Thomas Trenton argued that, compared with the American New Left, radicals at the University of Toronto could not be categorized as a "liberated urban-middle class generation."[101] Instead, the exact opposite could actually be seen. According to Trenton, the University of Toronto working-class students were more likely to be at the forefront of radicalism, as many issues (tuition fees, student aid, and day care, for example) were their direct lived concerns.[102] This is significant, especially once we consider the attention paid to the very pressing problems of universal accessibility and the vigour with which the student New Left took up these concerns. This helps us move away from the assumption of privileged students adopting the cause of the downtrodden, since not all students came from privileged families; many of the agents of change were themselves members of the working class.

Many working-class New Leftists may have moved to defend their interests, as in the 1971 strike vote, yet this cannot imply a causal link between working-class status and involvement in radical politics. Their working-class status did play a role for many important New Leftists, however. A surprising number described themselves as coming from working-class households, including several who played a vital role in pushing New Leftists toward a worker-oriented approach. Peter Warrian, who was president of the Canadian Union of Students, had been a technical student who worked in a telecommunications factory before entering the seminary. Stan Gray, a New Leftist and a prominent, controversial lecturer at McGill, credits his own perspective on social change and activism in part to his growing up in working-class Jewish Montreal.[103] The Moose Jaw Caucus in the Canadian Union of Students, a group of students instrumental in shifting electoral politics and direction within the organization in 1968, originated in a working-class high school in Moose Jaw, a location that influenced their own personal direction, politics, and ultimately engagement with the community.[104]

Most students and youth, however, were not radicalized. The middle-class nature of the majority of university students, who would then understandably provide the majority of the leadership of student and New Leftist movements, certainly alienated some students. Sharon Yandle, who founded SFU's Student Union for Peace Action chapter and was active as a student senator and activist, remembers some of these class tensions. When the Student Society called a student strike, she felt that many of the leaders did not understand the sacrifice that working people had made to attend university, forgoing other opportunities.[105] Hers was a case in point: a single mother from a working-class family, Yandle attended SFU straight through in continuous semesters. Apart from these anecdotes, however, the non-radical working-class voice is hard to capture: student papers were increasingly dominated by radical voices, as were student societies. They are cautionary notes, though, as we attempt to uncover this past.

One final connective tissue throughout the baby boom generation, forming a route to radicalism, was a general opposition to hypocrisy. Expectations had been set up by various people and institutions, from Dr. Spock to high schools, and by the general social idea of progress and fuller employment; the subsequent disappointing reality was a motivating factor behind social unrest. The prevailing rhetoric of consumerism held that the twin forces of mass consumption and mass production could create a richer, more equitable place to live.[106] These were the promises. But what was the reality? Many youth recognized (or were beginning to note) that inequality existed in Canada along lines of class, gender, and ethnicity. The gap between the rhetoric of liberalism and the reality of the state of Canada's First Nations, for example, was stark. So too was the dichotomy between those who held power and those who did not, between those who had to work and those who could profit from their capital. Youth also began to raise similar questions about women in society – did they really possess equality, even within ostensibly progressive oases like the New Left? As New Leftist attention began to focus first on race, and then emphatically on class, the neglect of women's rights especially became glaring.

Radical ideas were transmitted several ways. There were class distinctions in youthful exposure to radical ideas. Working-class youth, as reflected in the interviews cited throughout this section, were more likely to garner their ideas from music. As Winnipeg-based student activist Paul Graham noted, music could be a connective tissue between metropolitan commercialized youth culture and even remote peripheral locations.[107] Messages of resistance would have been heard not just in the often overtly political lyrics of the time but also in the energetic rhythms, the marketing campaigns, and the sheer energy that came from this culture. Middle-class youth would have drawn political energy from this source as well, of course, but because of their increased accessibility to the post-secondary milieu would have drawn more on political pamphlets, speeches, and ideologies.

Young people became politically active in the political milieu of the 1960s for numerous reasons. That there were disparate paths to radicalism, united by a shared sense that things were not as they ought to be, demonstrates that a homogenous view of the baby boom generation cannot be sustained. An earlier idea of being separate as youth, inculcated in the 1950s, developed for a minority into a radical political or cultural perspective. The Vietnam War and the civil rights movement provided an important context for their activities as they became aware of a much larger injustice that formed a constant undercurrent. Beyond these, however, a series of lenses gave these youth an ability to make sense of their lived experiences in a radical fashion. Familial factors, such as being a red-diaper baby, were key for some; for others, it was the disjuncture between liberal ideals and the reality of the university or workplace. Working-class youth may have become active because of their powerlessness within the workplace, aggravated by their sense that unions failed to support their demands for industrial democracy. These concerns paralleled the calls of student New Leftists for greater involvement in the running of the university. By the 1960s, then, there was a new youth subculture of radicalism, one that began to challenge the status quo and demand a better workplace, a better classroom, or a better world.

Conclusion

Youth unrest in the 1960s was more than just middle-class students rebelling against alienation and liberalism. Many Canadians believed that youth in general formed a broad cross-class culture. Working- and middle-class youth were both part of this culture, which was divided by divergent lived experiences of class, especially along the lines of who pursued post-secondary education and who went directly into the workforce. Despite this very real difference, these young people also shared important commonalities of mass experience, anti-authoritarianism, a belief in democracy, and being commonly constructed as a part of a youth culture. By the mid-1950s, thanks to mass schooling that prolonged adolescence, coupled with the ability to "buy in" through commercialized rock and roll, and the developing sense of something larger beyond their own schools, towns, or even region, a broader anti-authoritarian culture of youth separateness existed.

This anti-authoritarian spirit rejected the *in loco parentis* role of the university just as it did the tyranny of the foreman, lending the sixties its distinctive flavour as the demographic bulge reached these often paternalistic and authoritarian institutions. The sense of difference then gave way to a minority of youth actively challenging their conditions and structures, forming either student or New Left protest movements in the universities or oppositional wildcat movements within workplaces. They did so because of numerous discourses in several political, economic, social, and cultural contexts, which gave them lenses through which to view their circumstances. These were a diverse group of influences, from religious upbringings stressing a social justice seemingly divorced from reality, to the televised injustices of the Vietnam War, to lived experiences under the autocratic rule of university administrators or factory foremen. The story of the student New Left has been told elsewhere, but the narrative of their counterparts in the labour movement has not been similarly examined. In the next chapter, we explore this story, and see that the sixties was a much broader phenomenon than often assumed.

2

Punching In, Walking Out:
The Challenge of Young Workers

The spark was lit at the 2,200-foot level, in the Levack Mine, a remote and undesirable outpost of the International Nickel Company (Inco) outside Sudbury, Ontario, when a group of low-seniority young men opened their lunch pails in July 1966. Because of rising tensions between their union, Local 6500 of the United Steelworkers, and their employer over a recently expired collective agreement – languishing in Toronto-based conciliation hearings – they were forbidden to gather on the job. Their foreman stopped them, told them to close their lunch pails and carry on to work without eating; as the few old hands explained to the newer workers, this was a severe provocation. Miners worked "collar to collar," or surface to surface, and work assignments were always to be given underground during an initial break. The miners refused and were sent to the surface. Word spread, and the shift began to gather at the cages that would return them to the surface, taunting foremen, banging lunch pails, singing, and chanting. By the next morning, word had spread even farther, picket lines were up, and the union had lost control. It took almost a month of union and police effort to bring these young workers under control, and the incident led to enduring changes in union discipline within one of Canada's largest and most important trade unions.

Young workers took a militant lead elsewhere. Indeed, that same month, almost sixteen thousand members of Steelworkers Local 1005 went on a wildcat strike at Hamilton's Steel Company of Canada (Stelco). Young men had similarly been concentrated in undesirable low-seniority positions, and after being provoked by a foreman, ignored their stewards and walked out.[1] The next month in Toronto, a large strike of rail workers was ignited by youth: the *Toronto Star* ran pictures of young men who would not have looked out of place at the Woodstock music festival, and older members of the Canadian Brotherhood of Railway, Transport and General Workers Union denounced younger members for plunging them into a strike they and their families could ill afford.[2] These were not isolated incidents. Some 20 to 50 percent of strikes were wildcats in 1965 and 1966; although the numbers are unclear, there may have been as many as 575 wildcat strikes in the period.[3]

Young workers spearheaded rank-and-file opposition to managers and unions alike. A surging economy had flooded large industrial employers with new recruits who had no traditional connection to union or employer and little sense of material deprivation, which may have inhibited their parents' generation. They questioned poor health and safety practices, as well as archaic "traditions" that made no sense in this more affluent postwar world. They brought a new inquisitive energy to a labour movement that had become increasingly staid, refusing to accept the old ways and sending a strong message to their aging leadership.

A Giant Tamed? The Postwar Settlement

Writing in early 1964, *Canadian Dimension* editor-in-chief Cy Gonick wrote of labour leaders who were "lethargic in their maturity," attending hotel conventions and paying officials high salaries. Labour had become an institution rather than a grassroots movement, "rooted in bureaucratic routine, selling a service to the membership not unlike other service industries."[4] This perhaps overstated things, as unions had relied on bureaucracies for decades, but it did capture the difference between early unions, and their fight for basic legality and rights, and increasingly entrenched postwar unions. There was a growing division between leaders and the rank and file: the former spent more time on union activities, and the latter was insulated from his or her union outside of ratification votes and occasional strikes.

Strikes were rare. As the *Strikes and Lockouts* report put it in 1963, that year was "only the fifth year in the past twenty years in which the number of man-days [lost to strike or lockout] did not reach a million."[5] These reports until 1965 read as happy and satisfied, the Department of Labour manning a ship of economic prosperity, satisfied that the postwar settlement had calmed the seas of labour unrest. Harry Woods, McGill's dean of arts who would later lead a federal task force on labour relations, addressed the Ontario Federation of Labour (OFL) in 1963. Strikes had not wholly "withered away, but [have] declined," Woods declared; the new problem was instead going to be resolving the relationship between members and their locals, which would "become increasingly important as unionism settles down to administration as opposed to organizing and fighting."[6] These were prescient words.

The so-called postwar settlement, specifically a legal regime of industrial pluralism, formed an important backdrop to the decade's labour militancy. Official recognition and legal protections had long been a goal of the mainstream labour movement. The 1872 Trade Unions Act had legalized unions, albeit without any compulsion for employer recognition. Mackenzie King's 1907 Industrial Disputes Investigation Act, establishing a mandatory conciliation process in federally regulated industries, set in motion a move away from a conception of simple industrial legality and toward a model of industrial plural-ism that recognized the compatible interests of capital and labour. During the Great Depression, the federal state began to accept labour market restrictions, such as minimum-wage legislation and limited welfare provisions, but little was done to persuade employers to bargain with unions.[7] The watershed mo-ment came with federal order-in-council PC 1003 in 1944, a wartime measure subsequently made permanent in 1948 as the Industrial Disputes Investigation Act. This measure compelled employers to recognize unions and made collective agreements recognized legal documents. As labour historian Stuart Jamieson argued in 1969, "In no country, including the United States, have the two par-ties become so enmeshed in such a detailed, complex, and on the whole rigid web of legal regulations," and this contributed to disenchantment and illegal-ity.[8] Strikes were now allowed only on the collective agreement's expiration, with punitive individual and union fines imposed if the agreement was violated and not policed by the union.

One result of this framework that was significant during the sixties was that changes imposed on the workplace during the collective agreement, such as technological alterations, were difficult to deal with. Although mechanization had been common throughout the twentieth century, automation was rising to the fore of both worker and elite consciousness in the 1950s and especially the 1960s. As early as 1963, George Meany, president of the American Federation of Labor and Congress of Industrial Organizations, declared that automation was a curse,[9] and in 1964 the chairman of the board of US Industries addressed labour leaders, declaring that automation was emerging as "our greatest domestic problem."[10] Union members, leaders, and onlookers pondered the long-term dangers of automation: job losses, to be sure, but also on-the-job seniority, changes to work processes, and security. Labour leaders were at a crossroads. On the one hand, automation threatened their membership – both actual and potential; on the other hand, it represented a move away from the physical and mental drudgery of assembly work.[11]

This trend was linked to the continuing development of the theory of residual management rights, which granted employers rights over all issues not specific-ally delineated in the collective agreement. By 1964, OFL president David Archer decried this developing trend, noting that by 1964 "most Canadian arbitrators and every Canadian court" now subscribed to the theory.[12] Indeed, one of the explicit recommendations that jurist and academic Ivan Rand made in his 1968 report was the specific enshrining of residual rights, clearing up any remaining confusion.[13]

Another crucial change was the advent of the automatic dues check-off. In his arbitrated settlement of the 1945 Ford strike, Supreme Court Justice Rand granted union security to the United Automobile Workers (UAW): the Rand formula. All workers below the managerial level who were employed in a union-ized workplace would have to pay union dues, whether they were members of the union or not. This guaranteed a steady critical stream of union funds, but severed the critical and routine connection between leadership and rank and file. The onus of dues collection instead fell on employers, who could withhold funds from the union if the collective agreement was violated by an illegal strike. Unions would now have to work very hard to build connections with new members. David Patterson describes joining Local 6500 at Inco: "I sought out a union steward, who didn't even have a card at the time – [he] had to go get a card for me to sign" – indicative of his steward's lack of preparation, and a point that Patterson brought up several times during our interview.[14] Thanks to the automatic dues check-off, unions did not have a structural or financial impera-tive to reach out to their youngest members. It would take the wildcat to make them recognize the importance of doing so.

Wildcats were challenges to union authority. The OFL president defined wildcats at the Rand Inquiry as a situation in which "the workers have taken the bit into their own teeth and are running without permission or authoriza-tion ... There could be an illegal wildcat, but not necessarily so." They were "in defiance of the constituted authority of the union itself, rather than the gov-ernment law."[15] Crispo and Arthurs, both experts in the field, defined wildcats similarly. It was important, they said, to draw a distinction between unlawful strikes called by union hierarchies and the wildcats that they were concerned with. "The wildcat strikes to which we refer are authentic, spontaneous rank and file uprisings," they wrote; "They are essentially protest demonstrations against the authority of both employer and union."[16] Stewards would enforce industrial legality; wildcat strikes and unauthorized labour action would be met with stern reproach from local, national, and international officials during the period. Unions took this role seriously. As one UAW Canadian national director noted in 1965, they had "always been able successfully to restrain our membership in most cases from going on hair-brained [sic] strikes."[17]

The complexity of this system alienated many rank-and-file members, who were increasingly removed from their leaders. Matters had come to a simmering boil as an older generation of leaders was enshrined in their positions. When the industrial unions had rapidly grown in their process of becoming established, new talent had been absorbed quickly. By the mid-1960s, fewer openings led ambitious Young Turks to conclude that the path upward lay over the bodies of the incumbents.[18] Without strong union education departments, and little labour history to draw on, new members were unaware of the legal structures and circumstances their unions operated in. They had not known unions before the Rand formula or the postwar settlement, and many took their union's existence for granted. Seemingly minor issues of comfort might have seemed fairly insignificant to older workers who came of age among Depression-era fights for union recognition, but they seemed critically important to newer workers. When a steward came to break up an illegal picket line, the question was the oft-heard refrain of sixties youth: Why?

"The New Militancy": Youth Culture Meets the Mines, Mills, and Factories

As a response to broader currents of youth culture, a spirit of rebelliousness and anti-authoritarianism began to percolate among young male workers by 1965. This wave, which peaked in the late summer of 1966 with massive labour actions in Hamilton, Sudbury, and along the railroads, was concentrated in Ontario and Quebec. Central Canada saw a particular concentration of strikes, violence, illegality, and state intervention, while British Columbia and Atlantic Canada were comparatively quiet.[19] The uneven geographic distribution of strike activity in part reflects disparate provincial economies: Ontario was home to large manufacturing industries such as steel and auto, whereas British Columbia, for example, had a more resource-based extraction economy. There *were* significant strikes outside central Canada, notably the Lenkurt Electric strike in New Westminster, British Columbia, which would shape the provincial labour movement in that province for years to come. Yet these did not revolve around younger workers.

Case studies are particularly useful for understanding the wildcat wave, for pragmatic and historical reasons. Labour archives often say little about wildcat strikes save for legal complications or post-strike recriminations. Given the sensitive nature of an illegal strike and the role union officials played, this is unsurprising: records could be subpoenaed, or used by one faction against another; unions simply do not rely heavily on the written word. D'Arcy Martin, who moved from the student-based New Left into the union movement in the 1970s, remembers:

> As part of my acculturation, I almost stopped writing memos ... I had begun
> to see the written word as a last resort for internal communication.
> I came to realize the weight of history in this stance. In the early days of
> Canadian unions, activists communicated orally among themselves because
> their work was a criminal "conspiracy in restraint of trade."[20]

Government archives are useful, but even the RCMP archives have comparatively little on wildcat strikes: agents were concerned with Communist infiltration, for example, but once they determined the 1966 wildcat strike at Inco was not related to the Communist-led Mine Mill union, they largely stopped their investigation.[21] Beyond this, however, the key issue lies in the nature of these wildcat strikes. These were not organized groups, with spokespeople and platforms and flyers or manifestos. Instead, there was action, and if a historian is lucky, some graffiti left on the wall of a mill that caught the eye of a journalist. In some cases, these were spontaneous activities – often provoked by long-standing structural tensions or grievances, to be sure – that were borne out of daily, lived experiences and discussed over beer in taprooms, or steaming bunkhouses, rather than formal meetings. When the media tried to find spokespeople, they often found none, except perhaps the voice of a union official claiming that the union had control over the situation. The section that follows is based on interviews with a handful of individuals whom I have been able to track down, as well as on government documents from the Woods Task Force on Labour Relations and media reports.

The vast majority of youth, coming from the anti-authoritarian youth culture discussed last chapter, were now moving into the formal labour market. Some were shocked to discover that basic amenities in workplaces were sometimes lacking. Keith Lovely, who came to Sudbury in 1964 at the age of twenty-two to work in the Creighton Mine, recalls one story. Workers arrived at the mine with expectations of certain reasonable comforts, yet conditions were primitive and seemingly out of place in modern Canada. When it came time for lunch, miners would heat their soup by putting one end of an electric wire into it, then wrapping that wire around the refuge station light bulb to conduct heat. To Lovely, this seemed absurd. "The younger generation from the '60s and the '70s were challenging authority," he explains, "they didn't accept everything the authority said. So when they said, 'Put your soup up on the light,' they said, 'Hey, that's fucking stupid. Why do we have to do that?'"[22] Through the period, young miners fought strenuously for basic improvements: a proper place to heat one's soup and proper lunchrooms, a proper place to wash one's hands with warm water and soap, and even proper lighting so they did not have to rely on helmet lights alone. In my interviews, these all emerged as very real, pressing issues. Yet these issues had largely not been raised by an earlier generation of miners. Their own fights for union security and inter-union battles between Mine Mill and Steel had led them to see such issues as luxuries, hardly worth walking off the job over, especially if one had a family. Older workers had resisted in their younger days, but under different expectations of what a union should do.

Improvements in workplace amenities were actively resisted. Dave Patterson remembers a senior mine superintendent mourning, "Poor fucking Canada ... what has it come to in the mining industry when miners have to have hot water and soap underground?"[23] This appeal to working-class masculinity seemed to have little resonance with a new generation, with their new understandings of masculinity and expectations of good conditions. These young men, many of whom came from a male bachelor youth culture, must have chafed at these paternalistic attacks.

This boldness stemmed, in part, from full employment. Between 1965 and 1969, unemployment for men ran between 4 and 5 percent, and even lower for women. It was not until 1970 that the numbers began to creep to 7 percent and upward.[24] In Winnipeg, Dave Hall remembers the labour market: "It wasn't hard to find work ... I'd work until I got ticked off." Workers had the possibility of taking chances at their job, to be active and stand up to management, and not face enduring unemployment. In Sudbury, former United Steelworkers of America (USWA) vice-president Homer Seguin remembers that "if you could walk almost, you could get a job at Inco ... When they're hiring, and it's easier to get a job, you feel very independent. You feel ... if you lost this job, you'd go on to another job. It's easy to get hired, very easy to get a job." When Patterson moved to Sudbury from southern Ontario to work at Inco, he remembered the "great job opportunities ... the company was hiring like two hundred people a day, but one hundred people a day were quitting."[25] The unemployment rate reflected the booming economy in 1965/66, which was resulting in large wage increases across the country as unions went to the negotiating table.[26] In this context, young workers felt that they could ask for more – and get it.

In some cities, there was a natural gathering of radical young people. Social worlds may not have completely overlapped, but the worlds of political activism often did. "I think it was quite common," Dave Hall says of Winnipeg, "a convergence of young counterculture kick-ass working-class kids bumping into middle-class, better-educated young people who probably politicized a little earlier." Although there were tensions, many would come to work together in the city's New Democratic Youth. Hall considers this as "two streams" of the left. Winnipeg was not unique. John Conway would similarly recall thinking of a New Left of Labour in Regina and Moose Jaw: "Certainly, the young workers that I worked with saw themselves as part of the New Left. But they saw themselves as part of the New Working Class left," holding their ire toward older workers, whom they saw as "stodgy."[27] Yet the New Left label is elusive and far too sweeping, as many workers harboured suspicion toward intellectuals and felt a strong consciousness of their class backgrounds, especially when compared with more middle-class student-based New Leftists.

Around the same time, the *Globe and Mail* ran an editorial noting that union leaders now needed to consider that "union ranks have been swollen in recent years by a new and largely undisciplined force of younger men with little or no trade union experience or loyalties," a precarious situation that was compounded by the fact that they had not experienced the "sobering" unemployment of the Great Depression.[28] Of course, most were male, given the prevailing gendered division of labour and economic structures. These young men challenged prevailing responsible ideals. Just as young men took their parents' automobile culture and twisted it into rebellious hot-rodding – as Christopher Dummitt has observed – these workers took their parents' unions and tried to turn them into something else, challenging them and expressing their anger.[29] Although most (but not all) of the workers discussed in this chapter were men, they existed within family economies that saw women playing active roles. This was realized in the realm of supporting families but also during the wildcat wave, as seen in Hamilton and Sudbury.

These are just glimmers of an active youth culture within unions, however. It was with the early 1965 eruption of wildcat strikes that we begin to see the power of this new demographic. Undoubtedly, much more of the youth experience did not revolve around strikes but, rather, encountering stultifying and dangerous work, raising families on limited budgets, and coping with intrusive management and even company-town policies. Much of this is lost to history.

For a few explosive years, however, youth within unions rose to the national stage as these workers began challenging employers and complacent unions alike.

The Wildcat Wave

The wildcat wave was without statistical precedent. The comparatively quiescent labour movement suddenly exploded through 1965 and 1966, in roughly 575 strikes. Wildcats made up 20 to 50 percent of strikes during the period, although the OFL ran a campaign pointing out that 95 percent of all collective agreements were still settled without recourse to strike action.[30] Many of these strikes, however, cannot be traced directly back to youth. Some of the largest strikes were those that launched industrial action before strike deadlines. In January 1965, six thousand members of UAW Local 444 at Chrysler in Windsor walked off the job at least twice in advance of deadlines, in addition to a few other smaller walkouts.[31] Other large actions were prompted by changes to customary work processes and expectations. At the same Windsor facility in 1966, two thousand workers walked off the job because of a jurisdictional dispute involving welding torches. Workers expected their torches to be lit by the previous shift; when one group arrived and found them unlit, the men refused to light them themselves and walked out.[32] The Oshawa General Motors plant, organized by UAW Local 222, had its own series of wildcats. In 1965, the suspension of a co-worker prompted 150 men to walk out, an event repeated in September 1966, and the facility shut down for three hours in April 1966 when workers went off drinking at lunch and refused to return because of debates over overtime pay (which were resolved, perhaps demonstrating the fruits of their militancy).[33]

In Windsor's UAW 444, an inter-union battle was raging between two slates, one of which was challenging the incumbents, arguing in favour of term limits and a stronger approach in bargaining.[34] One member wrote to the national director that this group was ripping apart the union, along with "many of the young Brothers who don't know anything about the earl[ier] strife."[35] A week later, UAW 444 launched a final wildcat strike, on 14 December 1966: the local president declared to his members that he would be living up to his responsibilities by ordering the men back to work.[36] There had been fifty-five wildcat strikes at Chrysler Windsor in 1966 alone.[37] Much of the local's unrest during the period came from the engine line, with its cluster of low-seniority workers.[38] The level of unrest at the plant was so high that in early 1967, then UAW director George Burt wrote a denunciatory union newspaper article. "Wildcat strikes

[are] a denial of our democratic procedure," he said. "In practically every case it is engineered by a few 'hot-heads' in a department." Burt reminded readers that wildcat strikes were forbidden contractually and legally, and that these hotheads should not be followed.[39]

We have more information about several extremely high-profile youth wildcats that hit Canada in the summer of 1966. While militant young workers smashed onto the scene in the United States in 1972 at the UAW strike in Lordstown, Ohio, captivating a national audience, the Canadian story had emerged seven years earlier. This happened thanks to strikes in Sudbury by workers with Steelworkers Local 6500, in Hamilton by Steelworkers Local 1005, and across Canada with the railway workers in the Canadian Brotherhood of Railway, Transport and General Workers Union. These are significant for several reasons: they demonstrate the power of youth in the largest of Canada's industrial operations, they illustrate the different approaches taken by labour toward strikes, and most importantly, they present the largest amount of source material to draw on. They all took place at roughly the same time, peaking in August 1966. Furthermore, a large industrial union like USWA 1005 at Stelco is seen as a "classic case," setting national trends and, by virtue of its size and strategic position in the economy, assuming a great import.[40]

USWA 1005 and USWA 6500 were members of the same international union, which allows us good opportunities for contrast. August 1966 was a tough month for Steelworkers officials as they gathered in a climate of industrial unrest at two of their largest workplaces. At both, young men were the sparks that ignited large conflagrations, confounding union leaders, government agents, and managers alike. The strikes were also popular in the two locals, though some of this had to do with youth culture colliding into picket-line traditions. One could throw up a picket line and have it respected, albeit amid confusion. These were demographic concentrations of young people, feeling alienated and physically threatened, and seeking to change their conditions for the better.

At both locations, working-class masculinity played a significant role as managers challenged young workers' courage. As noted, these were overwhelmingly male work forces. Some women had been hired on earlier at Stelco, but this practice had ended in 1962 and the workforce remained overwhelmingly male. At Inco, it was a man's world until 1974, when young women were again hired. In addition, most of the workers were white, as was common in industrial workforces in central Canada before changes to immigration legislation in 1967 and 1976.

Women played a vital role in these events. In Hamilton, women held the picket line while men went to a ratification vote; in the aftermath of the Sudbury strike, much was made of educating the wives and girlfriends of union members to control them. This suggests a collective aspect: individuals did not make decisions on their own but in the context of solid working-class families and structures. If union leaders wanted to restrain young workers from hare-brained strikes, they sought to educate their partners; if they needed to hold the line, they had a ready, willing, and trusted group to do so.

Hamilton is a useful starting place in trying to understand this youth revolt. Here, Stelco was a significant and very large employer, with a long history of labour strife. The company had emerged in the early twentieth century as an amalgamation of several iron and steel corporations, growing into the largest and most successful steel corporation in Canada by the end of the First World War and remaining profitable through the Great Depression and beyond.[41] Although skilled men had a long tradition of resistance in the plants, they were unsuccessful in gaining union recognition until the Second World War.[42] Wartime legislation forced collective bargaining, and tensions erupted following the war in a hard-fought 1946 strike that saw union security won by the Steelworkers.[43]

Workers were organized into Local 1005 of the Steelworkers, a politically divided local from the beginning. These divisions were initially between Communists and social democrats (members of the Co-operative Commonwealth Federation), subsequently coalescing into quasi-formal left-wing and right-wing political factions before again splitting on the question of nationalism versus internationalism.[44] There was further tension as leaders were accused of sweetheart deals, especially the 1964 agreement that was ratified by a slim 10 percent margin.[45] The 1961 defection of the union president to management was seen as proof to many of a much broader cozy relationship.[46] In the archives, handwritten notes on mid-1960s union elections and negotiations indicate a tense working environment, with one stating that there was a breakdown in communication and threats of wildcats and work stoppages.[47]

Youth issues became a significant current in the sixties as Stelco expanded dramatically. In 1960, Stelco had 7,258 employees; by 1966, it had reached the then record level of 11,762.[48] Low-seniority employees, often the youngest, were geographically clustered in Stelco's newer mills, an "inter-generational separation of the workplace," according to Maxwell Flood.[49] Young people were disproportionately involved in the unrest: the average age of members who made court appearances was 28.6 years, as opposed to a much higher average in the broader workforce.[50] Most were wartime babies. Those involved were certainly seen as youthful by their elders; the local's recording secretary termed them the "young bucks."[51]

Tensions were growing throughout 1966, a bargaining year. Union officials had difficulty keeping their members under control. Early that year, members had stopped working after three members were fired for drinking on the job. In addition, the usual pressure for settlement was compounded by fears surrounding technological change and automation. Low-seniority men, most threatened by potential automation-related job loss, felt this acutely. On the hot summer evening of 3 August 1966, negotiators met with the provincial Conciliation Board, an instrument of the postwar settlement designed to cool tensions. It did not work.

That night, young men gathered in the lunchroom of the Hot Strip Finishing Department, a unit largely comprising low-seniority men. They were heatedly discussing the negotiating team's progress, decrying their lack of information. As tensions rose, another young man burst in. A foreman had told him "You guys haven't got the guts to walk out," he declared, setting the room off. "Let's show the ——!" the men cried as they began shutting down equipment and gathering others together. Their masculinity had been challenged, and they were not about to put up with it. A union steward came over to tell them to "go back and settle it the union way," but to no avail: members quickly set up picket lines.[52] The first line was about two hundred men strong and quickly grew, especially once the overnight shift arrived – many joined, swelling the line to about three thousand members.[53] Union leaders declared the strike illegal, denouncing it as irresponsible and futile, and ordered members back to work, but again to no avail.[54]

Confusion reigned as word of the shutdown spread. The Department of Labour could not find out what was happening, as the local failed to answer the phone and management simply placed the entire Stelco switchboard on busy.[55] Journalists came down to the plant to try to piece their stories together, a difficult undertaking. There were no spokespeople, no leaders, no press releases, and no manifestos, just picket lines and angry young men. One supervisor told the *Toronto Telegram* that management had been staying late in anticipation of the strike, and that the workers "wanted something but they didn't know what."[56] An older steelworker dismissed the wildcat as youthful troublemaking, telling the *Globe and Mail* that they were "young men who had worked at the plant for only six to nine months and were already up to their necks in trouble."[57] Flood would later argue that the wildcat stemmed from concerns over technological change, "job integrity," job security, and the contrast between rising profits and increasing numbers of contractors.[58]

This was, needless to say, an enormous industrial action. Some 10,992 workers were now on strike.[59] Workers honoured picket lines. The local president, John Morgan, arrived to make his stance clear: the men had to return to work, the lines had to dissipate, and penalties would be severe if they did not listen to him. "We're fed up with you, we don't want you," shouted one picketer, and several physically assaulted Morgan.[60] Police placed a tearful Morgan into protective custody, before 300 officers (out of a total police force of 420) broke the picket line to allow managers entry.[61] The street scene was remarkable. About five hundred men now milled around in front of Stelco, moving in and out of nearby restaurants and bars. Cars were burned. Thirty-three mostly young men were arrested for variously obstructing or assaulting police, or causing a disturbance. At one point, picketers sat down en masse, obstructing traffic.[62] Perhaps they were taking a page from the contemporary civil rights and anti-war movements, or from a previous labour history of sit-down strikes.

Police eventually restored order, and a city clerk–supervised vote at the Civic Stadium (today's Ivor Wynne Stadium) saw 4,319 members favouring a return to work, 1,142 against, and hundreds more leaving without voting. Wives held the line while the local convened its largest union meeting in recent history.[63] This shows the level of organization at work. The union was trying to control its members, but it seems that all involved agreed that the wives could be trusted. Working-class families were important components of resistance. Indeed, during the strike, the *Hamilton Spectator* noted how many wives had come down to the lines to bring lunches to their husbands; several told the paper that although they had been caught off guard by the strike and hoped for a speedy settlement, they still stood by their husbands.[64]

While wives held the line, the Civic Stadium hosted a tense meeting. Leaders were booed, divisions exposed. "We will cross any picket line in the morning if there is one," declared Morgan. Some asked what happened to the thirty-three arrested workers, but got no response.[65] The next morning, 8 August, the strike ended.[66] Negotiations resumed. Stelco announced that sixteen employees would be suspended and thirty-five fired because of their role in the wildcat.[67] Men again began walking out. The union implored the dismissed men to sign a notice calling on their peers to stay on the job, to be widely posted. Twenty-seven of the men signed. Peace was kept.

A tentative agreement was reached ten days later and presented. It would have made the men the best-compensated steelworkers in the world; it also included a new pension plan.[68] The first attempt at ratification failed by 557 votes because of the failure to get the fired union members reinstated, though a second attempt (which saw additional seniority language and an additional three-cents-an-hour raise) succeeded by 2,460 votes. The new contract was lucrative, but nineteen men were permanently terminated for their role in the strike.[69]

The strike would witness an irreconcilable parting between two large political factions. In the strike's aftermath, the autonomy faction was able to capitalize on the unrest and point to the suppressive role officials played. By August, the faction elected fourteen of twenty-one positions to the upcoming Canadian Labour Congress (CLC) conference and subsequently took over the executive.[70] In 1967, the left-wing group fully took power and substantially changed the union's direction. Local 1005 would play a supportive role at a host of progressive strikes, joining young New Leftists from across Ontario, as well as forming a hub of support for the Waffle.

In Local 6500 at Inco, we see more evidence of a youth revolt. Negotiations were ongoing for a collective agreement there as well for the local's 15,767 members. Inco had been operating in the Sudbury Basin since its inception during the First World War, growing into one of the world's largest nickel producers by the end of the Second World War. The Communist-led International Union of Mine, Mill, and Smelter Workers (Mine Mill) had been carrying out attempts to unionize workers since 1919, although it was not until the Second World War – and the example of the 1941 Kirkland Lake strike – that inroads were made; by 1944, Inco was organized as Local 598 of Mine Mill.[71] By the 1950s, however, as part of the broader Cold War context of anti-Communism, Mine Mill was expelled from the CLC and the United Steelworkers began raiding its Sudbury local. A disastrous 1958 strike by Mine Mill – demonstrating to some the need for broader links – had resulted in infighting between members who wanted to affiliate with the CLC and national Mine Mill supporters (who denounced mainstream unions), creating an opening for a raid.[72] By 1962, after a long fight between the two unions, USWA Local 6500 won the right to represent Inco workers.[73] It had been a close vote, with 7,182 for USWA versus 6,951 for Mine Mill, and 168 abstainers (whom the Ontario Labour Relations Board counted as Mine Mill supporters); the USWA thus won by only fifteen votes over the required 50 percent of membership level.[74] In 1965, Mine Mill attempted a raid on Steel, which failed by 2,000 votes. Local 6500 was on shaky ground.

Contract negotiations began in April 1966, before the 10 July expiration date. The atmosphere was tense, since Steelworkers saw an opportunity to take revenge on Inco for the 1958 defeat. As Seguin explains, "[The] '66 wildcat didn't start from '66 ... it got its origins in 1958."[75] Negotiations reached an impasse and the matter went to a conciliation board, meaning that workers would have to work beyond the expiry of the agreement before they could strike. Graffiti began appearing throughout Inco: "No contract, no work – July 10."[76]

Keith Lovely, then twenty-four, remembers June 1966 as his real introduction to unionism. That month, a slowdown began: work-to-rules, lost keys, sabotage, all of which hampered production. RCMP investigators described the ongoing sabotage, such as manipulating railway switches, cutting ladder rungs, slashing tires, and tampering with other equipment like hoses and gauges.[77] Lovely remembers that it was all about everybody sticking together, and he learned what happened to "some miners, older miners, who wouldn't slow down."[78] The offending miner would go down into his stope, only to find at the end of his shift that his ladder had been pulled up behind him; he would need management assistance to leave.

High wages led to a wide hiring zone. In 1966, Inco had recently hired a large number of young men from Atlantic Canada, particularly Newfoundland. In their interviews with Flood, several of these young men expressed resentment: they believed they had been brought in en masse and made financially dependent on the company so that they would stay. These unmarried workers lived together in communal residence-style company housing. Many worked together at the Levack Mine, a remote work site about forty-five kilometres from downtown Sudbury up Highway 144 toward Timmins. Levack was home to mostly young workers with no seniority; because of its remoteness, it was "mostly new hires [who] went there."[79] Many aimed to switch to a mine closer to Sudbury. Seguin remembers that some regarded Levack miners as "Local 6501" because of its "isolation and independence."[80] But there was a handful of older miners there as well, and the Newfoundlanders were thus susceptible to "events being interpreted for them by the 'old hands' in the mine."[81] Without much experience in industrial workforces, the young workers were open to having their elder counterparts explain and interpret traditions of resistance, but they also had their own notions of justice and action.

It was at 2,200 feet below the surface at Levack that the simmering tension boiled over. As noted, miners worked "collar to collar," surface to surface. A miner received the day's orders in the lunchroom; if received earlier, he still had a chance to have a cup of tea or coffee, or a sandwich, before heading into his stope.[82] Yet on 14 July, in light of rising tensions, the men were forbidden to gather on the job. Consequently, the foreman stopped the young men from eating, violating a twenty-year mining tradition.[83] The young men refused to start work as ordered, were sent up to the surface, and the shift followed in solidarity.

Word spread. Some miners were contacted by phone – the source of the calls remains unknown to me – and told to report being ill.[84] Seguin recalls that a single worker went to the Copper Cliff refinery, posted a sign that read Nobody's Working, and "they all just honoured the picket line. One picket! Because they wanted to get at the company, '58 – the hate that they had for this company that had beat them up so badly in '58."[85] Local officials were quick to condemn the walkout, and president Tony Soden went to Levack to implore workers to stay on the job, saying that there was no point in walking out.[86]

The union's position remains murky. Seguin claims that, officially, the union unequivocally condemned the strike. Others felt that the union did not mean it. "I think the union leadership didn't do everything they could [*laughs*] to stop this wildcat strike," Lovely says – that although the union did not support the strike, it did not stop it. "The members really ran this strike," he says. Norris Valiquette describes the meeting where Soden unequivocally declared the strike illegal – "He said that a number of times, he made it very clear that was his message" – but that a whisper campaign started to the effect that management felt the union did not have support. This was a provocative dare to the membership. Valiquette does not know who started the whisper campaign but suspects officials may have played a role. Flood cites an interviewee who claimed that Soden had actually told the workers privately not to listen to him.[87]

In any case, it is clear that, as RCMP agents noted, the union's executive board had lost control of the striking members.[88] Seguin, who was in charge of the local while Soden was negotiating in Toronto during much of the strike, clearly remembers that the union had almost no control in the strike's first days. He claims that the young miners had no understanding of industrial legality or of how unions worked, and that they spread the wildcat: they had "no education about unions, how the democracy in the union works, how you got to take votes to conduct these things."[89] Officials began to grow fearful; one noted to Flood, "We were reluctant to stop it – we could have been beaten up." Flood concludes that from 15 July onward, the union "had lost control of the men and the situation was 'wild.'" Officials were told to stay away from the gates lest they be physically assaulted. Another told Flood, "We lost control for three days. There really was no need for picket lines. Nobody wanted to go to work ... the three-day period was wild. I saw the Molotov cocktails, the guns and the dynamite."[90]

It is clear that youth played a significant role. Seguin is unequivocal: "The real militants at that time were the young guys. The young guys on the picket line were the most militant of any group ... There weren't many young guys who weren't part of that group of militants, real wild-eyed kind of guys."[91] These were violent picket lines. In one incident on the first day of the strike at Levack, an employee who had stayed inside the mine during the walkout viciously stabbed a twenty-nine-year-old picketer in the chest.[92] Apparently, he had a new car parked outside the plant, and when he came out of the mine he could not even recognize it because of vandalism. "I guess he lost it," Valiquette concludes.[93] Elsewhere, cars were overturned or had windows smashed, and police officers reported several fist fights. One worker described the evening of 15 July as "like a festival," with crowds of people, "Newfies" playing guitars, singing, dancing – and consisting of "mostly young guys. I don't think there would be one of them over 30 years of age."[94] RCMP officers also noted drinking, and that police feared that picketers would break into explosive storage facilities.[95] Helicopters were ferrying managers past picket lines, and shots were fired at them. Seguin had to go to those responsible and pretend he was about to report them to the police to get them to stop.[96]

The union tried to regain control. Nobody was being let in past the picket lines, contrary to law, and in several cases nobody was even being let out. Pictures of the strike show boulders strewn across roads, pickets manning these ad hoc barricades under the watchful eyes of Inco police force officers.[97] Management refused to negotiate unless its staff could return to work. Union leaders printed up passes that would get them through the lines, but rank-and-file members on the lines refused to accept them, and called for a meeting in response.[98] Lovely recalls a contractor at the Creighton Mine having a note signed by Soden to pass through the picket lines to pick up a pair of boots beyond the fence; one of the stewards responded by saying, "Tony Soden isn't running this fucking strike. We are. So get out of here."[99]

The union eventually regained control, harnessing the rank and file's ire. A large gathering of six thousand members met at the Sudbury Arena for a debate: four men spoke in favour of accepting the bargaining team's recommendation to return to work; four men spoke against it. Soden came to speak and was greeted by "jeers and boos."[100] Seguin explained the rationale behind holding the big meeting: "One thing about workers: they may not like the results of a vote, but once you have a democratically run vote, as long as it's run fair, they'll abide by it."[101] Workers decided by a three-to-one margin to return to work, but a proposed contract was overwhelmingly rejected three weeks later.[102] There was one more wildcat strike during the negotiations, prompted by their slow pace, but it was short-lived, ending three days later when a formal agreement was signed on 16 September.[103] In this agreement, management doubled its earlier wage offer; the nickel demand during the Vietnam War made any work stoppage too costly.[104] Concessions, however, were made by the union in return for rehiring workers fired during the strike.[105] In the aftermath, as we will see, the local would regain control over the youthful rank and file.

It was not simply the Steelworkers and the UAW that experienced youth unrest. In the summer of 1965, the Canadian Brotherhood of Railway, Transport and General Workers Union (CBRT) employees with Canadian National Railway (CN) began a cross-country wildcat strike, starting in the large Toronto rail yards represented by Local 327. There, workers accumulated demerit points for infractions, a sore point. On 3 June, a truck driver with five years' seniority on the job lost a shipping carton, received his fiftieth demerit, and was summarily demoted to a porter position. His fellow workers walked off the job.[106] This was followed by mass walkouts elsewhere in Ontario: in London, Oakville, Brantford, and Hamilton. In Hamilton, the local leadership explicitly condoned the walkout.[107] The next day, the CBRT prepared all locals for a solidarity walkout. This proved to be an unnecessary step, as by 8 June it had made significant gains: no discipline for walkout participants, a review of demerit points, and consideration of a labour-management committee. However, this was at the cost of the union explicitly pledging to never support or condone future illegal strikes.[108] This event was significant, as it bequeathed to workers a lesson on the fruits of militancy but also put the union in a critical position for disciplining employees. Younger workers were paying attention.

Through the summer of 1966, master collective agreements were being negotiated between CN, Canadian Pacific Railway (CP), and the CBRT. A previous collective agreement had expired in December; a conciliation board had been established even earlier but took nine months to deliberate, concluding its meetings in mid-July. Pressures were growing within locals for a settlement. In Toronto, Local 26 was under watch by the RCMP, which noted the emergence of militant groups and that "most of the rank and file is prepared to walk out." The "majority will need very little urging to fall into line with the more militant group," presumed to be Trotskyist, the RCMP continued.[109] By August, the Conciliation Board had still not issued its report. Workers were demanding a significant wage gain of ninety-seven cents an hour. On the evening of 2 August, three hundred men walked off their jobs in Toronto, expressing frustration with delays and their union.[110] Unlike the previous summer, however, the union moved to stop them, and the *Toronto Star* reported strikers' tension with their leadership.[111] Many milled around in front of the rail depots, leaving when they found no work.

This was not an officially sanctioned or endorsed wildcat. This was a strike of young people. The *Star*'s front-page picture on the second day of the strike was of young men in front of their depot. One has his hair cut fashionably, like one of the Beatles, and is wearing a blazer; the other holds a sign reading Poor Contract, No Money. According to the *Toronto Telegram,* older workers blamed younger workers for the strike. One was quoted as saying, "It's completely senseless. Many of us cannot afford to lose wages through an illegal strike. We only get $2.09 cents [sic] an hour to keep a family. A bachelor hasn't this problem."[112] The strike collapsed quickly. CN employees voted to return to work, while CP workers shouted "Chicken!" at them and accused them of being cowards. They did, however, return to the picket lines briefly for an additional day after wildcat leaders hinted at reprisals.[113] Employees decided to return to work on 6 August, but only after rumours that the entire executive was going to resign.[114] Before the legal strike deadline of 26 August, workers in Montreal, Windsor, Chatham, and Wallaceburg launched a brief wildcat on 18 August; the union made it clear that although they were not illegal strikes per se, they were certainly unauthorized.[115] A legal strike *was* finally waged, throughout late August and early September, before the government ordered the workers back to work with a guarantee of an 18 percent wage increase over two years.[116]

These examples highlight the key dimensions of this unrest. Tens of thousands of workers were involved, the weaknesses of the postwar settlement exposed. It was no longer just enough for youth to be happy with a tedious job and the ensuing pay; instead, they demanded respect, better working conditions, and the continued defence of customary rights. Workplace control was at stake and, buoyed by the surging economy that had hit fuller levels of employment, the benefits, the gains to be made, and the exhilaration outweighed the limited potential consequences of short-term wage loss or, at worst, the loss of a low-seniority job.

As 1966 ended, the upswing in labour unrest tapered off, though the amount of labour militancy continued at a far higher level than the pre-1964 figures. A good degree of continuity can be seen past the wildcat wave. The year 1967 saw over a million fewer hours lost to labour action, about 4 million versus the 5 million of the previous year, but this was still far higher than 1963's approximately 1 million lost.[117] Similarly, the distinct phenomenon of youth leading wildcats had also come to an end – though it continued through to the early 1970s and beyond on shifted ground. The reasons for the decline shed light on the exceptional nature of the wildcat wave, demonstrating the interplay between an anti-authoritarian youth culture and the labour market.

Some of the reasons for this decline lay in economics, others in improved control mechanisms. In Sudbury, for example, there was by the 1970s a crisis of youth unemployment, with many of the young men who had come for boomtime work finding themselves on the streets or living in tents, closets, and other transient places.[118] The unemployment rate for males aged twenty to twenty-four had been at its lowest point in 1966, but in 1967 it began to increase, peaking in 1970 at 10.5 percent.[119] The risks, so seemingly low only a few years earlier, were higher when the spectre of unemployment seemed more real. There were still instances of youth conflict within unions and on the streets, however. Ed Finn, the labour columnist, observed in 1971 that the "generation gap" was still present, that youth had learned to "reject authoritarianism in the schools, only to be plunged into an environment ... where their every act is dictated by someone else." He warned of a looming threat to union leaders from the rank and file, pointing out that the top officers were "still" in their fifties and sixties, conservative and cautious, and that "they bitterly resent the youngsters who are coming into their unions and telling them they may have to modernize their methods and outlook."[120] In December 1967, Harry Greenwood, the Local 1005 recording secretary, wrote to the USWA's public relations director and noted that there were only three stewards or committee-men less than thirty years old. "After witnessing all of the 'young bucks' in action last August," he wrote, "I'm surprised that we only have three in this category, so I guess the 'slate' will not be facing any threat for awhile yet."[121]

Even as late as 1973 there was still youth unrest within unions, though to a lesser degree. Through August and early September 1973, fifty-six thousand non-operational staff of CN launched a massive nationwide strike. Robert Laxer has argued that this was a significant strike in that it represented a cross-roads: the vital workers could have led the labour movement across Canada to improve living conditions, or be defeated and prevent a pattern of wage gains being set. A week after the strike began, the federal Parliament reconvened in a special sitting to legislate the workers back to work. After the legislation passed, both the CLC and the New Democratic Party (NDP) counselled compliance. There was widespread resistance to this among locals, from British Columbia's Lower Mainland to Calgary to Thunder Bay to Windsor.[122]

Thanks to *Canadian Dimension* and Cy Gonick's first-hand reporting, we have a good narrative of one such local at Winnipeg's CN Symington Yard. "I want it recorded that on Labour Day 1973, the union bosses ordered the workers back and the NDP sold us out for 4 an hour," declared an angry young man ("maybe 24") on 3 September at a union meeting.[123] His local had symbolically ignored the back-to-work order for two days over the weekend, and the young members were unhappy with the token gesture and the return to work without even a formal membership vote (as had taken place in some of the other locals, including that of New Westminster, British Columbia).[124] When workers returned to work, things appeared normal, but by 10 a.m. an illegal picket line was thrown up outside the shop by "a dozen or so young men," subsequently joined by "a few hundred others." For days, the yards were shut down.[125] Throughout the strike, mostly young men, bolstered by a handful of older ones, ran a picket line. One older worker looked at the line and declared, "[It's] the young guys that are responsible for this. They started it. If it weren't for them, we wouldn't be here now. They're different. They're fearless. They don't give a damn for the company or the government or the unions. It's a new generation."[126]

Much of the young workers' ire was certainly directed at their unions. When the local leader attempted to cross the line, he was turned back. One of the younger workers explained that there was "business management," "union management," and the workers: "The union is just the other side of the management coin ... And they wonder why we don't come to local meetings."[127] They operated a very different form of picket line: no leaders, no picket captains, no committees, no order, no scheduled picket times – people arrived, people left in a "spontaneous" manner. As *Canadian Dimension* reported, "There's no consensus as to why they are there. Mostly it's defiance of the union leadership." It was also opposition to back-to-work legislation. They did eventually go back to work. The enduring impact of such a wildcat is lost, but the magazine did note that there had been no plans for a sustained rank-and-file committee. The lack of organization may have been the movement's downfall. Yet Karen Naylor, a young worker who joined the union in 1973, remembers being invited to join the union executive after the wildcat period, around 1974. One of the "old guys" said to her, "Ooh, come in, we don't usually get many young people here" – then continued, "That's okay, we like young people, we have a position for you on the executive if you want it."[128] Although Naylor's tenure as political education chairwoman was marked by controversy, especially when the executive threatened to resign when her newspaper denounced the ruling provincial NDP government in an article attacking their support of strikebreakers elsewhere in the province, the very fact that she held that position demonstrates a degree of receptivity that had been absent earlier.

Beyond 1966, youth continued to play an important role in union unrest, albeit not on the scale that had characterized the earlier wildcat wave. As Cy Gonick wrote in 1974, young workers continued to be "conscious of the dehumanizing effects of their jobs," and "less willing to accept the arbitrary authority of bosses."[129] By 1974, however, a critical difference was the growing awareness of youth's role within union structures.

These young workers had challenged their employers and occasionally their unions in an economic and cultural context conducive to militancy. Fuller employment emboldened young workers to take chances with employment – if worst came to worst and they were terminated, there was usually work at the next factory or mine. But this alone does not explain the unrest. The development of an anti-authoritarian youth culture, realized in different dimensions by working and middle-class youth, certainly led many to challenge their conditions. There was also a belief in progress and hope, as explored in Chapter 1. These young workers were seeing material improvements on a large scale and thus had expectations: basic material conditions, respect on the job, health and safety regulations, and *control*. Battles were being waged for participatory democracy in universities, and a form of this battle was occurring within workplaces and unions. For reasons of timing and culture, however, there was little outreach between these disparate currents of youth unrest. The battles occurring within workplaces would have an enduring impact on union hierarchies as they moved to reassert control over their unruly members.

After the Wave: Governments and Unions Wake Up

As early as late 1966, governments and academics began studying youth unrest. The Ontario and federal governments launched commissions of inquiry into labour relations. Academics such as John Crispo and Harry Arthurs began writing about the wildcat wave and ruminating on youth militancy. Union officials also began publicly and privately considering the impact of youth on their unions, and began thinking of ways both to involve them and to mitigate their pernicious effects.

In December 1966, Prime Minister Lester B. Pearson established the Task Force on Labour Relations, responding to the elevated levels of labour unrest. Chaired by McGill University's dean of arts, Harry D. Woods, it consisted of three more industrial relations experts: Abbé Gérard Dion, founder of the Department of Industrial Relations at Laval University; John Crispo, founder of the Centre for Industrial Relations at the University of Toronto; and A.W.R. Carrothers, president of the University of Calgary and previously first director of the University of British Columbia's Institute of Industrial Relations. These four men had the mandate to "examine industrial relations in Canada and to make recommendations to the government with respect to public policy in labour legislation and on such other matters that were considered relevant to the public interest."[130] The task force would commission more than eighty reports, from histories of trade unions and studies of public opinion to constitutional legal opinions and notable case studies of various wildcat strikes.

The most significant study was Stuart Marshall Jamieson's *Times of Trouble: Labour Unrest and Industrial Conflict in Canada, 1900-66.* Jamieson, an economist and sociologist at the University of British Columbia and author of the classic 1957 text *Industrial Relations in Canada*, was commissioned to produce a history of labour unrest in Canada. This was an unprecedented, historically significant report. Jamieson's argument was that the wildcat wave was not without precedent and thus needed to be seen in a broader context. He maintained that Canada's labour history was actually marked by a tremendous amount of violence, "second only to the United States," and that the events of 1965-66 are unsurprising in this context.[131]

The period was, however, unusual in its proportion of wildcat strikes – a quarter to a third in Jamieson's estimation – and that these were especially marked by violence and by the reluctance of rank-and-file members to endorse settlements.[132] He noted that this was more characteristic of labour relations in the 1930s. He further noted the significant role young workers played. Unions had grown slowly through the 1950s and early 1960s compared with the broader labour market, meaning that there were lots of young workers without leadership positions; they would become Young Turks in the face of older leaders, who "tended to hang on to their posts."[133] Crucially, Jamieson wrote about the broader social role of youth. Demography, he stressed through rhetorical underlining, was the most important factor affecting Canadian industrial relations. More youth meant more unrest: "One does not have to overdo the clichés about youth being more radical and idealistic, more energetic and impatient for change, etc., to accept the validity of this broad generalization ... the mere fact of numbers alone is giving younger people a new sense of power."[134] These young workers, raised in affluence, were "*not* impressed with the appurtenances and status symbols that their elders have acquired" and instead followed nonconformist paths. He concluded that these youth "have contributed a particularly militant new element to the rank-and-file of some unions," with their higher schooling, propensity to question, and unwillingness to "accept, resignedly, the monotony, bureaucratic regimentation and submission to authority that is imposed by the discipline of the modern industrial system."[135]

This was a powerful statement connecting the wildcat wave to broader demographic changes. Other academics raised similar points. In his report for the task force, H.C. Pentland of the University of Manitoba noted that leaders had failed to "keep in touch with their memberships, especially the younger part." By continuing to represent older, conservative workers, they were growing increasingly far from their younger, aggressive ones.[136] Pentland was not alone in observing this generational divide. Arthurs and Crispo noted the increasing level of education in the labour force in a 1967 speech addressing the recent labour unrest. They contended that this was a "healthy sign of renewed trade union vitality," as unionists, "like so many in our society, seem less disposed today to accept the status quo."[137]

Responding to this insecurity, union leaders began making strong statements about the need to involve rank-and-file youth. The UAW had a strong response. In early 1968, newly appointed national director Dennis McDermott pointed out how young workers were different from his own generation: "The young worker of today is not servile. He was not raised in an environment of fear and virtual industrial slavery, as many of us were. He knows his civil rights and liberties. He will not be intimidated."[138]

At the local level, USWA Local 6500 moved quickly after the disastrous wildcat experience. Seguin identified education as a key problem: young people had no education about unions, and did not realize the laws that governed bargaining, strikes, and picket lines (as evidenced by the boulders strewn in front of mine gates) – and this needed to be fixed. He became local president in 1967 and instituted a training system: all stewards and committee people went through a union course, and future picket captains were educated. The union also recognized the importance of families to working-class members, focusing on wives and girlfriends: "We even educated their spouses or girlfriends about how a proper union operates," he says, "and how a strike is conducted and how it occurs and who runs the stuff." The result: "No wild stuff, and control, you know ... in fact, the union is running the strike, not the workers! ... Ever since then we've had disciplined strikes."[139]

When Local 6500 went on strike again in 1969 over improved wages, benefits, and health and safety legislation, it was a different story. Dave Patterson, briefly picket captain at the Copper Cliff North Mine before being fired when he refused to let anybody in or out ("What's the sense of being on strike if you can't do that?"), remembers how 1966 loomed large: "In '69, the union kept stressing that it doesn't matter what happens, you can't walk out. If we wildcat, that's what they want, it'll hurt us, we can't win."[140] The 1969 settlement was controversial: a pre-strike slowdown had left Inco without a nickel stockpile, and prices were high because of the Vietnam War. The leadership, including Seguin, thought that the proposed settlement was good and voted to accept it – especially given its groundbreaking language on health and safety committees. A dissident faction, however, felt they could have received more.[141]

The following years saw a greater involvement of younger workers in leadership positions. This culminated with the 1975/76 election of twenty-seven-year-old Patterson to the position of local president. Norris Valiquette, who later came to support Patterson, describes many members' reaction: "Holy geez, here's a long-haired hippie going to become president of our local, that's just impossible!"[142] This was a notable development, culminating in Patterson's election as District 6 director and the subsequent "civil war" within the broader international union.[143] Some young men had found places within the union, coming up through labour education, but they would come, in the late 1970s, to butt up against their aging leaders once again. But as we have seen, the young members of Local 1005 did not play a significant role in the aftermath of the strike.[144]

The move toward youth education came at the local level within the Steelworkers, at least until the appointment of D'Arcy Martin as national education director for the USWA in 1978. The UAW took a different approach. By early 1968, the groundwork began to be laid for a youth conference within the UAW to address the growing perception of a crisis. At the conference, the differences between the Canadian and American experiences would be illustrated. Young members would be brought together in Detroit in April 1969 to get them to describe "the special problems they have as union members" and to help leaders learn.[145] Personally planned by UAW president Walter Reuther, this endeavour involved the entire executive board.

Who would the delegates be? Many of the selections were from a youth "establishment." UAW Region 4, representing midwestern workers, sent one young man who was secretary of a local county Democratic Party committee, as well as another member of the Iowa Democratic Party. Region 8, in the southwestern United States, sent a recording secretary and a local president. The other regions did the same: local members of the Democratic apparatus or officers within influential union locals were sent.[146] Canada took a different approach, with McDermott selecting two young men, Mike Lyons and Claude Petelle. His rationale for this selection is fascinating, and provides a window onto the issues facing Canada.

Mike Lyons, from the Northern Telecommunications factory in Bramalea, Ontario, and an officer with Local 1535, was selected for interesting reasons. As McDermott explained, Lyons was a "very well educated young man, an office worker, a socialist and an active member of the New Left. He represents a new breed of cat which we can expect to emerge in our more sophisticated white collar units."[147] This was a remarkable difference from the approach American regions took, and demonstrated the degree to which McDermott was dealing with the issue: through engagement and respect. Indeed, Claude Petelle, his second nomination, was chosen because he "represents the not so quiet revolutionary from Quebec. He is reportedly a separatist and whether we like or dislike his views, again he represents the young generation in Quebec."[148] A third nominee was suggested, Dorothy Heck, a "drop-out" who had begun working at seventeen and represented the "not-so-educated" female workers that were becoming more common. This represented thoughtful engagement with the youth crisis. It was not an abstract sentiment but an extension of McDermott's statements on the youth problem – just as he had told participants in the 1968 Labour Day parade about the "same sociological bag"[149] into which he would throw the wave of strikes and university unrest. By sending these individuals to Detroit, McDermott was explicitly recognizing youth culture.

Reflecting the rather staid origins of the majority of the youth delegates, the conference itself was unremarkable. Delegates were broken into small groups to brainstorm recommendations, which were subsequently personally presented to the executive. Delegates discussed several issues: youth barriers, collective bargaining goals, which broader social issues should be engaged with, and general social and economic questions about youth in the workplace.[150] An extensive list of recommendations was presented to the international executive, several pages long. Some recommendations were significant. There was widespread disengagement with union newspapers, which needed to provide for dissent and the voices of young people; there needed to be more communication with the rank and file, and limits on executive power; and the union needed to organize more white-collar workers.[151]

The UAW was the most receptive to these recommendations, but other unions and federations took action as well. By 1971, OFL president David Archer was clear in several speeches. In his annual address to the OFL, he held that unions needed to provide more opportunities to youth and women so that they could "play their full role in the trade union movement," and that union activities had to be made attractive and meaningful.[152] Indeed, Archer explicitly declared during his Labour Day address that "younger members are coming into our ranks. They are questioning the old collective bargaining procedures and the slow-moving grievance technique. They are demanding, and rightly so, more say in the company decision-making policy."[153] Even USWA national director William Mahoney, who had emerged as a vocal and outspoken opponent of the New Left-inspired Waffle movement, made public pronouncements that youth needed to be reckoned with in the unions. He told the *Globe and Mail* that "younger workers are far more concerned than were their fathers about such fringe benefits as frequent and adequate breaks," and employers – especially in resource towns – needed to factor in the possibility of such pent-up strikes in their financial calculations. Yet he did not dismiss the union's role, stating that unions needed to "work like hell" to persuade their members to adhere to industrial legality.[154] At the CLC, the director of the legislative and government affairs department observed that young workers "are better educated, less awed by authority. They will not accept tamely the low earnings that have been the lot of many tradesmen."[155] The federal minister of labour was sympathetic toward youth as well, and in 1970 astutely summarized the problems facing them in the labour movement: "We have taught our children to be responsible citizens, but have given them a value system that is too often contradictory. Their disagreement is not with the aims, but with the practices of our system."[156]

Compared with the United States, it is remarkable how early much of this had occurred in Canada. Young workers had been part of a broader rank-and-file rebellion in the United States from the late 1960s onward, but it was not until 1972 that the experience of young baby boomer workers really crystallized in the public consciousness.[157] That year, UAW Local 1112 struck the General Motors plant in Lordstown, Ohio, as young workers rebelled against line speed-ups and called not for wage increases but for control, justice, and a better quality of work life.[158] As Barbara Garson wrote in *Harper's*, "More and more young workers now seem to be fed up with the whole ethos of the industrial system."[159] As media armies descended on what *Newsweek* called an "industrial Woodstock," they described what had been established years earlier in Canada as new challenges to the labour movement.[160] Although the ethos on display at Lordstown did not grace Canadian media coverage, this current was present on the lines and in the mines of Canada.

By 1972, Canadian union officials had at least taken hesitant steps toward recognizing the importance of young workers. According to Finn, there was increasing recognition of the growing gap between old and young within unions.[161] The *Globe and Mail*'s Wilfred List convened twelve union members, mostly young, to provide their impressions in a 1972 group interview, with the goal of exploring youth's "new militancy within organized labour" and beginning with the premise that "younger members are more impatient, less docile and question the union leadership more than their elders."[162] Their narrative was change. One young Local 1005 member noted that more young people were now involved, taking over union offices and bringing a new inquisitive attitude. The consensus was that the most militant workers were still young people, and that more change was needed.

Conclusion

Youth unrest extended from factories to mines to university campuses, albeit divided by several factors. These young workers had refused to "grow up" and accept their assigned role in the postwar economy, instead continuing youthful traditions of resistance and anti-authoritarianism. This youth culture collided with a healthy mid-1960s labour market, reducing fears of unemployment and facilitating risk taking. On the shop floor, many realized the merits of direct action, unconstrained by notions of industrial legality preached by union leaders. Their leaders, however, moved to bring them within the mainstream house of labour and in some cases opened up avenues for promotion into the labour hierarchy. In addition, the increasing levels of youth unemployment throughout the decade, trending upward from its low of 1966, reduced the appeal of direct action – there might not be another job to move to. As many of these young workers moved into leadership positions, they would again encounter a renewed pushback from their elder counterparts within the movement. Here, as we will see, they would meet colleagues who had emerged from the New Left and were now making homes in the labour movement.

This would be in the future. Now, however, youth unrest declined amid rising youth unemployment and better education and control programs. No rank-and-file movement emerged out of the period's unrest – there was simply no opportunity or network for this between locals. Without proper communications methods, transportation, or something to forge a broader connection, these were isolated flashes of youth unrest, contained individually.

The irony would be that just as young workers were rising up against managers and industrial legality in record numbers, their New Leftist counterparts were writing them off as ineffective agents of social change. Instead, these largely middle-class youth were looking toward the nebulous "dispossessed." As described in the next chapter, only by 1967 would many look again toward the traditional working class as key to altering society. Yet the large explosion of youth militancy within unions was tapering off. Only by the mid-1970s would New Leftists begin moving into labour, bringing a transformative energy to the organization.

Through the mid-1960s and beyond, however, young workers were heard throughout the mills, factories, railroads, and other industrial operations of English Canada and Quebec. Questioning old norms and archaic ways of performing their duties, this generation brought a new vigour to a labour movement that was becoming an increasingly staid institution. They had grown up amid greater affluence than their Depression-era parents (though they were far from privileged), and they refused to accept the old ways. Although inevitably defeated by a combination of union, management, and state intervention, their revolts sent a message to unions and managers that they had a new generation to reckon with. As these young workers grew up through the 1970s and began to contest for positions within unions, a shift would begin.

3

Say Goodbye to the Working Class?
New Leftists Debate Social Change

Despite eruptions of youth anger within the factories, by 1965, New Leftists had largely written off workers as a force for social change. In his 1960 "Letter to the New Left," post-Marxian sociologist C. Wright Mills decried that New Leftists still clung to the working class as "*the* historic agency, or even the most important agency, in the face of the really historical evidence that now stands against this expectation."[1] Similar arguments appeared from other prominent theoreticians. Much of the Student Union for Peace Action (SUPA), Canada's pre-eminent New Leftist formation of the mid-1960s, took this injunction to heart. Its members engaged in debates that resulted in a loose consensus that, instead of the working class, social change would be found in the dispossessed – a nebulous concept that variously included students, First Nations, urban poor, and racialized minorities. Rather than pursuing an Old Left strategy of mobilizing the traditional working class, New Leftists went into depressed urban and rural areas, worked among First Nations, and sought to radicalize professionals.

This strategy eventually became a primary reason for SUPA's dissolution, as the approach crashed against the dual shores of a disappointing reality – community organizing was not leading to a revolution – and a growing global shift toward Marxism. The need to agree on an agent of social change, and the failure of New Leftists to arrive at any cohesive sense of self on this essential issue, led to splintering and factionalism. The umbrella group of SUPA, as well as the Canadian Union of Students (CUS) on its 1969 collapse, was replaced by a plethora of New Leftist groups. Yet even subsequent groups such as the

Toronto Student Movement fell apart over this essential issue. Gendered divisions, from inequities in how work was distributed to explicit sexism, also played a key role. A constant irony was that many of these young men, so focused on class and eradicating structural inequities, further perpetuated them in their own organizations through sexism and misogyny. Indeed, even though my focus is on the classed dimension, an undercurrent of gendered debate and division runs through the issue discussed here. The focus on class as a category of analysis, coupled with simple misogyny, contributed to the sundering of these New Leftist groups.

The sixties question regarding what agent of social change would reshape the world emerges as crucial to the understanding of English Canadian New Leftists, and it lies at the heart of this history's narrative. In Quebec, the story was very different. There, labour rose to prominence in a radical milieu considerably influenced by ideas of decolonization and subsequently became centred on the Conseil central des syndicats nationaux de Montréal. In contrast to the story that follows, as explained by Sean Mills, there was marked overlap between Montreal New Leftists and labour unions. Drawing on a historic tradition of anti-war resistance and political agitation, labour unions encouraged people to participate with them, leading to a fusing of left and labour interests in the city.[2] The English Canadian story was no less fascinating. New Leftists in English Canada knew they wanted change but could not agree on how to get it. These fractures became increasingly interesting and important. In this chapter, we explore the debates, discussions, and fractures that underpinned this aspect of a decade of labour.

A New Intellectual World

New Leftists engaged with a world of new ideas, distinguishing them from the Old Left. This was necessary, as they did not have a sense of a larger cohesive Canadian left tradition, making it difficult to place themselves in a narrative beyond that of the Communist Party of Canada and the Co-operative Commonwealth Federation (CCF). There were regional differences on this point, notably in Saskatchewan, where the 1962 medicare strike loomed large in the minds of New Leftists. It suggested that change *could* come against all odds, that citizens could self-organize (as seen in the community health clinics set up during the doctors' strike), and that coalitions with labour or the NDP could be fruitful.[3] As seen in the next chapter, this resulted in a distinct approach to social change. However, it is important to realize how generally unknown Canadian labour history was. Doug Ward recalls his wonder on learning of the Winnipeg

General Strike in a fourth-year Canadian history course.[4] Standard issues that Canadian history undergraduates, steeped in social history, now take for granted were largely absent from the curriculum and historiography of the early 1960s.

Just what was the intellectual context underpinning English Canadian New Leftist thought? Several authors and works continually appeared during debates, adding credence to one view or another. There were several central figures: Herbert Marcuse, C. Wright Mills, André Gorz, and the husband-and-wife team of John and Margaret Rowntree. In Canada, further inspiration also came from John Porter's seminal *Vertical Mosaic*. Other figures were also important, especially Frantz Fanon, who saw the working classes as "pampered" and unsupportive of the great decolonization struggle,[5] but it was Mills, Marcuse, Gorz, and the Rowntrees who featured most prominently. In this we see a key difference between Québécois activists, operating within an emerging context of decolonization, and the rest of Canada – Fanon was more important there, less important outside Quebec. That is not to emphasize too strict a division, though, as a chief means of intellectual transmission was the Montreal-published *Our Generation*. English and French Canadian New Leftists occupied a similar intellectual world, but with differing emphases.

It is notable too that, except for Margaret Rowntree, these central figures were all men. New Leftists also, importantly, read and understood the works discussed below through the prism of class. That many male New Leftists did not mention the disproportionate gender mismatch of these intellectuals speaks to the lack of attention paid early on to gender as a category of analysis. In this respect, the seeds of eventual conflict were laid at a very early stage.

The roots of the debate over the agent of social change had their origins in American sociologist C. Wright Mills's "Letter to a New Left." Among Canadians, this was Mills's most-cited, discussed, and distributed work. It directly addressed the role of the working class, as opposed to that of intellectuals, in social change. Mills noted that although the working class had long been considered the traditional agent of change for socialists, the context was now very different. "I cannot avoid the view that in both cases, the historic agency (in the advanced capitalist countries) has either collapsed or become more ambiguous," Mills wrote, continuing to indict New Leftists for clinging "so mightily to 'the working class' of the advanced capitalist societies as *the* historic agency, or even as the most important agency, in the face of the really impressive historical evidence that now stands against this expectation."[6] There simply was no evidence that the working class should be seen as such, and its central position in social change needed to and should be interrogated rather than taken for granted. Mills instead would look to radical intellectuals.

Mills's letter gave focus to a generation of Canadian New Leftists, across the linguistic divide. Dimitri Roussopoulos sees the letter as critical within SUPA and *Our Generation,* especially for those without a "red-diaper" background: "The preoccupation with agency for historic change, referred to as 'the agent for social change,' finds its source in Wright Mills."[7] Mills was an important starting point for a generation of activists, leading many to read his other important publications. Indeed, Mills had an entire body of work contemplating the agent of social change in postwar society.

Much of Mills's criticism of labour came out of his critical works concerning American elites. In particular, he saw labour officials as members of the elite, a distinctive bureaucratic stratum of the labour movement. They thus became not "representative of workers, but a new participant in a world of powerful, contending elites."[8] His 1956 *Power Elite* developed this further, asserting that labour leaders were sensitive about prestige, walking a tightrope between their constituency and their elite role: "They feel a tension between their publics: their union members – before whom it is politically dangerous to be too big a 'big shot' or too closely associated with inherited enemies – and their newly found companions and routines of life."[9]

For those at *Our Generation* and the Montreal SUPA office, this work was essential. According to Roussopoulos, the working class did not fit into the new analysis of elites (corporate, political, and military) advanced by Mills. "Where does that put the traditional working-class analysis? A working class that in North America at least was officially at the top, had certain social democratic proclivities, but at its base was often as right wing as one can imagine," says Roussopoulos, adding that he and his colleagues concluded that "one's relationship, as radicals, one's relationship with working class organizations of whatever profession, cannot be any different from one's relationship to the cooperative movement, or the credit union movement."[10] This was instrumental in the subsequent development of the New Left thinking of the working class as *an* agent but not *the* agent of social change, a crucial distinction.[11] Unfortunately, Mills would not live to see his ideas discussed and developed: he was felled by a heart attack in 1962. The man who had presaged a "New Left" when there was none in 1960 would not see its rise and fall.

Mills is important, but no discussion of New Leftist ideology and theory is complete without a discussion of the German philosopher Herbert Marcuse, who also explicitly dislodged the working class as the agent of change. Marcuse's 1964 *One-Dimensional Man* became a critical component of New Left philosophy, and Marcuse came to identify with the New Left, achieving heights of academic popularity while assuming the role of guru for an idolizing counter-culture and New Left.[12] As an important figure in Europe and North America, he was thus a connective tissue to the global sixties. Marcuse was at one point extolled by *Canadian Forum* as having "influenced current political conditions more than most other living persons."[13] Stan Gray suggests that Marcuse's thought was a "common ideology that united a good part of the New Left."[14]

Marcuse believed that the traditional working class had been integrated into the capitalist system and bought off with material affluence. A 1968 *Canadian Forum* article explained: "Marcuse postulates that in modern highly industrial-ized states workers no longer feel exploited; since they own large consumer goods and in many cases their own homes they consider themselves 'part of the establishment.'"[15] Indeed, by 1971, when students had again turned to the traditional working class as an agent of change, Marcuse was negative in an address at the University of Toronto, bemoaning the New Leftist "labour fetish." Looking to blue-collar workers might have made sense when they were the majority (as when Marx wrote), but this was no longer the case – and the New Left should widen its search.[16]

Yet if the agent of change was not to be the traditional working class, who would be? Marcuse had not initially specified an explicit revolutionary strategy, or a particular agent of change, though as the decade's upheaval became pro-found, he began to engage with those questions. In his writings and lectures, he called attention to the crises of liberal capitalism, arguing that fundamental social change could come by attacking capitalist pillars through the university, the Third World, or black liberation.[17] By 1965, Marcuse was looking to ethnic and racial minorities, radical intellectuals, and outsiders more generally as agents of change.[18] Through this, he could bring together radical student activ-ists and the seemingly apolitical hippies living contrary to mainstream society in locales such as Haight-Ashbury and Yorkville. Students played a special role. As *Canadian Dimension* explained, since the exploited did not realize they were exploited, "the students who have the necessary intelligence and know-ledge should revolt first, take control of the universities and establish them as centres of information for the misled masses. This would create the necessary psychological climate for the revolution which would then overturn the estab-lished order."[19] Students could spark the bigger conflagration that could prompt the revolution. For one former student leader, this message was key: "He spoke to *us*, because we had a role now ... Students, the former colonials, women, minorities, are all part of this grand coalition. Forget about the working class. Because it's been bought off."[20] Yet the rhetoric of the "misled masses" also had a dangerous ring to it – that of an elitist approach that could inhibit coalition building with others.

Students could not achieve a revolution alone. Marcuse saw opposition to capitalism in the underprivileged ghettos as well as among the most privileged, among those who were materially starved as well as among those who had the intelligence and knowledge of the system.[21] By finding common ground for the underprivileged and the privileged, Marcuse gave ammunition to affluent young baby boomers. The working class would not have to play a role, especially in North America, where it had been willingly integrated.[22] This was controversial. Gray maintains that Marcuse presented a stereotype of complacent workers as "dopes, a tabula rasa, that they believe whatever they're told, and are backward." It was "crap," stemming from middle-class stereotypes.[23]

The final foreign significant intellectual influence on many New Leftists was the Austrian-born and naturalized Frenchman André Gorz. He was an influential theorist on questions of both students and workers, and his work was reprinted and discussed extensively throughout the New Left milieu. Gorz's work concerned questions of power relations and the self-management, or industrial democracy, of workers, and spoke to New Leftist concerns with labour without abandoning them altogether as an agent of change.[24] If unions had begun as radical workers organizations, their transformation into officially recognized institutions had ended that.[25] Gorz explicitly maintained that labour unions had accepted disciplinary responsibilities and thus behaved as "institutional mediators within the capitalist society."[26] The wildcat strike was significant, as it demonstrated that "an untapped potential of combativeness and radicalism exists," to the fears of managers and labour hierarchy alike.[27] Gorz's overall strategy of social change revolved around reducing alienation and increasing autonomy, giving individuals the ability to achieve socialism through collective self-determination.[28] Workers' control, as well as others being able to control aspects of their own lives, would open up a space for social change through social autonomy.

There were other thinkers with particular Canadian influence. The most notable were the husband-and-wife team of John and Margaret Rowntree, accurately described by Levitt as the distinctly American response to the global Marxist shift.[29] The Rowntrees came to Toronto from Berkeley in the late 1960s; John taught economics at York University, and Margaret taught political science at the University of Toronto.[30] In 1968, they published a "major, provocative piece"[31] in *Our Generation,* contending that youth should be understood as a class. For the Rowntrees, the new proletariat consisted of "(1) the masses of the backward countries; and (2) the young of the United States." Youth were seen as trapped by the choice of education or the military, with freedom being taken away by conscription or the unemployment stemming from under-education. The authors found the "real revolutionary potential in the youth arising out of their role in production," which was either producing knowledge in the university or serving in the military, a choice forced by labour market pressures.[32] Their argument was enthusiastically received. At SFU, it spurred further discussion of class, as Jim Harding emphatically recalls: "Old working class, new working class, and youth-as-class. We're reading the Rowntrees!"[33] The influence of the Rowntrees was mentioned in several interviews as generating further discussion of youth and the working class, as well as of the idea of the new working class.[34]

Their attempt to find a role for youth within a Marxist framework met with criticism. Roussopoulos says that it failed to establish that youth had become "self-conscious of itself as a class, and therefore as an agent of social change."[35] Yet the article spurred discussion and provoked New Leftists to think further about the role of the working class and youth in social change. The Rowntrees had attempted to update class as a category of analysis for a new generation of young activists, and whether the argument itself was necessary, it appeared at about the same time as this broader intellectual shift back toward class politics.

While New Leftists increasingly thought more and more about subordinate classes in Canadian society, their understanding of a class structure was becoming focused on questions of power. Most would agree that there was a ruling class holding power over subordinates. New Leftist thinking on these questions was helped by the work of John Porter. His 1965 *Vertical Mosaic* was extensively discussed and well received by many New Leftists.[36] Echoing Mills, Porter posited that elite theory was a better means of understanding society than Marxism. Porter demonstrated how class as a category of analysis continued to matter in the ways in which power was distributed in society, writing that "class differences create very great differences in life chances, among which are the chances of individuals reaching the higher levels of political, economic, and other forms of power," yet dismissed Marxism as "quasi-religious," saying that "only the most dogmatic ... would cling to the theory of proletarian revolution."[37]

Porter also addressed the labour elite. Organized labour would not be a force for social change, he said, because of conflicts of national versus international unionism, and francophones versus anglophones, as well as because of the formation of a trade union elite. Porter convincingly demonstrated class, education, and material differences between the leadership and the rank and file.[38] He was read and discussed, especially by those within SUPA, and these ideas can be seen seeping throughout the debates on the agents of change and the specific role to be played by labour.

These works all focused on power issues. Although there may have been sympathy toward workers, it was based on an analysis of power possession; the working class had no special privilege in the new dichotomy of those with power and those without power. The comfortable, unionized worker was seen as part of the system, relatively empowered, and thus accorded little sympathy. These theories were also largely ambiguous and created a space for middle-class New Leftists. Moving away from prescribed doctrines allowed debate to take place on a wide range of serious, deep questions about the nature of Canadian society and how change might occur.

Debates under the Umbrella: New Leftists Debate the Working Class

The first round of concerted debate over which agent of social change could play a role in a social revolution occurred within the Student Union for Peace Action and the Canadian Union of Students. This debate raged throughout SUPA's short life, especially at federal conferences held in Saint-Calixte, Quebec, in 1965; in Waterloo, Ontario, in 1966; and in Goderich, Ontario, in 1967. The influences of these theories are also seen in the activities of CUS, which had considerable personnel overlap and continuity with SUPA.

SUPA was the pre-eminent English Canadian New Left formation, despite its short three-year existence. At its 1965 peak, SUPA's formal membership never exceeded 450 (though journalist Peter Gzowski speculated that the informal circle around it was double that).[39] Yet SUPA had a far larger impact than these numbers suggest, thanks to student and mainstream media attention and its activities. It grew out of the Combined Universities Campaign for Nuclear Disarmament (CUCND) at its December 1964 conference in Regina. There, members argued that "the goal of a warless world cannot be separated from other fundamental social issues. Economic exploitation, racism, and war cannot be understood in isolation."[40] Peace would still be important, but the conference was seen as "a broadening of the orientation of SUPA from [a] one issue peace group to a social action group with interests in all aspects of society."[41] SUPA had transitioned from a nuclear disarmament "issue-oriented" group to a "radical" one.[42] Doug Ward, who chaired the Regina meeting, says that CUCND "led almost seamlessly into the New Left. And what it did was [transition] from a single-issue movement about nuclear war to a full societal analysis of the power structure." Judith Pocock similarly recalls the consensus that "the whole society had to change."[43] Many would now seek fundamental social change: this approach was the only way to improve the lives and security of everyday powerless Canadians.

The other nexus of New Leftist activity was the Canadian Union of Students. It had transformed itself from the National Federation of Canadian University Students in 1963, consciously choosing the name in a nod toward the labour movement.[44] Initially a service-oriented organization, by the time of Ward's activist presidency of 1965/66, CUS was seen as an important New Leftist formation, a view maintained during the presidencies of Hugh Armstrong (1966/67), Peter Warrian (1968/69), and Martin Loney (1969).[45] From its inception, CUS looked beyond the campus. Goals of universal accessibility resonated with labour, and as early as 1965, President Patrick Keniff had written to the Steelworkers, expressing his interest in continued cooperation between the two organizations.[46] By 1966, there was a renewed emphasis on recognizing the need for off-campus allies, especially in the labour movement. From 1966 onward, CUS joined SUPA and its Québécois counterpart, the Union générale des étudiants du Québec, in arguing that "students should be agents of social change." This reflected the adoption of student syndicalism, which conceived of students as both workers and citizens, as a driving force, and saw a greater degree of political activism within CUS, as opposed to it being a service-oriented federation.[47] The argument that students need to be active advocates for change would dominate much of the New Leftist activity discussed in this and the following chapter.

A final group that was part of the New Left milieu is the Company of Young Canadians (CYC). Formed by a 1966 Act of Parliament as a Canadian domestic version of the American Peace Corps, the CYC focused on disadvantaged areas in the country, helping with social ills while placing youth under limited adult oversight.[48] The CYC soon became independent and, in the wake of the 1965 Saint-Calixte SUPA conference, began to recruit SUPA members, providing salaries.[49] The CYC played a significant role in dividing the movement: it increased the tension and accentuated the ideological debates that crippled SUPA. As some took federal money, they moved out of SUPA. Among those who remained, there was suspicion over who took money and who did not. In 1970, the CYC was effectively recaptured by the government with the appointment of a new board, leaving no large independent New Leftist group to return to.

How were ideas and theories of social change mediated and discussed in Canada? These discussions are difficult to recover today. As noted, New Leftists operated in an oral culture. Many students were not reading the work of the aforementioned thinkers directly. Instead, they read about them in the student or left press, or learned about them at the bar. Doug Ward remembers the pub as a central site of debate and intellectual development between annual CUS meetings.[50] At SFU too, much of the theoretical discussion was transmitted orally at the pub.[51] Discussion took place in communal houses, kitchen-table debates that would range late into the night. As nationalism became more widespread throughout the movement, there was also increasing dissatisfaction with the foreign nature of thinkers such as Mills and Marcuse.[52]

Although much of the discussion took place in an oral context, more formal outlets and webs of networks did stitch New Leftists together across English Canada, solidifying a transnational community. *Our Generation against Nuclear War,* founded in 1961, evolved into just *Our Generation* in 1966 and was an important and influential theoretical journal. Roussopoulos, its editor, had become involved with the British nuclear disarmament movement during his graduate studies in England and thus brought many ideas home to Canada. *Our Generation* was an important component of the pan-Canadian web of connection and a key link to the francophone left by virtue of its being based in Montreal.[53] It was widely read and discussed. Internal SUPA discussion could be carried out through the monthly *SUPA Newsletter,* allowing debate to continue between physical gatherings.

Cy Gonick's Winnipeg-based *Canadian Dimension* was another important publication. Founded in 1963, it provided a space for relevant discussions and debate. Gonick had been a student at the University of California, Berkeley, in the early 1960s, and was involved in a New Left journal there. He returned to Winnipeg (by way of Saskatoon) to find little comparable taking place in Canada. *Dimension* had a diverse readership, from left-wing intellectuals to New Leftists to labour. The array of articles reflected this. Martin Loney, leader of the Students for a Democratic University at SFU and subsequently CUS president, describes it as being "another link" between students and workers.[54] It was briefly joined by *Canadian Alternatives,* a short-lived publication out of Regina, which presented itself as a distinctly New Leftist version of *Dimension.*[55]

Finally, there was also SUPA's Research, Information, and Publications Project, which supplied literature to subscribers, providing information on a diverse range of topics, including political economy, economics, labour history, and various other projects. After SUPA collapsed, CUS took it over and continued its activities largely unchanged.

The annual CUS congress and seminar were national gatherings of New Leftists and student leaders. The seminar was a point of radicalization for many and an opportunity to discuss and exchange ideas. Andrew Wernick, who went on to be a founder of the Toronto Student Movement, was radicalized at the

1968 Winnipeg seminar: "That seminal week really was transformative for a lot of the people that were there." Jim Brophy, a member of the radical student council at the University of Windsor, had a critical moment at that Winnipeg congress as well: it changed "everything" in his personal development.[56] These were important connections for the movement. They also led to rapid ideological development, perhaps *too* rapid, as a letter written to the CUS leadership in 1968 noted: "People who have their minds fucked at Seminars, Congresses, expect to give birth to a minor revolution by October."[57]

Another important avenue was the Canadian University Press (CUP). Student journalists involved with CUP had a similar annual meeting, where they spent a "weekend or longer in the run of that battle over student politics ... most everybody came back with new and dangerous ideas."[58] Unlike with CUS, which elected student politicians, one did not have to be elected to be part of CUP – activists and radicals could just show up at the offices of the student newspapers. Given the developed mandate of the student press acting as an "agent of social change," the annual CUP meetings were especially significant.[59] Furthermore, CUP was a valuable transmission belt for radical ideas between campuses, syndicating important news and disseminating theories among various student newspapers.

SUPA's most notable organizational and ideological meeting took place in Saint-Calixte, Quebec, in September 1965. SUPA rented a summer camp, and members gathered from across the country to discuss their ideology, the organization, and the organization's future. Meetings were held sitting on lawns, or lying in sleeping bags. Here, several intellectual tendencies collided. The CYC actively intervened in the conference, commissioning SUPA member and University of Toronto's *Varsity* editor Harvey Shepherd to write a report on the various community projects being undertaken; in return, the CYC paid for a substantial portion of the conference costs. This intervention was controversial; as Shepherd later recalled, "The leaders of SUPA and so on had to answer the criticism ... this new radical movement was already being bought out by the government."[60] The question of whether to take government money led to fragmentation and distrust.[61]

Saint-Calixte also represented a lost opportunity to clarify SUPA's strategic approach. Without a cohesive sense of self, the organization would be ripped apart by the tensions within the movement – especially over the agent of social change and the working class in particular. Roussopoulos remembers Saint-Calixte as being a turning point for the CYC because of the absence of sustained analysis. In his view, the failure to define, redefine, or refresh the organizational philosophy led to a lack of strategy, be it short, medium, or long term.

He further stressed that the meeting did not accomplish "a re-evaluation and refurbishing of the organizational framework of SUPA, so that it could continue to work in the period ahead."[62] Subsequent events bore this out. Without a unity of purpose, the movement was open to a divisive break. Member Rainer von Königslöw suggests that the organization did not have a clear focus or mission – having "not much to tie the pieces together." Jim Harding echoes this, recalling SUPA's lack of a cohesive narrative.[63]

Of course, there was still heated debate over many questions at Saint-Calixte. Participants debated the name of SUPA itself. Some urged for "student" to be dropped, to emphasize the off-campus issues being raised.[64] Others held that the name should remain unchanged, as the university was still the organization's main base. Perhaps in response to this comment, participants decided to launch an outreach project in British Columbia that would "connect up the unions and particularly young people in the unions with questions such as Vietnam, democratizing of the union structure, automation, and so on."[65] Here was the first glimmer of a New Leftist understanding of some of the complexities of the union movement: youth, the rank and file, and the need for democratization of union structures.

A tendency arguing for a turn toward the working class reared its head at Saint-Calixte. Yet this remained a minority view against the majority emphasis on community organizing. Stan Gray emerged as a pivotal figure for the working-class tendency. His own personal history gives some sense of why. He had grown up as a red-diaper baby in working-class Montreal and later studied in England, where he became familiar with the Marxist historian E.P. Thompson, André Gorz, and others.[66] At Saint-Calixte, Gray led a discussion on the working class and the role of working-class youth in particular, but although the "problem was recognized, ... no solution or potential solution was found."[67] This failure to arrive at a solution, or even a way to incorporate the working class into analyses, proved to be divisive. SUPA's activities (discussed in the next chapter) remained focused on community organizing among the dispossessed, such as the working poor in Kingston, the blacks of Halifax, and the First Nations people of northern Saskatchewan. Marcuse's theories were put into action.

CUS was similarly embroiled in debates. Its 1966 congress was a defining moment. A fight erupted between universities with more conservative student bodies, including the University of Alberta, McGill University, and the Atlantic universities, which wanted CUS to eschew social issues and become a service organization. Newfoundland's Memorial University withdrew at the meeting, which also saw Hugh Armstrong elected president. The left wing of CUS saw this as a victory, as the president-elect declared that "students must take a

Chapter 3

consciously radical political position ... it is students' duty to society to be intellectual and political leaders."[68] Indeed, in the aftermath of the Congress, a fieldworker explained to the University of British Columbia student government, which was waffling on the question of CUS membership, that CUS had become a "radical student movement in the true sense of the word – a movement that analyzes the educational process more critically."[69] Several important policies were passed at the 1966 congress, including one mandating CUS "to establish working relations with various unions in order to gain support for universal accessibility."[70]

Despite rhetoric, little was done at the national level for unions or working people. There was no overall shift, which may have reflected some misgivings toward labour. Hugh Armstrong was a union supporter. However, as he remembers, there was criticism of unions' general acceptance of the postwar compromise, notably their willingness to "accept lousy work conditions in return for good wages and the acceptance of management rights." Pat Armstrong says that CUS recognized "their rigidity, their structures, their sexism, and a lot of other things, that were true of most organizations in the country."[71]

John Cleveland, then a member of the national CUS office, picked up on the lack of action in spite of lofty resolutions. In a working paper, he pointed to the middle-class backgrounds of student activists, as well as to a generation gap separating young students from the older labour leaders, to explain why little progress had been made. Cleveland responded to students who criticized labour as reactionary because of its economic and material focus by noting the similarity of CUS issues (universal accessibility, quality of the work environment, and university control) to those of labour.[72] The interests of students, New Leftists, and labour were not so different. With all this discussion of class, some New Leftists were beginning to note the mismatch between reality and ideals when it came to questions of another category of analysis: gender. Much of this would begin to strike close to home in both main New Leftist organizations.

A resolution was passed at the 1967 CUS congress recognizing the social and economic subordination of women, from the labour market to marriage, and acknowledging the "legitimate demands of women for liberation from the social, economic and sexual subordination and exploitation prevailing in Canada." It also called for the formation of women's liberation groups.[73] Although they were small steps, CUS was having a more promising discussion than SUPA was.

Within SUPA, the nascent Canadian second-wave feminist movement was beginning to note the glaring gap between the organization's rhetoric of participatory democracy and its perpetuation of internal discrimination against females.[74] At the 1966 SUPA federal council meeting, the conference committee noted: "In this era when women are moving forward into their rightful place in the movement ... it is indeed gratifying to be reminded that the ancient, healing arts of womanhood will not be absent from the revolution."[75] Pocock recalls the "brutal" sexual politics within the organization, how horrible it was; indeed, this was the biggest debate within SUPA that she remembers. Clare Booker, who was involved with the student movement at the University of Toronto, similarly recalls, "These male chauvinist pigs who said they were all for equality and society, but uh, could you get me a coffee, clean the house, and have kids."[76] This rhetoric led to the famous Canadian feminist manifesto "Sisters, Brothers, Lovers ... Listen ..." wherein several prominent female New Leftists declared that they were "going to be typers of letters and distributors of leaflets (hewers of wood and drawers of water) NO LONGER."[77] These tensions existed throughout the period and would come to a head in the late 1960s as large numbers of women left these New Left formations. We will return to this shortly.

As these issues percolated, debates over class and social change continued to range within SUPA. Throughout 1966, there was much discussion about the need for social analysis within SUPA. Harding and Tony Hyde both called for "a detailed analysis of youth during the transition from an industrial to a technological society," as a way to "transcend the 'micro-politics' so common among radicals," foreshadowing SUPA's subsequent sectarian implosion.[78] These debates took concrete form in mid-1967, when SUPA tried to bring the issues together in a comprehensive manifesto, to achieve that analysis that had thus far eluded it. SUPA member Donald McKelvey had called for a Canadian equivalent to the Students for a Democratic Society's 1962 Port Huron Statement, and this would be as close as SUPA would get.[79] The momentum for ideological clarification came at the December 1966 federal council meeting in Waterloo. Members gathered to clarify their future directions as well as their definition of the agent of social change. SUPA now explicitly moved away from viewing the industrial working class as the primary agent, looking toward the dispossessed instead of toward a working class that, as Myrna Kostash says, had begun to resemble a "selfish" middle class.[80] The movement was too fragile to sustain this explicit renunciation, however. SUPA was on shaky ground.

Statements were being made by some New Leftists that expressed a totalizing perception of the world and how change would be achieved. Harding realized what was happening. His efforts had been with organizing the dispossessed, but it had not been as if they were the "sole agent of change." Others, Harding realized, were increasingly taking a narrow vision: "They were seeing the blacks as the liberation of all, or the women as the liberation of all, or the youth as the liberation of all, and the notion of agency was dissecting history rather than integrating it." Many were similarly unconvinced by this turn away from the working class. Harding was in the middle, between these poles, maintaining that gender, class, and race had to be interconnected, that one could not develop a totalizing class-based analysis.[81] A similar argument was advanced by Roussopoulos, who saw the forces as being interconnected: "Ethnic minorities, the large 'other world' of poverty, the student, the young industrial worker, and more particularly the Negro people in the USA, the French-Canadian in Canada[, were] faced with the same sense of powerlessness and hence frustration."[82]

In Regina, John Conway thought the debate unhelpful: "We agreed to do all of the above [that is, working with the working class and the dispossessed]. We were not sectarian in that sense. I think that was why we were successful for a time." Hyde, who had grown up in a working-class Ottawa neighbourhood, thought Marxist theory seeing the working class as an agent of change was "a more reasonable starting point."[83] Gray continued to favour a return to the working class.[84] Others, such as Harvey Shepherd and Clayton Ruby, wanted "something that would be newer and not so dependent – we had a great deal of suspicion of more traditional Marxist and non-pacifist points of view, so there would have been a fair degree of resistance to that."[85]

The clarifying manifesto was finally written in 1967 at the University of Waterloo. Seven men – Jon Bordo, Ted Folkman, Jim Harding, Tony Hyde, James Laxer, Donald McKelvey, and Jim Russel – were asked to "set in motion the development of a coherent, wide-ranging, hopefully even profound, statement of SUPA's history and origins, our values, the way we approach political and social questions (methodology), our analysis of Canada and the rest of the world, and our strategy and tactics."[86] That seven men were selected speaks to the state of gender politics within SUPA. It raises questions of how representative the manifesto can be taken, a point balanced somewhat by the high regard in which each of these men was apparently held. This attempt at a Canadian equivalent of the Port Huron Statement is important, especially its role in precipitating the ensuing debates within SUPA; its exclusion of women equally speaks volumes.

The manifesto focused on discussions of class and Marxism. The working class was largely written off as comfortable and stable, possibly "the result of union activity," but lower-range managerial and clerical jobs were seen as being lost to automation. The authors then explicitly looked to a new working class, a class "defined by their relation to the means of production training[, which] brings them into contact with society's contradictions – inclined towards liberal views but alienated from power." Here finally was a definition of the agent of social change, with the manifesto stating that the "working class [*was*] the agent for change." Change would be led by "a particular group in the working class, the 'new working class,'" and would finally see an "integration of Marx and new left theory." Indeed, this new class could "come to power and achieve their goals without maintaining the alliance with the poor and the traditional working class."[87]

SUPA was torn apart by this attempt at clarity at its final 1967 conference in Goderich. The meeting was seen as an explicit last attempt to develop a clear direction.[88] Debates came to a simmering boil. Members debated whether SUPA should turn to Marxism, whether there was a new working class emerging. They could not reach any agreement on these crucial questions. SUPA, already tremendously wounded by debates over the CYC's role, fell apart over the question of the agent of social change. This destroyed any hope for a united English Canadian New Left umbrella group. Kostash is unequivocal: "[By] rejecting the organized industrial working class as the most promising agency of social change, SUPA was stuck with a group of social 'marginals,'" people who could not provide much prospect for revolution, as they were isolated from important places in the economy.[89]

At the Goderich meeting, it was decided that SUPA had no future viable role to play; it was formally dissolved. A much smaller New Left Committee (NLC) was formed to assume the organization's debts and to continue with a mission of laying groundwork for further New Leftist undertakings.[90] As it declared in its first public pronouncement, "SUPA is dead. Long live the revolution."[91]

"SUPA Is Dead, Long Live the Revolution": The Umbrella Begins to Fold

The twelve-person NLC could no longer claim SUPA's national base. Eight of the twelve members, all former SUPA members, hailed from Toronto, seven of them from Toronto's Annex or Yorkville neighbourhoods. A further two members were in Montreal, one in Kingston, and one in Ottawa. Apart from one member's secondary address in Edmonton, the NLC was overwhelmingly Ontario-focused.[92] Balancing that somewhat, four of the twelve were female, as opposed to the more male-dominated SUPA, as witnessed by the all-male author list on its final manifesto. Although the higher degree of female participation was not emphasized in the NLC literature, which focused on class oppression, it spoke to the earlier gendered debates. NLC was more representative. Pocock observed the importance of the "women's question" within the organization, in marked contrast to SUPA.[93] The committee certainly represented a dramatic break with the beliefs of SUPA. Several former SUPA members remember the NLC in a poor light. Harding recalls the organization as being a "joke," and Roussopoulos as a "pathetic little endgame."[94]

True, the NLC would not amount to much. Yet its understated significance lies in its commitment to the traditional working class as an agent for social change, representative of a broader shift toward more Marxist forms of analysis. The impact of the Rowntrees' aforementioned youth-as-class theory was being felt. Some New Leftists, such as Conway, sensed that the older working class might not "come willingly, but they could be dragged by the younger working class."[95] Perhaps the two solitudes of the Canadian New Left and the working class were not as completely cut off from each other as previously thought.

In the first issue of the new group's *New Left Committee Bulletin,* the group issued their statement of purpose. They began by denouncing their predecessors, stating that SUPA had been "greatly hampered by its failure to seriously consider Marxist analyses and socialist perspectives, and by its isolation from and ignorance of working class life and institutions." SUPA had not entirely erred. It had discovered some "truths" the NLC deemed essential, such as the role of mass movements, direct action, and "speaking to people's immediate concerns." Yet it had been "side-tracked by myths: the myth that revolutionary change can be a result of spontaneous popular rebellions, the myth that capitalism can be made to fulfill its liberal pretensions, the myth that radicals can ignore working class struggles and dismiss socialist perspectives."[96] The NLC would instead look to the working class and especially working-class youth.

NLC members Peggy Morton and Myrna Wood expressed this view even more vividly in their manifesto "1848 and All That or Whatever Happened to the Working Class?" SUPA was again dismissed, this time as a product of middle-class alienation: "They [SUPA members] had in common a rejection of their own class and their own affluence – the comfortable life that failed to give them a sense of purpose or a reason to be alive." These New Leftists had rejected the middle-class lifestyle, putting them at odds with a union movement that sought affluence; students could return to affluence whenever they cared to.[97] Morton and Wood argued that they had to reconceptualize middle-class Canadians as workers and move beyond the "false consciousness" of a middle class, returning to proper class analysis.

Cracks began to appear within the NLC from almost its very inception. Shepherd, a prolific contributor and author of the "SUPA is dead" declaration, wrote in a resignation letter to his fellow committee members that ideology was being used as a panacea to remedy "organizational problems which are really and fundamentally structural, programmatic, and personal."[98] That said, Shepherd recalls it as an amicable split.[99] Don Roebuck, who resigned a month after Shepherd over his complaints that other members were not doing their fair share of administrative office work, echoes this.[100] In late January 1968, the remaining Toronto members gathered and decided that the NLC "has no useful role to play at present, besides, it is not capable of any[;] ... the active existence of the NLC shall not and ought not to be pursued."[101] Indeed, the lack of energy in the organization was expressed by the decision to communicate the collapse of the NLC to the remaining non-Toronto members by letter, explicitly in lieu of a meeting. The organizational strand that had stretched from CUCND to SUPA to the NLC had ended.

Many of the ideas raised by the NLC would soon be echoed by CUS, demonstrating that the NLC was not wholly unreflective of the broader New Leftist milieu. Discussions over the role of the working class saw added impetus throughout 1968, as many attentively observed the events of Paris 1968. At the time, it seemed as if Parisian students were serving as a revolutionary vanguard to lead the workers out to the street, prompting many to wonder if the same could happen in Canada. Initially, the fact that French workers appeared to be supporting students forced some New Leftists to further explore the notion of a worker-student alliance and to consider abandoning the idea of a co-opted working class.[102] In Vancouver, Jim Harding recalls the excitement behind the events, seeing them as something that could happen there as well. Jackie Larkin, then with the New Democratic Youth, remembers that Paris 1968 was a "big deal," happening around the same time that unions were becoming "more meaningful" to her. In Toronto, Phil Resnick remembers the huge influence the events had on the burgeoning Toronto Student Movement, reinforcing notions of student syndicalism.[103] The events also confirmed the preconceptions of some, as countercultural challenge in Paris had spurred the workers into action: a deliberate strategy need not be employed, but rather just a continual challenge.[104] Along with sit-ins and other demonstrations, Paris 1968 formed part of a practical education for English Canadian New Leftists.

With the election of Peter Warrian, who would be president from 1968 to 1969, CUS tangibly turned toward the working class. Among CUS personnel were many former SUPA members. Warrian had been active with that group, and some saw his election at the 1967 CUS congress as a "grand conspiracy."[105] Indeed, Warrian was significant in this shift to the working class. Born in Toronto to working-class parents, he worked at Toronto's Northern Electric (later Northern Telecom) factory after graduating from the technical stream of his secondary school. Later enrolling in a seminary, he was able to transfer to an undergraduate program at the University of Waterloo, despite his technical-streamed background.[106] Although he was elected by a vote of sixty-seven to thirty-seven, the election was chaotic, and debate continued over whether CUS had a mandate to engage with off-campus activity or whether it should focus instead on being a service organization.[107] The Declaration of the Canadian Student, issued at the 1967 congress and an integral part of Warrian's platform, held that students needed to immerse "themselves in intellectual pursuit but also to engage in fundamental action to confront society with discoveries and to promote consequent action to bring reforms into practice."[108] In his own writing, Warrian maintained that CUS needed to move out into the community. He was quoted in the "bourgeois media" as referring to "burning buildings if necessary."[109] In a working paper, Warrian asserted that a "link between students and the working class is an obvious necessity. However, this link must have a functional basis, it cannot simply be based on an abstract sentiment of fraternal solidarity."[110]

Warrian's ideology was put into action on his August 1968 assumption of the presidency. Throughout the next winter, these abstract ideas were enacted at the *Peterborough Examiner* strike, when, as we will see in Chapter 5, CUS threw its full support behind the striking journalists. CUS thus became connected to a broader tendency of New Left picket-line support in Ontario and Nova Scotia. These student leaders moved beyond the mere rhetoric of the working class and engaged in concrete and sustained action. This opened CUS up to criticism from the more conservative elements of its on-campus base, which argued against CUS in general on the grounds that many "don't quite like the idea of having someone with a 'workers uniform' (blue jeans and a blue jeans jacket) manipulating your consciousness."[111]

For the March 1969 national council meeting, Warrian invited delegates to discuss "a national strategy for social change in Canada and for the CUS ... what kind of role did the National Council see for CUS in the future[?]"[112] Andrew Wernick, then a graduate student at the University of Toronto, advocated that students had to play a specific independent role as an agent of social change; however, they could make alliances with other groups. Following Wernick, the council discussed who they could possibly ally with to achieve social change. They considered farmers as a possible ally, over the issues of falling grain prices, higher costs, and the corporatization of agriculture. They then turned toward workers, looking at labour history before turning to strategy, and raising ideas such as allying with workers on issues of wage freezes, compulsory arbitration, and injunctions. This demonstrated an awareness of the major issues facing the labour movement in mid-1969, but little would come out of the subsequent proposals.

By 1969, CUS was divided, caught between the more conservative and liberal members of its university base and the more radical members. Harding, for example, denounced CUS for not being radical enough and instead focusing on the delivery of student services.[113] Motions were passed supporting the Vietnamese National Liberation Front, which compounded the earlier inflammatory rhetoric about burning buildings. Martin Loney took over the presidency in August 1969 and sought to restrict the aims and goals of CUS to "specific issues which affected university students more closely, such as housing, student unemployment, universal accessibility, and course content."[114] This was a dramatic change from Loney's rhetoric when elected at the 1968 congress, which had explicitly concentrated on students focusing on "our wider constituency [throughout] the world ... I'm talking about liberating the people of the world."[115] Harding publicly challenged Loney's "accommodationist stand" on his assumption of the presidency, declaring that CUS was "irrelevant, centralized, elitist, and undemocratic."[116] Most observers would agree that the group was pulling back from some of its more radical positions, especially on international affairs and "revolutionary strategies."[117]

By then it was too late. CUS had been on increasingly shaky ground since 1968. Universities had been withdrawing at an alarming rate. There had been thirty-nine member universities in early 1968 and twenty-seven in late 1968; by late 1969, there were only nineteen. A 1969 referendum on whether to continue CUS membership at the University of Toronto, by far the biggest member, was intensely debated. CUS had been attacked by the more conservative elements of the student body, especially engineers, but had also found itself on the wrong side of more radical factions, such as the New Left Caucus.[118] This referendum was critically important not only for the political legitimacy conveyed by the University of Toronto's mass membership but also because the university's fees paid the national office overhead.[119] With the defeat of the referendum at the University of Toronto – 5,434 to 2,222 – that was followed by separate referendums at other universities throughout the country (Dalhousie and Carleton left the same week), CUS voted itself out of existence in late October 1969.[120]

The Cycle Continues: The Case of the Toronto Student Movement

In place of these umbrella groups came a plethora of smaller, independent local New Left groups. Groups continued their radical actions on several campuses, such as at Regina, SFU, and the University of Waterloo, and independent New Left groups appeared in several cities. Around this time, at the University of Windsor, Jim Brophy began realizing that although unions were part of the establishment, "I see some good people [there] ... I recognize that it's not just the youth revolution or whatever, it's got to be something way beyond that."[121] He would soon move to Toronto and work with the United Farm Workers Union, before eventually going to the Windsor Chrysler plant.

One group that serves as an important illustration of these local New Left groups was the Toronto Student Movement (TSM). It is noteworthy as it shows how independent New Left activity continued after SUPA and CUS in an organizational form and also how the working-class question remained both predominant and destructive. This question was not the only one, however. The TSM would ultimately be partially undone by its misattention to gendered issues, a consistent current that unites many of the groups discussed in this chapter.

The TSM was founded in Toronto in late 1968. Its name was chosen by Andrew Wernick, a sociology graduate student, to head off attempts by the Maoist Canadian Student Movement that was giving birth to groups throughout the country – the Hamilton Student Movement, the Peterborough Student Movement, the Vancouver Student Movement, among several others. Wernick pre-empted them, figuring that their approach to organizing would be thrown off.[122] The TSM was an amalgamation of many forces. As one of its flyers claimed, it was an "association of radical students at the University of Toronto. [They were] self-confessed members of the left (New, Old, and Psychedelic – but mainly the neo-Marxist New Left), [whose] strategy and tactics for the university [were] placed firmly inside a revolutionary perspective."[123] The TSM represented a merging of the counterculture and the New Left in a way that previous formations such as SUPA had not. Its focus was on democratizing the university and opening it up. Adhering to an ethos of direct action, its members intervened in campus orientations to politicize them, and disrupted speakers such as Clark Kerr, president of the University of California. The night before, in an on-campus lecture, Kerr had said that "an alliance between students and workers [was] inconceivable," as workers had a responsibility to their families and had to make a living, whereas students could be irresponsible with demands.[124] Disrupting the Kerr event brought headlines in the *Varsity* and crowds – about three hundred people – to the group's next meeting, although TSM's infighting would quickly drive many away.[125]

The TSM was drawn into the working-class question, reflecting the broad intellectual shift underway. It had a general strategy, calling for "an alliance of many sectors in Canadian society: students, blue-collar workers, white-collar workers, and technical workers."[126] Wernick describes it as "a bit of an umbrella group, but it was basically direct action, minority action, some notion of this minority/majority dialectic ... it wasn't particularly ideologically closed."[127] Unions and workers were critical, but other groups would have to play an important role as well to reflect the massive changes in society. Phil Resnick reflects on the debates, saying, "A simple black and white, worker versus owner, simply did not capture the reality of the more complex society that we lived in." Workers would be part of a coalition to change society, but the definition of the agent of social change was now much broader, "given the emergence of students in large numbers and the new middle class in society."[128] The TSM had three main lines as identified by Wernick: campus democracy, fighting the bourgeois university, and forming a student-worker alliance.[129]

A growing split loomed within the group over the specific role that the working class would play. Again, we see the divide between those who saw the working class as *the* agent of social change and those who saw the working class as *an* agent of social change. As Wernick explains, his faction did not exclude workers but saw them alongside students, women, and others – and he felt that the students drawn to an explicitly working-class struggle were "stuck in the 1930s."[130] Students with a traditional Marxist working-class orientation were joining the TSM, attempting to influence it in a doctrinaire, Old Left direction, and to take it over. This divide became clear during the TSM 1969 open summer courses, Theories of Revolution, Contradictions in Canada, Bourgeois Identity, Student Strategy, Cultural Oppression, and Worker-Student Alliance. This last course is significant, as it presaged the split within the TSM.

The Worker-Student Alliance course drew on Gorz, Lenin, and Mao, as well as Martin Robin (*Radical Politics and Canadian Labour, 1890-1930*) and the Woods Report. The Old Left line became clear: "The readings are an attempt to link Leninist theory with the Canadian historical experience and contemporary strategies." The TSM would put theory into action if a strike happened in Toronto.[131] When the United Steelworkers launched a first-contract strike at the Wiener Electric Company in mid-June 1969, the TSM went out for a practical education. Daniel Wiener, the owner, was an outspoken opponent of unions, declaring that he would rather close his plant and live off his investments than sign a collective agreement.[132] Pickets were organized, and groups such as the Women's Liberation Group and members of the University of Toronto's Students' Administrative Council came. Some sixty-five students tried to convince strikebreakers to quit. Negotiations broke down in part over the role of students. Management wanted them gone from the pickets; union leaders protested that they had no say over them.[133]

Wiener was a defeat for the Steelworkers. The owner was fined $200 for unfair practices violating the Ontario Labour Relations Act, but this was a miniscule victory of principle for the unemployed workers.[134] Yet the lessons learned from the strike were impressed upon these Worker-Student Alliance students within the Toronto Student Movement. The union was criticized far more than was management: for failing to press for Unemployment Insurance for their workers, arrange mass pickets of other workers, and, ultimately, win.

After the TSM's taste of action and a summer of debate, a document was circulated, calling on the group to develop a conscious worker-student alliance in the 1969/70 school year. The strategy was to reach out to workers, demanding free admission to universities for the working class and minorities, the establishment of a people's college, the end of streaming, and free tuition and books.[135] Further platforms called for the removal of capitalist "agents" such as John Crispo and his Centre for Industrial Relations at the University of Toronto, as well as for the support of working-class struggles, such as on-campus unionization.[136] A series of essays was produced: Steve Moore's "Building a Student-Worker Alliance at University," Bob Dewart's "Students and Workers: Building a Real Alliance," and Bill Johnston's "The Revolutionary Party, Students and Worker-Student Alliance." These authors saw themselves as revolutionary vanguards, with Bob Dewart asserting that students had "several things to offer the workers; namely, time, research skills, and Marxist consciousness. When I add this all up I arrive at the conclusion that we can best perform a research and revolutionary propaganda function within the working class movement."[137] This workerist group was aware that the rest of the TSM might disagree, as it published the essays to "stimulate internal discussion."[138]

Two caucuses had now emerged within the TSM. One put forward a working-class perspective, and the other presented an "autonomous student movement-type perspective."[139] This latter group became known as the New Left Caucus (NLC). By August, the NLC was having its own separate meetings as they explicitly rejected the "workerism" of the Worker-Student Alliance (WSA) caucus. On 13 August, Wernick announced that the split was formal and that the NLC would be doing its own organizing and recruitment.[140] The WSA then institutionalized its ties with the Canadian Party of Labour, a Marxist-Leninist organization.[141] The TSM was no longer.

Both groups carried on. WSA adherents cut their hair short, abstained from drugs, and adopted a "straight" lifestyle to emulate the lifestyle of an idealized blue-collar worker.[142] In contrast, NLC members wore their hair long over their denim jackets, as self-described "Freaks."[143] They were denounced by the WSA as "toadstools," engaging in "showbusiness" and being too frivolous.[144] In return, the NLC denounced the workerists for using a 1910-era definition of class, "an ossified definition of class, which seeks to restrict basic revolutionary potential to the industrial working class (presently shrinking in size due to the changing nature of the means of production)."[145] Yet we see here a fundamental agreement that was lacking earlier. Workers and students would need to ally, workers were not dupes, and the language of Marxism was pervasive.

The NLC ultimately fell apart in 1970 over gender issues, splitting into two groups, one male and one female.[146] The split was precipitated by male sexist behaviour, the boiling point an internal document making fun of women activists as "clucking, gossiping hens in a knitting circle" (with "cluck-clucks" interjected among banalities in an imaginary transcript – as opposed to the statements by serious men). This prompted a crucial response manifesto by a group of women who used the derision in their new name: the Knitting Circle.[147] Their manifesto was entitled "Destruction Is the Highest Form of Creation, or The *Real* Contradictions in the Social Relationships in the New Left Caucus (Back to the Materialist Knitty-Gritty) or Cluck Cluck Titter Titter Tee Hee Tee Hee (Sigh)." In it, they skewered the men's behaviour, demanded that community issues be politicized, and called for an open discussion. And a gauntlet was thrown down: "Any man who portrays us as you do is part of our problem too. ('Tee hee tich tich tee hee titter titter tee.') We will not work with men who caricature us."[148] This point was repeated throughout the paper. This continuing strand of inattention to the gender question continued after SUPA and into left formations such as the NLC, leading to understandable disintegration. The caucus thus split apart, though individuals continued in radical activities, especially around the May Fourth Movement in Toronto that emerged from large protests over the invasion of Cambodia and the Kent State shootings in May 1970.[149]

After the collapse of SUPA, a new emphasis was placed on the working class by the remnants of the New Left. Although this was most manifest in the New Left Committee (despite its short existence), with its explicit denunciation of SUPA for failing to adhere to a working-class model, this could be seen in other left groups as well. Just as SUPA had fallen apart over the working-class question, so too would the TSM split, into the New Left Caucus and the Worker-Student Alliance. The continuing theme of gender also appeared, with male members of the NLC failing to heed earlier lessons and continuing to perpetuate sexual discrimination. Yet class was a significant part of the story: the Toronto

Women's Liberation Movement fell apart in 1969 with a split between Marxists, who held that a broader revolution was necessary, and New Feminists, who emphasized the oppression of women.[150] The collapse of these groups, exemplified here by the Toronto Student Movement, signals that, by 1970, there would be no substantial ideological agreement on the agent of change in society (or whether fundamental social change was even necessary). Most agreed, however, that the working class was important and would play a role.

Conclusion

At the end of the decade, English Canadian New Leftists had undergone significant intellectual transitions. Initially inspired by a host of political philosophers and their own take on the postwar economy, many had explicitly broken with the Old Left tradition of working-class struggle and resistance. Indeed, not only would workers not be an agent of social change but many would be seen as sellouts and complacent members of mainstream society. Debates over who the agent could be, of the role that the middle or working class would play, tore SUPA apart. Failure to achieve consensus at the pivotal Saint-Calixte meeting led to severe internal debate that could not be transcended; the September 1967 Goderich conference would see the collapse of SUPA and its replacement by the more doctrinaire and worker-oriented New Left Committee. CUS was similarly beset by debates, searching for allies but unsure how to effectively do so. This was not the only issue: debates on gender and the treatment of women were of significant importance as well. Yet it was a critical one, underpinning the story of Canadian New Leftists, as this chapter has argued.

Throughout this period, there was the perceived emergence of the dispossessed as an agent of social change: a *lumpenproletariat* of the unemployed, youth, and ethnic minorities. The question of what role a blue- or white-collar worker could play was contested, with increasingly more emphasis being placed on a "new" working class than on an industrial working class that was seen as affluent and content. SUPA was marked by ideological confusion, and there was little resolution. Opportunities to develop a cohesive sense of self on these essential questions were missed, a situation compounded by consistent myopia among many male New Leftist leaders and thinkers on questions of gender. Late attempts to obtain unity were too little, too late. SUPA crumbled in part over the working-class question. In its wake, subsequent left formations were profoundly influenced by working-class questions and strategies. Even when the New Left Caucus and the Worker-Student Alliance divorced in 1969, they shared fundamental agreement on the importance of workers and unions to any schema of social change – despite their enduring disagreement about whether there had to be *one* or whether there could be *several* agents of social change.

In stark contrast to C. Wright Mills's sentiments, by 1968 and 1969, students were flocking to picket lines and expounding on the need to support the working class. Marxism, or neo-Marxism, was becoming increasingly *de rigueur*. Yet this support was qualified by the debates over the working class as an agent of social change, particularly a suspicion of economic demands, of union leaders versus the rank and file, and of the postwar compromise more generally. This suspicion would shape the events to come.

Examining these debates is essential not only for understanding why the New Left fragmented, leading to the subsequent rise of the revolutionary left that so characterizes our understanding of 1970s radicalism, but also because they provide the context for the concrete actions taken when New Leftists actually reached out to labour. In 1968, students began to take to picket lines and engage in supportive action. In some ways, this represented a continuity of community organizing and joining demonstrations. Yet it was these debates, which saw the working class virtually abandoned in the early 1960s as an agent of social change and then quickly returned to a few years later, that would set the groundwork for subsequent activities. This set in motion a series of events that would change the face of the labour movement for decades to come. As we will see in the following chapters, these views on social agency shaped SUPA's community organizing projects, as well as the subsequent relationship between New Leftists and labour in the late 1960s and early 1970s.

4

Leaving Campus:
The Outward-Looking New Left in Ontario,
British Columbia, and Saskatchewan

The strike of Simon Fraser University's Political Science, Sociology, and Anthropology (PSA) Department began in September 1969. Precipitated by concern over departmental autonomy in staffing decisions, the strike owed at least as much to the unorthodox conception of the university's role in society held by many PSA faculty members and students. They proudly declared that the PSA Department was "grounded on the philosophy of participation and control from below and designed to serve the needs of the PEOPLE OF BRITISH COLUMBIA."[1] As Mordecai Briemberg, then departmental chair, says: "It was dangerous, the outward form of it. That somehow the university comes off the mountain, and actually goes to see what it can do in relation to ordinary people's working lives and their needs."[2] When eight striking professors were dismissed and an injunction ended the strike, New Leftists moved off campus. The actions at Simon Fraser University (SFU) would have a longer-term impact: the development of the Service, Office and Retail Workers Union of Canada, which grew out of the Vancouver Women's Caucus and other institutions, including the Community Education and Research Centre.

Two years later in Saskatchewan, a different form of community outreach occurred. Standing before six thousand people in Regina's Exhibition Stadium in April 1970, Don Mitchell, representing the University of Saskatchewan's Regina campus, received a standing ovation as he voiced students' support of the militant National Farmers Union (NFU). That Mitchell stood alongside the NFU president, the Saskatchewan Federation of Labour (SFL) president, and a number of other prominent speakers at the rally reflects the outward-looking culture of involvement that New Leftists had forged in Regina. As Mitchell spoke, students circulated through the audience, organizing and taking pictures of police plainclothesmen who were in attendance.[3] Labour had stood with the Regina students during an earlier crisis over their student newspaper. This brought the two groups together and diminished the normal cultural gulf; labour and New Leftists were curious about each other, and a working relationship emerged.

These vignettes show that New Leftists, while still largely based on university campuses, had begun to look outward to find ways to collaborate with working people and unions. As early as the mid-1960s, they had launched projects aimed at working-class communities. This pro-worker perspective often translated into cultural misunderstandings or resulted in little more than somewhat strained dialogue with labour leaders at regional or provincial levels, such as in Ontario. But in the late 1960s and early 1970s, in Saskatchewan and British Columbia's Lower Mainland, dramatic public events erupted that brought together New Leftists and their allies among organized labour and farm movements.

Early Steps: The Kingston Community Project and Student Neestow Partnership Project

An outward-looking perspective was key to the inception of the English Canadian New Left and a defining characteristic of its ethos. As previously noted, the decision to organize the "dispossessed" appeared as early as SUPA's founding 1964 conference, where New Leftists decided to organize around Canada's Aboriginal population, the poor, and youth in general. For some activists, such as Judith Pocock, these sorts of activities were already, "in some ways, a turn – certainly the anti-poverty work and all that – a turn to the working class."[4] Two major projects illustrate the attempted realization of this outward-looking culture: the Kingston Community Project (KCP) and the Student Neestow Partnership Project.[5] This community organizing underpinned subsequent action.

With the KCP, members of SUPA's Queen's University chapter headed into the city's working-class north end. They would live alongside the impoverished residents of north Kingston, a world removed from the comparatively comfortable life of Queen's students, predominantly located in the city's south end. Living together in two communal homes, the organizers worked with their new neighbours, helping them confront abusive landlords.[6] Joan Kuyek, who quit the CYC to work for the KCP, learned quickly about class: "We were very conscious that we were working with the working class." John Conway remembers the KCP as being part of a broader attempt to link up to the working class.[7] Throughout, there was a conscious attempt to focus on local community issues among the powerless, rather than focusing on the class relations generated in the workplace.[8]

Accordingly, the relationship between organizers and working people, as well as their organizations such as unions, was one of pragmatism. Sweeping change was not attempted, at least not all at once. Significantly, for example, it became clear that the conservatism of the local labour movement would keep workplace politics largely off the table. Yet as the KCP developed, it was able to garner support from the Canadian Union of Public Employees (CUPE) and United Electrical Workers (UE) locals for establishing a tenants union, challenging property ownership rights, and showing the power of cooperation.[9]

CUPE and UE were outliers, however, as other unions were generally unsupportive.[10] Although some New Leftists would see unions in a mistakenly monolithic fashion, the divergent responses of different unions and locals would help some of the students realize the diversity of views within the labour movement. UE was particularly important, since it was a large union outside mainstream labour. The Communist-led union had been purged from the Canadian Congress of Labour in 1949.[11] At a host of high-profile activist events throughout the 1960s, UE played a significant role: when mainstream labour turned its back on nationalist unions or other unpopular strikes, UE was often there to lend support. In a similar vein, New Leftists in British Columbia and Nova Scotia discovered that the United Fishermen and Allied Workers Union was similarly estranged from mainstream labour and thus looked toward New Leftists as allies. UE provided meaningful support to the KCP, but its unique nature meant that it was hardly representative of the Kingston labour movement as a whole.

The lack of cooperation between mainstream unions and the KCP may have stemmed partly from the frustration and growing divide between organizers and residents. Despite some cooperation over local issues, many KCP members were becoming frustrated. Some felt that they were acting as social workers rather than facilitating self-directed community work; Kostash has suggested that they were perceived as the "middle-class interlopers [that] they were."[12] SUPA activist Peter Boothroyd further lamented that "the Kingston poor seek housing for its status value ... and allow themselves to be dehumanized in an anachronistic welfare system." Summing up, he noted how difficult it was for the Queen's students to relate to the Kingston poor. They became cynical and anxious, and had trouble empathizing: "We call ourselves radical and become self righteous about this and they are not radical."[13] These issues and tensions were a continual theme.

With the end of summer, most organizers moved back to school and out of the KCP. Some stayed, however. Kuyek continued to work with youth and tenants, and on Kingston's waterfront revitalization, developing along the way a long-standing suspicion of summer projects. She went on to become a municipal politician in 1968, raising awareness of housing issues and the problems with the Landlord and Tenants Act, before moving to Sudbury to work as a union organizer. Out of Kingston, she developed her perspective on unions, recognizing that "each place was a site of struggle." "One of the things I found really irritating about SUPA and a lot of the New Leftists as things went along there," she says, "was that lack of analysis about the internal struggles of these institutions."[14] It was through experience that Kuyek moved away from a monolithic idea of organized labour. The KCP was significant not only because it had a valuable impact on the lives of the city's working people but also because it bequeathed a legacy of single-issue cooperation with the working class as well as an appreciation for the sheer complexity of unions.

In Saskatchewan, another project took shape. This began with discussions at the University of Saskatchewan in February 1965, when local SUPA members decided that they had to act in light of poor Aboriginal social and economic conditions. They would live in Native communities on welfare rates, learning and hopefully giving guidance on how Aboriginals could "gain greater security and independence over their economic, social and political lives."[15]

They were largely unsuccessful. The nine activists became embroiled in "more basic problems instead of starting a grassroots political revolution."[16] Kostash notes the gap that quickly became apparent as the clash between idealized Aboriginals and reality appeared: organizers began to see themselves as intruders.[17] Several organizers grew frustrated with local culture, seeing it as trying too hard to integrate itself into the dominant society: "The Indians have little respect for their heritage except for the superficial pride in a commercialized Indian festival and the like."[18] The organizers' focus on poverty downplayed the importance of culture when dealing with such a group and is illustrative of implementation problems.

A look at these projects helps us to understand the first stage of New Leftists venturing into the community, and the lessons they learned. New Leftists discovered the complexity of the projects and the importance of culture. They were not resounding successes, at least according to the majority of participants. A minority stayed in Kingston and effected meaningful change, Kuyek among them. Despite intellectual moves toward the dispossessed as a potential agent of social change, for most, action had not yielded positive results. This would leave some New Leftists sympathetic to a wholesale move back to more traditional working-class politics, especially in light of the ongoing intellectual debates over the agent of social change.

As those discussions led many New Leftists toward a more pro–working-class position, other attempts at forging this outward-looking culture emerged. In Ontario, the New Leftist leadership of groups such as the Ontario Union of Students and CUS began to make hesitant overtures to labour hierarchies. Unlike earlier community projects, these efforts involved leaders speaking to other leaders, but there was a hope that they could perhaps move beyond that and down to the rank and file. They would begin to understand the labour movement's complexity, and that forging a worker-student alliance would be harder than they first suspected.

Ontario: Formal Relationships

Early formal communication between CUS and the labour movement was restrained, limited to information sharing and supportive resolutions. Some of this came through personal connections. Laurel Sefton MacDowell, daughter of USWA national director Larry Sefton, was active in the University of Toronto's student movement and arranged a meeting between campus leaders and her father. The meeting was not fruitful, as MacDowell describes:

> I remember my dad saying that one of the problems with the student movement was that of course people were going to move on. I mean, they're not workers in the sense that you're going to stay in a plant, and so while we had all these ideals and we were going to democratize the university, which to some extent we did, we of course were then going to move on.[19]

We can see a glimmer of this perception in tensions between activists and workers during a 1968 University of Guelph support staff strike. When the Marxist-Leninist Guelph Student Movement attempted to support the strike by trashing residences, plugging toilets, and joining the pickets, they were rebuffed by workers who feared that they would incite violence. "In a few years, I suspect, many of them will get into the establishment and do a 180-degree turn as far as their attitude to labor is concerned," one worker declared to the *Globe and Mail*.[20] Although the Guelph students involved probably would not have adopted the New Leftist label themselves, this cautionary tale reminds us to not overly romanticize ties across the class divide.

Indeed, along these lines, further tensions between New Leftists and organized labour appeared at formal gatherings, such as those held at the UAW's Port Elgin educational centre. By spring 1967, labour leaders were interested in youth issues in part because of their own youth-driven challenges, and brought student unionists together at Port Elgin so both sides could figure out what each other was about and to establish contacts.[21] A vigorous discussion ensued about international unionism, with students bringing their anti-imperialist politics to the fore. There was tension under the giant Canadian and American flags in the main hall where the meeting took place – especially when students began talking about removing the flags, says Hugh Armstrong. Union members were "proud of their internationalism," whereas the students were strident English Canadian nationalists and opposed to American imperialism and the Vietnam War.[22] These initial contacts did not lead to sweeping agreement between labour and students in Ontario, and it would take another two years before a comprehensive attempt was again made. In lieu of this, the link in Ontario then took a single-issue perspective: student scabbing.

Addressing an NDP riding group in 1973, for the release of his book *The Strikebreakers*, *Toronto Telegram* labour reporter Marc Zwelling declared that "students are a tremendous problem during strikes," going on to say that they had been generally ignorant of the issues at stake in labour disputes.[23] Indeed, the issue had been a critical one over the previous several years, in Ontario and beyond, as the realities of student under- and unemployment met the rising tide of labour militancy.[24] Yet unlike the scorn normally meted out to strikebreakers, New Leftists and even union officials expressed sympathy for student strikebreakers. Few argued that students would engage in the unpleasant act of crossing a picket line if they had better options. A common approach when dealing with student strikebreakers was to frame the issue as part of broader economic and educational issues; individual responsibility was not stressed.

The first high-profile incident in Ontario was in early 1968 at Etobicoke's Thermotex glass plant, though elsewhere other incidents of student scabbing had received some attention (one incident occurred with SFU students, as we will see). The Steelworkers had organized Thermotex, but negotiations broke down and the local launched a wildcat strike without going through the proper strike procedure, a distinction that some students later claimed influenced their decision to cross the line. Student strikebreakers were hired and paid a substantially higher starting wage than the permanent employees, which became a hot-button issue during the strike. Workers and other activists showed up on the picket line with signs that read "Student Scabs Get Out" and "Per Quanto avete venduto vostra dignita? $1.85 per hour."[25] One positive result, however, was that the University of Toronto's placement advisory committee passed a motion that it would not place students in such strikebreaking positions.

The Ontario Union of Students (OUS) took a leading role in this controversy, perhaps because of president Monique Ouelette. She had been invited in March 1968 to give a keynote address at the UE annual convention, where she spoke on universal accessibility, the growing awareness of student social responsibility, and the need in society itself for the same changes students were trying to achieve in the university. After a standing ovation, UE delegates voted their support for student unionism and accessibility.[26] Given this, it is perhaps unsurprising that the OUS issued a strong statement about the Thermotex strike, attempting to persuade students that social responsibilities trumped financial need. Although the release was sympathetic to students' plight, taking the opportunity to condemn inadequate provincial student assistance, the OUS firmly stated that "students, as full members of society, must support the workers in their struggle for decent human and working conditions."[27]

By late 1968, the issue began to gain traction in several student outlets. The issue hit the front page of the *Varsity*, and the New Democratic Youth paper *Confrontations* commented that "student scabbing is getting worse," rhetorically pondering why students were so contemptuous of unions.[28] According to the article, students were made to feel superior to working youth, and that this feeling of entitlement led to the sentiment that they could take jobs from workers. *Confrontations* suggested placing students in menial and unskilled jobs, away from skilled labour's bailiwick. The *Varsity* also noted the inherent tension between students and workers: "Workers cannot raise protests about scabbing without someone accusing them of trying to deprive these students of their education."[29]

This was an issue elsewhere, too. In Vancouver, a columnist for the University of British Columbia student paper, the *Ubyssey*, condemned students for working at BC Tel (the provincial telephone company) during a bitter strike over the summer of 1969: "The students who scabbed did not encourage joint action between unions and student employment groups."[30] An open letter was written to the students by the Federation of Telephone Workers, claiming that students were essentially "taking food from our families' mouths," and noting that "28% of our tax assessment is going towards education costs."[31] In Waterloo, the issue was again brought to the forefront with the revelation that students were taking jobs from Ontario Hydro corporation workers through the summer of 1972. They were reading meters and taking all their direction over the phone, allowing them to never cross a physical picket line. CUPE noted that the University of Waterloo was responsible for placing students in these positions;

the Ontario Hydro Employees Union and others subsequently blacklisted the students.[32]

A fairly unified, relatively sympathetic line thus appeared in various responses to student scabbing, seen as a product of the worsening job market and financial instability of many students, the growing importance of the working class, and the competing social and financial responsibilities of students. It highlighted the financial need of students, given the danger and unpleasantness of picket-line crossing, but it also highlighted the competing values. Ultimately, this line of discussion was quite limited, being largely restricted to the level of official dialogue with labour leaders. Student journalists and OUS leadership cooperated with their labour counterparts in publicizing the issue of student strikebreaking, perhaps spurring some students to reconsider their summer employment situations and prompting minor policy changes in student employment centres, but a meaningful and comprehensive relationship did not emerge from these hesitant steps.

One final attempt was made in 1969 to forge a comprehensive relationship between student New Leftists and labour in Ontario, through a conference organized by the University of Toronto's student council, the Ontario Federation of Labour (OFL), and the OUS. It focused on the difficulties of labour organizing in the wake of the Woods and Rand reports and the necessity of continued organizing, as well as on issues of Canadian nationalism, foreign ownership, and the role of international unions. From the first organizational steps, it was clear that the relationship between students and unions was to be conducted through official channels: "If a dialogue is to begin at the local rank and file level," the organizing notes stated, "then the student unions should contact the local Labour councils in their respective areas." In any case, there was some tension and distance between the two bodies, with OUS minutes noting considerable misunderstanding on both sides and that "whether grounds for common liaison exist remains to be seen."[33] The conference aimed to reach a turning point in this relationship and to develop a better rapport.

The conference was held over the weekend of 18-19 October 1969. OFL president David Archer opened with a keynote address, remarking, "There are many aspects of your activities which strike a sympathetic note with us." By this he was referring to a shared desire to end poverty and achieve a higher standard of living, among other things. He went on to emphasize the importance of universal accessibility, and note that students were still generally an elite group within society. Finally, he defensively stressed that this was not a "labour brainwashing" session, pointing out the shared organizational responsibilities among OFL, OUS, and CLC.[34] For the rest of the weekend, the delegates discussed student and labour union organizing, labour history, and legislation, as well as the looming question of international unionism. The UAW's Dennis McDermott addressed the students on this question.[35] Unfortunately, no notes of what was actually discussed survive.

This lack of documentation coming from the conference is telling. No resolutions of note were made, at least none that led to enduring and concerted cooperative action. The conference was never referred to afterward, despite the continued involvement of student groups in labour issues. The meeting did not change the relationship between labour and New Leftists. They remained on working terms over such specific, circumscribed issues as student scabbing. But no systematic alliance was pursued between the two groups. Brian Switzman, then OUS vice-president and subsequently president, recalls that students were invited to union events, "but they were just so suspicious of us because, again, these are people who are still of a generation where you have to drive the commies out of the union movement, and you have to protect the CCF or NDP kind of stuff."[36] The gulf between the leadership of the labour movement and of the student movement was simply too profound: it was a generational gap, but also an ideological gap over the need for social transformation and the role of extra-parliamentary opposition. This was to be the last formal high-level attempt at bringing the two sides together. Ontario New Leftists would eventually move out toward picket lines, as discussed in the following chapter. It would be in Saskatchewan and British Columbia's Lower Mainland that this relationship would come to fruition, thanks to unique political cultures and captivating public events.

Defending the Public University: Coalition Building at the Regina Campus

The University of Saskatchewan's Regina campus saw one of the best examples of an outward-looking culture that helped develop a New Leftist and labour coalition. It had a dramatic effect not only on the individuals and groups involved but also in shaping provincial politics. As the home of the first North American socialist government under Tommy Douglas, the political character of Saskatchewan shaped student experiences. With a brand-new modernist campus opening on the shores of the man-made Wascana Lake, the Regina campus was an instant campus.

Labour played a role in its creation. The Regina Trades and Labour Council was the first group to contribute money to building the new campus, and additional political support came from the nearby Moose Jaw and District Labour

Council. These two councils drew attention to the fact that the smaller city of Saskatoon had far more students than Regina. This crucible gave birth to a distinctive on-campus political culture. Some students from working-class backgrounds could now attend university, and they brought a different perspective to the campus than their middle-class peers.[37] This would lead to a distinctive New Leftist formation both on and off campus.

Several influential individuals help give a sense of the importance of this culture. John Conway, Don Mitchell, and Don Kossick were important players at the Regina campus. Conway and Mitchell were both editors of the *Carillon*, Mitchell was a CUS vice-president, and Kossick was a national CUS field-worker. All of them were part of the aforementioned Moose Jaw Caucus within CUS that helped elect Loney to the 1969 CUS presidency. They all attended high school in Moose Jaw's South Hill neighbourhood, the Eastern European working-class district that stood in contrast to the establishment North Hill neighbourhood. According to Mitchell, this was a formative environment that helped shape subsequent events; South Hill children were taunted by the "elitist crowd" north of the tracks, feeding Mitchell's "instinctive sense of solidarity with the underdogs in society at a pretty early age."[38] This background was also critically important for Kossick and Conway. As Kossick says, there was a "grouping of us who came out of those kind of backgrounds, the kind of working-class labour or working-class farm ... and also had a whole set of values around that."[39]

The 1962 Saskatchewan medicare struggle formed another critical backdrop for the events that were about to unfold. Occurring just as young baby boomers were in high school and becoming politically aware, this was a formative experience.[40] Douglas had defied the doctors, the political establishment, the reluctance of the Saskatchewan Liberal Party – and won, securing a single-payer insurance system that would eventually spread to the rest of Canada in 1967. Those who had grown up through the doctors' strike would not discount the power of progressive peoples and organized labour to effect meaningful change and improved conditions for working people. Certainly, organized labour and the NDP had their fair share of problematic issues, but they could not be entirely written off. Many New Leftists recognized the history and the continued relevance of labour and farmers, and worked with them on that basis. "I think it was unique to some extent," says Conway. "[As it] was just a continuation of Saskatchewan's progressive history, an effort to revive the old coalition together that brought the CCF to power."[41] Unlike in Ontario, there was an active engagement with a continuous provincial left history. In Saskatchewan, many New Leftists had been politicized by the doctors' strike.

"There are actual people who have been doing this very mobilizing," Harding remembers thinking, "[yet student activists from the rest of Canada are] talking about starting anew. The disjuncture."[42] Activism and progressive politics were not dusty old books from the 1930s but something that these youth had been exposed to. There were pre-existing active networks to be re-established and a shared sense of possibility, a belief that change could happen.

Change could not happen on a campus alone, however. New Leftists realized, especially in the context of Saskatchewan, that community mattered. This orientation was present throughout the history of student activism at the Regina campus, giving events there a distinct orientation. Although progressive change had been seen in the Douglas government, the defeat of the provincial NDP in 1964 led to the reign of the pro-business Saskatchewan Liberal Party, headed by Premier Ross Thatcher. Thatcher provided a common foe for student New Leftists, labour, and farmers alike: autocratic, sympathetic to user fees, and an interventionist in campus and labour disputes.

The year 1968 was the turning point for the Regina student movement, and it is also significant in that it saw campus New Leftists moving toward greater cooperation with labour. A key moment came when Alwyn Berland, dean of arts and sciences, resigned. He was concerned about the Regina campus's lack of autonomy from the main Saskatoon campus, the poor facilities, and, perhaps most importantly, the failure of the university to defend academic freedom in 1967 when the premier attempted to intervene in the university budget.[43] Berland was an expatriate American who had come to Canada in part because of his opposition to the Vietnam War, and he was known for his sympathy toward students. A search was mounted to replace him, and students won representation; they wanted another amenable dean. This led to massive involvement: some nine hundred students showed up at the student union's annual meeting, which revolved around the perception that Thatcher was attacking several groups, including labour, teachers, and now students.[44] A common foe had been found. Discussions took place with the Regina and District Labour Council and the Canadian Labour Congress about the Students Union becoming a subtenant of a new labour centre being built downtown. This did not bear fruition – the campus would have no permanent centre until 1997 – but it demonstrates a commonality of interest, as well as the campus leaders' attention toward community issues.[45]

It was a controversy over fees for the student newspaper, the *Carillon*, that cemented the emerging coalition between labour and New Leftists. In December 1968, the *Carillon* published an explicit image of a woman giving birth, prompting the administration to withhold student fees from the paper.[46] Nearly

40 percent of the student body came to the defence of the paper at a mass meeting, a staggering figure that speaks to students' level of engagement. Off-campus supporters were a critical factor. Students rallied around the *Carillon,* printed 100,000 special issues, and "connected with the farmers union [and] trade unionists to help on that issue," says Mitchell. The newspapers were sent back with students to their communities, and a special trip was organized to Moose Jaw, and the entire city blanketed with newspapers.[47] Kossick explained why the students took this route of action: "That's what we believed: you have a right to partake in a decision over a major learning institution in your province, and it's a public university, you have a right to defend the public nature of that university."[48] RCMP surveillance noted that the Saskatchewan Federation of Labour (SFL) and the Saskatchewan Farmers Union both supported the students.[49]

This was a successful issue-based coalition, tapping into the goodwill built up by students in the community. New Leftists were brought into contact with the Moose Jaw and District Labour Council, remembered by Conway, Kossick, and Mitchell as a very significant site of connection. Young workers ran this labour council. President Jerry Hudson was only about only five years older than the students.[50] Conway recalls that "in Moose Jaw, the whole labour council was taken over by young workers who were quite militant."[51] They became aware of Conway thanks to his high profile at SFU and Regina, as well as through common NDP links. The *Carillon* crisis had been framed as an issue of free speech for the community, and as one against Thatcher, and thus united people. As a result, an issue-based "socialist, nationalist" alliance emerged, framed around issues of class. When students pursued a distinct issue, appealing to traditions of free speech and portrayed in a non-radical manner, an effective alliance could form. Together, New Leftists and the labour council ran educationals and rank-and-file mobilizations, and cemented political ties that would emerge in 1970-71. Conway recollects this as being part of a common New Left, as young workers and students could identify through a shared antipathy toward their elders.[52] Kossick was invited by Hudson to labour council meetings: "They wanted to know what we were doing at university, what the issues were, so it was really good alliance building," he says.[53]

This coalition helped transform left politics at the Regina campus and throughout Saskatchewan. Links with the provincial NDP were strengthened, as party leader Woodrow Lloyd had supported the *Carillon.* Lloyd feared that Thatcher was attempting to use the Board of Governors to shut down a significant avenue of criticism. Lloyd emerged as a friend of students, many of whom were active in the provincial party. Indeed, at the 1969 Winnipeg NDP convention, Lloyd voted for the left-wing Waffle manifesto.[54]

In 1970, a crisis erupted over anti-labour legislation. A piece of legislation from 1966, the Essential Services Emergency Act, allowed for compulsory arbitration (through back-to-work legislation) and circumvented collective bargaining procedures.[55] It gave cabinet the power to legislate an end to strikes in essential positions, such as public utilities and health care.[56] In the summer of 1970, the government attempted to extend the act to cover private-sector construction workers.[57] Large rallies took place throughout the province and especially in Regina, bringing together the student movement and labour supporters from the SFL, CUPE, the CLC, and local unions.[58] New Leftists supported the fight, understanding its broad implications. The *Carillon* claimed that the bill was "an undemocratic piece of legislation which invades civil liberties and deprives thousands of our fellow citizens of democratic rights."[59] Union and student leaders made speeches, and students distributed flyers reading "Your Fight is our Fight."[60]

These protests helped contribute to the momentum that led to the 1970 defeat of the Liberal government. According to Kossick, these were large gatherings:

> That protest in '70, '71 actually showed the work that had been happening
> between farm, labour, and students. It really was a massive turnout, and
> showed the outwardness rather than the inwardness of the strategies at that
> time ... [And] the fact that you could align all those social movements at the
> time and create a manifestation.[61]

Lloyd had worked to build a coalition of youth, feminists, young workers, and farmers throughout this early period.[62] An alliance formed between them and the Saskatchewan Waffle. The group's candidate would be Mitchell, the former *Carillon* editor and CUS vice-president, with substantial support from younger workers around the province.

A host of socio-historical forces had led to Reginan New Leftists being less estranged from the NDP than their counterparts elsewhere in English Canada. Crucially, labour was not as powerful a presence within the Saskatchewan party as in Ontario, where international unions were instrumental in defeating the Waffle. As noted, Lloyd had signed the manifesto. This would precipitate an internal party fight.

Through early 1970, cracks began to appear in the party. Conservative NDP members were agitating for Lloyd's resignation; he obliged them in March, setting in motion a leadership race. That same month, Conway returned from SFU to run for the NDP nomination in Moose Jaw South. On 27 March 1970, the Saskatchewan Waffle was founded by several activists: Mitchell, Conway, and a professor at the Regina campus, John Warnock. They decided to run Mitchell as the unofficial Waffle candidate in the leadership contest (they feared official status might be a hindrance). His platform focused on the agricultural sector, calling for reforms allowing farmers to sell produce at above-market prices to the province, the nationalization of the machinery, food processing, and agricultural service sectors, as well as the creation of a Land Bank.[63] Mitchell's campaign literature stressed not only his agricultural credentials (beyond his National Farmers Union [NFU] work, Mitchell studied agricultural policy for his MA thesis) but also his national profile as a former CUS vice-president.[64] It also noted his experience as an on-campus activist, which, he explained, was where he saw the rhetoric of the just society flounder as working-class children found themselves unable to pay for education.[65]

A campaign decision was made to emphasize Saskatchewan's earlier left history, and to use the campaign to create a coalition for fundamental change. This too was evident in the campaign literature. This was an attempt to return the provincial NDP to its agrarian, community-based origins and away from slick, image-based professional politics. Indeed, even the RCMP had noted internally that the "right wing" was then in control of the party.[66]

In recollections, supporters emphasized their attempts to bridge gaps between various groups. Conway saw the Waffle as a "coalition of farmers, workers, students, and progressive intellectuals." Kossick remembers that it was "an absolute fusing of the student movement and the energies of that alongside the farm movement and the labour movement."[67] Mitchell agrees, recalling his decision to run: "I was a candidate for that coalition of youth ... the farmers union network, labour left contacts, and the student movement." The Waffle had the support of the NFU, as well as such influential labour members as SFL provincial secretary Bill Gilbey, and the Moose Jaw and District Labour Council.[68] While Mitchell was unsuccessful in his leadership bid at the provincial convention in July, he made it to the second ballot with about a quarter of the votes.[69]

We can see the coalition at work in Mitchell's campaign. Labour leaders, farm leaders, and student movement leaders joined together to effect a common enterprise centred on the recovery of a provincial left tradition. Indeed, its true victory came in its influence on the provincial NDP platform during the 1971 election. The Saskatchewan Waffle had resource nationalization and greater agricultural supports included in NDP leader Allan Blakeney's platform. Yet afterward, the group became fragmented and marginalized, eventually forming an independent Waffle in 1973.[70]

The Waffle was not the only avenue for this broader coalition in Regina between New Leftists and the broader community. In Saskatchewan, it was necessary to reach out to both workers and farmers, and an opportunity soon presented itself. The NFU was founded in 1969 as a merger of the Saskatchewan Farmers Union, the Ontario Farmers Union, the Manitoba Farmers Union, and the Farmers Union of BC.[71] By 1970, its membership was approximately thirty thousand across the country. Although it included only 10 percent of Saskatchewan farmers, it was seen as being ascendant by the RCMP, who were paying it increased attention.[72] It was an idealistic organization, inspired by concepts of collective bargaining for both farm inputs and farm outputs, and founded on an idea of direct democracy.[73] This idealism encouraged young people to get involved. Mitchell and Kossick worked as NFU organizers, Mitchell before throwing himself into the Waffle and Kossick sticking with the organization for years afterward. "The fact that we were brought into the farmers union with our whole long hair and everything [was very significant]," says Kossick. "They wouldn't have approached us unless they'd figured us out and saw us as allies, eh? I think it was actually a brilliant stroke on their part. They took all this energy we had. We were young, really motivated, able to speak to large groups and design education."[74]

From its inception, the NFU reached out to students. A large rally was held on 8 April 1970, bringing together important speakers to deal with the farmers' plight: the NFU president, Premier Thatcher, the mayor of Regina, the SFL president, the president of the NFU's Women's Branch, and Mitchell on behalf of the Regina campus. Mitchell, along with the mayor and SFL president, received a standing ovation and "warm round[s] of applause" from the audience, whereas Thatcher was jeered and interrupted.[75] Although the RCMP report of the rally is redacted, mention is made of activists circulating throughout the protest, taking photographs of police.

Beyond police reports, relatively little has been written on the NFU. I have therefore leaned heavily on interviews and a 1972 documentary entitled *Down on the Farm,* in which a filmmaker follows Kossick around southern Saskatchewan. Kossick drove long distances, dropping into farmhouses, having kitchen-table meetings with farmers, and otherwise organizing for the NFU. Produced by the Unconscious Collective in Toronto, there is an obvious agenda behind the documentary's production: highlighting the valuable community work done by the NFU and by Kossick, with a presumable aim to demonstrate a promising avenue of political organizing. It provides insight into the day-to-day activities of NFU organizers. The NFU sought to organize small family farms, an important economic and political force. In the film, Kossick introduces himself as he drives:

My name is Don Kossick, and I was born and raised in Moose Jaw. I did the standard thing. I went to university. I sorta got turned on there. Got actively involved in student politics, in the sense of that period, that critical period where we started taking on the institutions, you know? ... Then right around, I guess it was in November, I came into the farm movement ... we're talking about the same thing in a way. We're talking about the exploitation of groups, how power has left the people and it's concentrated with the corporations and so on, how these corporations control the government and make policy, which give them all the money they want.[76]

There was a conscious attempt to build something more than just a farmers' union, as Kossick points out at a farmhouse gathering of a few dozen farmers; they sought to build a *movement*. Throughout, Kossick stresses the need for a coalition, which garners a surprisingly favourable reception from farmers.

A few scenes of the film are illustrative. Kossick is in a farmhouse, washing dishes with a farmer's wife and daughter, discussing the need for transformative change on the farm. The daughter then expounds on the need for cooperation: "You've got to take one where the other is, and the other where the other is. You gotta take the students where the farmers are, and the farmers to where the students are." The wife smiles supportively. Kossick enthusiastically agrees, "You know we can't solve our problems just as farmers, right? I think this is obvious. And the next question is: How can we link up our farmers movement with the youth movement and what is going on with labour and so on?" This is coalition building, waged from one kitchen table to the next, from small-town diners to high school classrooms.

Nothing encapsulates this spirit better than a discussion captured in the film. Roughly two dozen or more people gather in a farmhouse, listening raptly to Kossick but frequently interjecting, asking questions, beginning a dialogue. The former campus newspaper editor and organizer commands the respect of the audience and is explicit about the next steps required for the NFU. Part of the problem, Kossick explains, is that the fishermen hate the farmers, the farmers hate the fishermen, with "everybody hating youth. And everybody is divided up from each other – you're never going to get anywhere." A farmer enthusiastically agrees: "It's just a matter of all getting together!" As Kossick drives away, he explains to the cameraperson the reasoning behind the farmers movement in a way that any New Leftist would have recognized. Farmers needed *control:* as it stood, they were held down on the farm, controlled by corporations and agri-business, stuck in debt without any control over product prices. But there was still hope: "The cynicism that you can get when you're just in the city, when you're cut off, you're isolated, you're alienated in the mass society, that's getting wiped out, man. They're breaking down the mass society thing. They're saying, 'Yeah, people can be good, people can work at things.'" After this film, Kossick became the national coordinator for the NFU's Kraft Foods boycott, launched on 19 April 1971 after Kraft refused to collectively bargain with the union over dairy prices, and which spread from coast to coast.

From Regina came a relatively successful approach to New Leftist organizing. A powerful coalition was built: young workers, New Leftists, students, and farmers. When the *Carillon* was threatened by a Liberal-appointed board of governors, workers from Moose Jaw, social democrats from Regina, and students gathered to save it. This set in motion a process of alliance building that culminated in the Saskatchewan Waffle and Don Mitchell's influential NDP leadership bid. Those individuals would have substantial impact on policy, resulting in meaningful social change and improvement for the lives of Saskatchewanites. In the NFU, another coalition was built and continued across the country. The NFU recognized the power of students, as would other unions in British Columbia, allowing the creation of a broader coalition.

Coming off Burnaby Mountain: Simon Fraser University's Outward Focus

SFU was an instant campus in decidedly working-class Burnaby, opened in September 1965 to accommodate baby boomers. The university's normal operations were disrupted between 1967 and 1969; according to the RCMP, it was the "best example" of radicalism in Canada.[77] Despite being geographically isolated on the top of Burnaby Mountain, literally in the clouds at times, many New Leftists there developed an outward-looking, community focus to their politics that sought to bring SFU "off the mountain" and into the service of the surrounding community. Notably, this outward community focus also significantly heard the voices of, and would eventually be led by, women. These young men and women tried to put the refrain "The university is for people" into action.

The media created a buzz around SFU's opening by building an "exciting" public image, highlighting its round-the-year trimester system, a teaching focus, and its modern architecture.[78] SFU sought "non-traditional" students, and endeavoured to encourage their participation in higher education through various means, particularly the trimester system. SFU differed markedly from the more established University of British Columbia and its more affluent student body. Briemberg remembers the rhetoric of bringing "ordinary working people" into SFU and providing them with the same opportunities they would have received at a more elite university such as UBC.[79] Yet SFU was not a class-free utopia, as noted earlier with the example of Sharon Yandle.

Early campus debates involved the role of students in society. In May 1966, during a Vancouver municipal workers' strike, twenty students crossed City Hall picket lines to cut the lawn in an act of strikebreaking. When the SFU Student Society chair declared his concern that this would lead to worker-student resentment, the on-campus newspaper the *Peak* responded that the student council was overstretching its campus-derived authority.[80] Student activists were thus concerned about relations with the broader community from an early stage, as well as being initially politically polarized. Later that year, a campaign against an on-campus Shell gas station prompted students to gather 350 signatures from the broader community and try to persuade area residents to support them.[81] Despite SFU's geographical isolation, student activists looked outward.

Student politics became increasingly political by 1967, thanks in part to an influx of new graduate students. Martin Loney was one. He came from Britain to study with the Marxist sociologist (and dean of arts) Tom Bottomore. Loney had been a member of the British Labour Party, had worked with the National Union of Students, and had been involved in anti-apartheid work.[82] Another Bottomore student was the aforementioned Jim Harding from Regina. John Conway also made the trek from Regina to SFU for his PhD.

In March 1967, events at Templeton Secondary School, in East Vancouver, presented New Leftists with an opportunity "to link up to the working class, a working-class school." According to John Cleveland, then a PSA graduate student, what followed "was a very conscious political choice based on pre-existing socialist politics that were pro–working class."[83] Five graduate teaching assistants learned that a Templeton student had been expelled for parodying and criticizing a teacher. They wrote an open letter to the high school, imploring students to stand up for their schoolmate through any "legal action," including a strike.[84] A visit to Templeton by the signatories to distribute pamphlets and speak to the students ended with the arrests of two.[85] The five teaching assistants were also all immediately fired by SFU's board of governors, as they had "discredit[ed]" the university and "recommended contempt for the law."[86] After Bottomore's resignation over the lack of due process followed, and the subsequent threat of a strike by the Student Society, the teaching assistants were reinstated.

The increasingly energized campus became fertile New Leftist ground. Inspired by a similar organization at McGill, Students for a Democratic University (SDU) was founded in January 1968. A poster summed up the group's initial areas of focus:

1 the structure of the university
2 the role of the university in society
3 collective representation of student interests
4 coordination of student action aiming at greater involvement in the
   control of the university.[87]

Much of this avid New Leftist activity was due to the influence of the PSA
Department, which was calling for community involvement and reaching out
to "working people, poor people, Native people, women ... [to show them] how
we could relate and meet the needs of those people as opposed to corporate
needs."[88] SDU would flirt with student political power in 1968: between March
and September 1968, Loney, Conway, and Harding formed a short-lived – and
controversial – SDU student government.[89]

In November 1968, the student council at Vancouver City College (VCC)
(later to become Vancouver Community College) protested the inequities and
challenges facing college students when they attempted to transfer to university:
the admissions process was opaque, and there was no transparency in the transfer
credit–granting process. Drena McCormack, a VCC Council vice-president
approached SDU in light of its radical reputation. By her account, "We didn't
even think they'd meet with us. ... And the funny thing was that the way they
looked at us was 'oh good, a new issue we can latch onto and run with.' And we
were just thrilled."[90] In the ideological milieu of the move toward the working
class, it is not surprising that SDU students were receptive to the VCC students
and their admissions issue. According to Guy Pocklington (who came to SFU
as an undergrad after hearing that Bottomore "attracted interesting people" and
became involved with SDU), the SDU was "interested in linking the student
movement with the larger society, the working class, so this particular struggle
– which was demands of working-class students ... was perfect [for us]."[91] In
interviews, other former SDU members echoed this. As John Cleveland put it,
these were "working-class kids trying to get into the middle-class university, so
again this was our attempt to take a class perspective."[92]

SDU members and VCC students drafted a manifesto, making four key
demands:

1 Freedom of transfer and automatic acceptance of credits within the BC
   public educational system
2 An elected parity Student/Faculty Admissions Board
3 The opening of all Administration Files

4   More money for education as a whole and equitable financing within post-secondary education. This involves the immediate end to the current school construction freeze.[93]

Three hundred SFU and VCC students attended a special meeting of the SFU Senate, called to discuss the demands. McCormack from VCC went into the meeting thinking that the administrators would recognize the folly of their policy, but SDU members were less sanguine.[94] After the demands were rejected, they effected a preplanned occupation of the SFU Administration Building and refused to leave until their demands were met. SFU president Kenneth Strand called the police. On the occupation's third night, negotiations broke down and the RCMP was ordered to move in. The occupiers were given the option of leaving, and some fearing immigration issues did so.[95] At three in the morning, the police moved in and arrested the 114 remaining people.

In support, CUS printed a special issue of its newspaper, *Issue,* aimed at working people. This was an opportunity for them to build on their recent ideological shift toward the working class. One hundred thousand copies were printed and distributed to factories and unions across BC.[96] Conway says that the paper was also distributed to other schools across Metro Vancouver, as well as door to door in Burnaby, to explain "our case to the working class."[97] The issue was entitled "Special Edition for the People of British Columbia," with the headline reading "Simon Fraser Concerns You." The lead story began:

> The BC government has shown in its policies that it does not represent the working people of this province. Attorney General Peterson was Minister of Labor and Minister of Education, as such he attacked both workers and students. With Bill 33 he sought to prevent unions fighting for the interests of their members. Now he is pressing criminal charges against 114 young people. (Under BC labour laws they have imprisoned labour leaders like Homer Stevens. It seems they intend to do the same to students.)[98]

The broadsheet pointed out that lawyers, business people, and financiers were on the SFU board of governors, and workers, students, and educators were not. The CUS Student Means Survey was used to show the disproportionate number of working-class students at SFU. The broadsheet emphasized that the SFU 114 were arrested for the rights of future students: "Your children today, our children tomorrow." Cleveland remembers there being some traction around these demands: "The unions could see 'hey, my kids have more access to university if they win these issues.' It resonated really well."[99] A second broadsheet, *Trouble at Simon Fraser,* was also distributed to union and community members. It was apparently a product of the PSA Department. It ran articles such as "Trouble Is ... You Pay for the University – They Run It," it reprinted what the PSA stood for, and it encouraged unions and community members who needed help to contact Briemberg.[100]

A Committee to Aid the SFU 114 was quickly established. It included a vice-president from the International Woodworkers' Association and the president of the Nelson, Trail and District Labour Council.[101] British Columbia Federation of Labour secretary-treasurer Ray Haynes called for the charges to be dropped, and agitated for a committee to look into student grievances regarding admissions. It was essential, he said, that the committee include union members, teachers, students, and other representatives.[102] Haynes also wrote to the minister of education and the attorney general in support of students.[103] Harding remembers the leader of the United Fishermen and Allied Workers Union (UFAWU), Homer Stevens, becoming actively involved. "I believe it was mostly ... fishermen," Harding says of the labour supporters. "We took the position of access of their children to higher education and, of course, that's part of their Old Left reason for working!"[104]

When the 114 were sentenced in March 1969, the *Peak* ran an editorial comparing student protest to earlier struggles, including the New Westminster fishermen's strike broken up by the militia in 1900, and picket-line attacks in 1930 and 1935.[105] A document entitled "Why They Occupied the Building" declared that the charges against the 114 paralleled the ongoing harassment of labour unions, and that being charged with "obstruction of private property" was similar to an injunction.[106] Harding and his fellow New Leftists began to see connections "between what we're doing and trade unions fighting for their rights. In fact, the same laws that were used against the early trade unionists in BC [were] used against us at Simon Fraser."[107] Although the comparison was apt in principle, the sentences meted out to the 114 for disturbing the peace were comparatively light. When the trials came up later that month, all but one student faced fines: $250 for most, $25 for two who apologized. Only one student faced a three-month prison sentence, for breaching an earlier bond.[108]

The last New Leftist activity of relevance at SFU was the PSA strike, which occurred after the administration overruled departmental tenure and promotions decisions. On 15 July 1969, the PSA Department was placed in trusteeship by the administration; one reason for this was that the move toward faculty and student parity on committees violated regulations.[109] The department countered by pointing out what it felt was the real reason behind the trusteeship: the PSA Department was "grounded on the philosophy of participation and control from below and designed to serve the needs of the PEOPLE OF BRITISH COLUM-BIA."[110] A full-page *Peak* spread discussed the common struggle of workers and students:

> More and more, official and wildcat strikes make demands for control over speed-ups, control over what happens on the shop floor, in the office, control over automation, control over the polluted atmosphere ... Students too are no longer willing to be bought off with a degree-packet. They want to control how they work, when they work, the conditions in which they work.[111]

It went on to say, "You meet the same excuses, the same tricks and sometimes even the same people in your struggles in the factory, in the office, in the apartment, in the school. And these struggles are not just yours. They are our struggles too." The department invited community members who needed research, teaching workshops, or other help to contact them. To this day, Briemberg believes this is why it was attacked:

> Some faculty and students are working with people in unions, or unemployed in demonstrations, and those things ... And it was dangerous, the outward focus of it. That somehow the university comes off the mountain, and actually goes to see what it can do in relation to ordinary people's working lives and their needs.[112]

Serving the public was a central issue throughout these events. The PSA student union agreed, saying that it supported the department's push to be "more involved in the community," and that greater decision-making power was necessary to "ensure that the university is responsive to all peoples [sic] needs, irrespective of wealth or power."[113]

In September 1969, the PSA students and faculty voted to strike for the return of local decision-making control.[114] Pickets targeted professors who continued teaching. Attempts were made to reframe the events into a broader, community issue. Briemberg addressed the Vancouver and District Labour Council, saying that the "same people who control the university also control the major businesses in this province, and used the same tactics as are used against the labour movement."[115] The council pledged its support. However, there was no mass mobilization of labour, no groundswell of rank-and-file support. The RCMP concluded that, with exceptions, "the reaction of the labour movement to the SFU problems was one of restraint and non-involvement."[116] This subdued reaction may have stemmed in part from the media; according to Briemberg, the papers "smear[ed] us as wild-eyed, crazy people who were chaotic, creating a mess ... And our time of working with people in the unions had not been sufficiently long enough that they were in a position ... to really rally their memberships in any way to speak out."[117]

While counter-courses were briefly established by striking students to "opt out of the business-university complex and 'do research for the people,'"[118] the PSA strike was short. The provincial Supreme Court, at the request of the administration, issued an injunction on 23 October aimed at preventing unlawful picketing, coercion, and intimidation. Facing arrest if they continued the strike, the Joint Strike Assembly (composed of students and professors) voted on 4 November to end it.[119] Although the students held on for ten days between the injunction and ending the strike, it was clear that the students were largely alone, that the state was marshalled against them, and that there was little reason to persist. In this context, students were not prepared for imprisonment.[120]

The strike's true significance for the long-term development of SFU's New Left lay in how it provided the final push for many to move off campus and wholly involve themselves with off-campus activities. As Briemberg explained to the *Peak* in early 1970:

[The PSA strike] made many of us more conscious of the necessity for alliances with oppressed groups off campus. It is easy to know this rhetorically, it is another thing to know this from the experience of a strike where the absence of a developed alliance is critical to success and failure of one's own specific struggles ... Secondly, and in a complementary way, having engaged in a strike, having fought for and not just spoken about community integration, makes it easier to work with oppressed groups off-campus.[121]

Briemberg's words would be put to the test, as many students left SFU entirely in the wake of the strike: for some, their supervisors had been terminated, or the rationale behind attending the PSA Department was gone; others were burned out from years of disruption. The student movement and on-campus New Left had been broken, a point raised in all my oral interviews and also noted by the RCMP and the *Peak*. SFU would become, as the *Peak* put it, a "hotbed of quietism."[122]

The continuity of the off-campus orientation can be seen in three projects: the Community Education and Research Centre (CERC), the establishment of the *Western Voice*, and the emergence of the women-led Service, Office and Retail Workers Union of Canada. CERC represented a direct continuation of PSA policies.[123] The fired faculty, led by Briemberg, established the centre in downtown Vancouver. Building on earlier promises, the centre was intended to host workshops on historical and contemporary issues, conduct research for unions, publish broadsheets, and assemble a public library of useful documents.[124] New Leftists also came to assist. An organizational meeting in December 1969 aimed to establish "a working relationship" between labour and PSA members. About a hundred unionists attended, including members of the Canadian Ironworkers Union, Telecommunications Workers, International Brotherhood of Electrical Workers, Marine Workers, Carpenters, and the Vancouver and District Labour Council. The RCMP was surprised by the turnout, though it noted that most appeared to be "students or long-haired hippie type youths." It also noted that the Pulp and Paper Workers of Canada made use of CERC's resources and facilities.[125]

The second meeting at CERC in early 1970 was more promising. Briemberg put the number of attendees at between 175 and 200, with about 75 unionists. This was "encouraging, given the usual alienation that exists between the two groups, the workers and the university." He drew a strong continuity between the earlier goals of the PSA Department and CERC:

> These major institutions within our society, the factory and the university, must be transformed and made to serve the needs of the working people of this province and this country. To accomplish that, people must be situated within them and struggle for those aims. But we must build links between the various struggles, between the campus struggle and the community. This is what PSA was always attempting to do.[126]

Despite the involvement of unions such as the Pulp and Paper Workers, these links, Briemberg says, were akin to "little seeds that never grew into plants," as CERC was too transitory to develop long-standing ties and projects. The fired professors had initially stood together and agreed to collaborate, but most soon left CERC to pursue academic employment elsewhere. By the summer of 1970, CERC's activities had almost completely ceased.[127]

Briemberg and several former students, including Pocklington and Cleveland, then found their way to other pro–working-class groups. With some contributors from the local newspaper *Georgia Straight,* which was going through an internal crisis, they helped establish a newspaper called the *Yellow Journal.*[128] This "yippie Marxist" production, as Pocklington refers to it, was a melding of the local hippie counterculture with the New Left line. The *Yellow Journal* eventually morphed into the *Georgia Grape* (and then simply the *Grape),* reflecting discontent with the mainstream *Straight.* The *Grape* combined a focus on municipal politics and the cultural counterculture, with an emphasis on working-class and union struggles.

Eventually, the *Grape* was transformed to reflect the increasing dominance of working-class and labour issues. As the paper noted in June 1973: "The name doesn't fit anymore. We're not an underground paper. We have changed our content. We have changed our style. So now we have decided it was time to change our name."[129] In September 1973, the paper was renamed *Western Voice: A Newspaper of Working Class Struggle*. For the next three years, the *Western Voice* threw itself into regional working-class issues: the conditions of service workers in British Columbia and Alberta, municipal politics, and more importantly, strikes, lockouts, international shenanigans, and struggles throughout the region. For Cleveland, the *Western Voice* represented continuity:

> [It was] kind of a continuation of CERC-type politics as opposed to SDU-type politics, where we were trying to link up to progressive community groups and unions. So it's more the kind of version of left-wing politics that Mordecai [Briemberg] was principally associated with ... [We] practised a kind of united front politics.[130]

Briemberg spoke of the class orientation of the *Western Voice*, and how the editors tried to report on and support both organized and unorganized workers' struggles. The paper attracted those who "had a more class orientation to struggle."[131] In 1976, however, the *Western Voice* folded, and many of the members moved into the national Marxist-Leninist group In Struggle/*En Lutte*.[132]

Perhaps the most enduring legacy of SFU's off-campus orientation was the Vancouver Women's Caucus (VWC) and the eventual establishment of the Service, Office and Retail Workers Union of Canada. The VWC had its origins in a PSA course that asked students to rewrite the *Communist Manifesto*. Marcy Toms and Dodie (Doreen) Weppler wrote a manifesto calling for the establishment of a Feminine Action League, and then, with the thought, "We've written a paper, maybe we should have a meeting?" brought people together.[133] The league, closed to men, held its first meeting in early July 1968; it eventually renamed itself the SFU Women's Caucus and began meeting regularly off campus.[134] According to Toms, the group was responding to gender inequities within the SFU student movement, where "you kind of felt that you were just an appendage, rather than somebody who would have the opportunity to develop as a leader."[135] A conscious decision was soon made to become a politically oriented group. Some women who attended the meetings were focused on psychological aspects, being involved in consciousness raising and preferring to "disclose and discuss" – Toms derisively explains that they wanted "to sit around and say how bad things are" – and they eventually "went on their way." The remaining women were focused on being "more explicitly political right away ... organizing and acting around a variety of specific concerns," including reproductive rights.

By July 1969, the SFU Women's Caucus recast itself as the Vancouver Women's Caucus, reflecting a new off-campus focus. SFU students were the majority, but VWC also attracted other students and women from the broader community, housewives and clerical workers among them. The RCMP observed that the group's majority was young students, though "about 10 members" were over thirty years of age.[136] The VWC approached women at other post-secondary institutions, as well as in the workplace, to join. As McCormack remembers, there were "people who had some sophistication about politics and class, so I would say that there were probably more working-class people in the Women's Caucus than there were in SDU."[137]

They began meeting downtown and developing a class-based orientation. Frances Jane Wasserlein sees this as unsurprising in light of the personal biographies of the individuals involved, and that the VWC's attention to class as a category of analysis made the group unique.[138] The members continued to write articles for the *Peak* through 1970, wherein they drew attention to the discriminatory labour market position of women, their unpaid labour, and their limited opportunities for class mobility.

The VWC's most famous activity was the Abortion Caravan, which pre-occupied the group in early 1970. Through late April and early May, the Abortion Caravan travelled from Vancouver to Ottawa in an attempt to repeal anti-abortion laws and raise awareness about the toll illegal abortions was taking on women. Political differences emerged. For example, the slogan "Smash Capitalism!" appeared on the side of one of the vans, and the women debated whether this "revolutionary demand" was appropriate; the women in favour of removing it eventually prevailed.[139] Factions had emerged within the VWC, notably the Working Women's Workshop in January 1970; it carried out picketing at the Vancouver General Hospital and rental car companies at the Vancouver airport in support of striking workers, and boycotted a drugstore that was being struck by women workers trying to garner a first contract.[140]

On the return of the caravaners to Vancouver, political debates boiled over, revealing the tension between a broader, working-class orientation and a more abortion-focused approach.[141] There were three factions, McCormack explains: one that wanted to focus on abortion as a galvanizing issue; one that was concerned with economic equality, pay, and access; and "a faction that said, you know, we need to organize women around their class and their gender. And women in working-class jobs, women who are home being housewives, all of that stuff." Toms recalls that while the Young Socialists faction of VWC was focusing on abortion as a coalition-building approach, the other groups wanted "to focus on issues pertinent to working women, who aren't in trades unions, try to get them organized, and to improving working conditions and pay for women who are already employed and/or in unions."[142] The RCMP noted the debate between the "practical" group and the others who were using the group as a "political gambit." Some members "always managed to turn the discussion around to political strategy, i.e., the importance of reaching the working class women, especially those whose husbands are now locked out in labour disputes ... and of making people aware of the 'social system they are presently suffering under.'" Indeed, "there was even talk about starting up unions for women workers!"[143] This group, which had its nucleus in the Working Women's Workshop, broke off to pursue a working-class women's orientation as the Vancouver Working Women's Association.

The association focused on strike support, encouraging women who wanted to organize to join unions such as the Hotel Employees and Restaurant Employees Union and the Office and Technical Employees' Union; it also distributed educational material. Based on their experiences, members argued that a new type of union was needed, as unions often had undemocratic structures and were led by men willing to sell out their female workers. In 1972, the Vancouver Working Women's Association formed the Service, Office and Retail Workers Union of Canada (SORWUC): "Since 80% of working women in BC were not in unions, it was felt that an independent union run by women workers themselves was necessary."[144]

SORWUC adopted New Leftist principles: all decisions had to be approved by a majority of bargaining-unit members, recall procedures were instituted for union officers, dues would stay in Canada, and every effort was made to develop a truly democratic union.[145] The majority of union positions were also unpaid and always elected. Beginning in 1973, SORWUC worked to organize workplaces, beginning with a legal office, then a shelter for female victims of domestic abuse. By 1975, it had organized fourteen sites, and by 1978 represented forty-one workplaces.[146]

When SORWUC collapsed and disbanded in 1986, it left a significant legacy.[147] It may have been small in size, but it was part of a broader women's trend within the trade union movement (including public sector unions and the provincial federation of labour) that pushed for the advancement of female issues. SORWUC attempted to organize the hard-to-organize service sector, took a radical approach to unionization, and is exemplary of a movement that used class politics to achieve social justice aims.[148] As such, it reflects an important class-based extension of SFU's off-campus orientation.

The history of SFU's New Left is unified by a single theme: off-campus community engagement, especially with working people. Reflecting a consistent class focus, we can see this commitment in the struggles for free speech at a working-class East Vancouver high school, in the fight over class-based admissions and transfer policies, and in the mission of the PSA to bring academics off the mountain and to the people. The transfer battle ended in tangible gains: a month after the Administration Building occupation, the Academic Board for Higher Education in British Columbia met and realized that if it did not resolve the "perceived problems" itself, the government might do so in its stead. Formalized transfer guidelines were published after this meeting, subsequently leading to the 1974 Post-Secondary Articulation Coordinating Committee and eventually the 1989 British Columbia Council on Admissions and Transfer. Indeed, a report by this council on its official history mentions the Administration Building occupation in its timeline.[149] The PSA Department's quest to become a community-focused department in the service of the people may have failed with its destruction by the university administration, but this did not end its outward-looking trajectory.

Conclusion

This chapter has argued that New Leftists' debates about the need to work with the working class and for working people to serve as agents of social change were not simply abstract intellectual exercises, but rather concrete policy put into place in various ways. In Ontario, Saskatchewan, and British Columbia, New Leftists sought to forge a broader movement that encompassed and was responsive to working people, and attempted to build a broader coalition with them. In Ontario, a deep relationship floundered because of the power of large international unions and more entrenched anti-radical sentiments. Yet in Saskatchewan and British Columbia, where traditions of labour radicalism were more pronounced, New Leftists were able to tap into these broader historical currents. Saskatchewan New Leftists took their place alongside labour, farm, and urban progressives to help bring down the Saskatchewan Liberal Party; they then played influential roles in determining NDP policy and were actively brought into organizations such as the National Farmers Union (NFU). This was enabled in part by formative youth experiences during the 1962 doctors' strike and a tradition of provincial social democracy, leading to a different understanding of parliamentary, versus extra-parliamentary, change. In British Columbia, an outward-looking New Left culture was developed, as seen in the case of SFU.

These were concerted efforts; however, New Leftists were generally unsuccessful in achieving a true broad-based movement alongside large numbers of working people. On specific issues, from strikebreaking to the case of the SFU 114, New Leftists did find sympathetic common ground with union leaders. That these were decidedly non-radical issues, often revolving around long-held liberal traditions such as freedom of the press or broader arguments surrounding *in loco parentis,* helped forge single-issue coalitions. Subsequent developments such as SORWUC, or the move into more traditional political organizations such as the NDP or the NFU, represented an effective continuance of worker-based politics. Although the end-goals may have been radical and idealistic, these activities demonstrated pragmatism.

Despite these limited successes, even the single-issue coalitions saw caution and hesitation from working people and unions. Many on-campus leaders may have had working-class roots, yet the gap between the quadrangle and the union hall was not fully bridged. Some of this can be ascribed to external factors: established social democrats in the NDP were hardly warm to many New Left concerns, as seen in Regina; university administrators were quick to denounce New Leftists while co-opting their more broad-based demands; geography could isolate students from the broader community; and the media often painted the New Leftists unfavourably.

Yet external factors alone cannot account for the overall inability to secure a broad-based working-class alliance. The countercultural heritage and outward appearance of many New Leftists hampered an alliance with some elements of the labour movement's rank and file. There was a generational divide *within* many unions, and this must have been felt toward New Leftists as well. New Leftists were also hampered by some of their views toward the working class, often founded initially on an ideological view of their integration into capitalist society.

However, there were meaningful outcomes from these events for New Leftists and for working people in Saskatchewan and British Columbia. These must not be downplayed. In Saskatchewan, the eventual establishment of a New Left-farmer-labour coalition was instrumental in bringing down the Liberal government in 1970-71 and subsequently influenced the NDP's platform and governance from 1971 onward. At SFU, New Leftists, including many who had migrated from Saskatchewan, developed an outward-looking community focus to their politics that sought to bring students "off the mountain" and into the service of the surrounding community. Subsequent developments such as SORWUC greatly contributed to the daily lives of ordinary working people in the province, and CERC and the *Western Voice* represented attempts to do the same. This experience helps us reach a different understanding of the New Left, especially in the less-studied post-1968 period. Far from a retreat to the campus, we instead see a dynamic movement out into the community in an attempt to foster meaningful change. Interacting with regional traditions, New Leftists reactivated old notions of radical histories.

5

Cold, Slogging Solidarity: Supporting Labour on Picket Lines in Ontario and Nova Scotia, 1968-72

Ontario and Nova Scotia witnessed a different story of New Leftist and labour outreach centred on picket lines. Although cautious labour hierarchies would thwart any attempt at a deeper, lasting student-worker alliance, this did not preclude local connections. Beginning with a hardscrabble group of journalists who stood up to the global Thomson empire, young men and women woke early in the morning, took school buses off to industrial cities, slept on the cold floors of churches and union halls, and attempted to make their ideology a reality. The strikes were all framed around issues that resonated with New Leftists: nationalism, dignity, poverty, and power. These were issues that re-deemed unions in the eyes of many New Leftists who, only a few years earlier, had scorned them. On the picket lines at the *Peterborough Examiner,* at Dare' Foods in Kitchener, at Texpack, and among the fishing outports along the Strait of Canso, New Leftists encountered labour.

Beginning in 1968 with the *Peterborough Examiner* strike, this connection manifested itself with New Leftists moving off campus to support striking workers. These were high-profile strikes where the opportunity for an alliance presented itself. New Leftists had been on picket lines before these instances, of course, but they had participated as supportive individuals. These activities were different, as New Leftists now came as a community. These strikes were fought around fairly consistent issues: strikebreaking, exploitation, national-ism, and the role of the police. New Leftists became increasingly aware of gendered issues within workplaces. Strikes in both Peterborough and Kitchener involved pay equity dimensions, an issue that by 1972 – but not in 1968 – was a key point of contention. New Leftist thought evolved during this period, with ramifications for the support actions taken. This support would come to profoundly matter. Although they represent only a fraction of all strikes and man-hours lost to labour action, these events captured the interest of people across each province.

The Newsmen versus the Empire: The *Peterborough Examiner* Strike

In April 1968, the Thomson Media empire acquired the *Peterborough Examiner*. With modest beginnings in North Bay and Timmins in the early 1930s, Thomson had grown to encompass nearly two hundred newspapers as well as assorted other media holdings. Roy Thomson was a paternalist in the finest sense, known as "Lord T" or "Uncle Roy" to his employees.[1] Resistance came quickly in Peterborough, a small city about 125 kilometres northeast of Toronto. The Toronto Newspaper Guild had been active in Toronto, securing collective agreements with the *Toronto Star* and the *Toronto Telegram*. In May 1968, the guild organized the *Examiner*'s editorial employees. Negotiations reached an impasse and the guild struck on 2 November for a first collective agreement. Twenty of the guild's twenty-two employees joined the picket lines.[2] Wages were a key issue, though the guild raised other issues as well: Thomson had offered minimum-salary scales below existing rates; also it had failed to end the gender differential, provide job and union security, ensure a five-day, thirty-seven-and-a-half-hour workweek, and guarantee that the employees could not be unilaterally transferred to a non-union Thomson newspaper.[3] The lack of attention paid by strike supporters toward the gender differential issue shows how some New Leftists were still grappling with an understanding of the significance of that category of analysis (as borne out in their internal politics, discussed in Chapter 3).

Picket lines were crucial, as the *Examiner* continued to operate using managing editors and strikebreakers from other newspapers. The guild hoped to reproduce their earlier 1966 experience when they had prevented the *Oshawa Times* from publishing through mass picketing.[4] New Leftists such as Andrew Wernick were aware of the Oshawa lesson, seeing it as a model.[5] The picketers needed external support as their small numbers alone were ineffective. The first obvious call for support was to the Peterborough and District Labour Council. The 1966 Tilco strike had galvanized the labour movement in that city around the issue of *ex parte* injunctions, and the newsmen must have expected solidarity – yet little was forthcoming.[6] The lack of support was surprising and the *Hamilton Spectator* questioned why Peterborough labour – which had stood behind Tilco workers so solidly – had failed to rally behind the newsmen. They speculated that in the wake of Tilco arrests, many rank-and-file members were afraid of incarceration, especially in light of the widespread use of police photographs. The timing was poor, as the strike began in deer-hunting season, and then continued through the winter holiday season. Furthermore, in the eyes of some onlookers, white-collar journalists were not "real" workers.[7]

There was limited support. Steelworkers did occasionally join the picket lines.[8] The Peterborough United Electrical Workers (UE) local, which had been instrumental in the Tilco strike, helped, though its picket support was limited to certain periods.[9] The strikers' union instead turned to students, especially student journalists, at nearby Trent University and with the Canadian University Press (CUP). The exact reasons for the union's decision are unknown but may have been rooted in the general lack of support from mainstream labour and the amount of attention New Leftists had been garnering in the media. In addition, many student journalists aspired to become journalists themselves, and saw their futures at stake.[10]

New Leftists had an education on the cold, slushy picket lines of the *Peterborough Examiner* through the winter of 1968 and 1969, as they took their first steps in putting the rhetoric of finding allies into concrete action. Indeed, as Jennifer Penney – who became CUP president the next year – explains, it was significant for students to actually get involved: "We would probably have been talking about it, big time, but not really getting involved."[11] New Leftists elevated the strike into the national news, put a focus on media concentration and strikebreaking, and ultimately helped acclimatize students to the unique issues that would face them as they reached out to labour. The Ontario Union of Students said that it was especially critical for students to be involved because "it is the first time that students in Ontario have manned a mass militant picket line ... It is vitally important to dispel the myth that all students are privileged middle class kids who either identify openly with management or just don't give a shit."[12] It was certainly a beginning, and came at the end of extensive debates over the agent of social change within the English Canadian New Left. As Peter Warrian says, "Hey, we've been talking about this stuff ... the opportunity presented itself."[13] Given all the rhetoric surrounding the New Left and labour, New Leftists had to test their resolve in an actual off-campus strike.

New Leftists soon encountered a world very different from their familiar world of direct action. Sit-ins, protests, demonstrations, and university occupations were central to their politics, and their picket-line behaviour reflected this. Yet picket lines were tightly regulated spaces. Union officers, unlike protest leaders, had an obligation to police their members or face fines and legal penalties. This would lead to complications.

A selective picket strategy was initially adopted with the goal of hindering the production of newspapers for the all-important Friday and Saturday editions. By achieving a critical mass, the picketers hoped to stop typographers, who because they were under a collective agreement were being forced to cross the picket line.[14] These picket lines quickly grew. By 9 November, twenty Trent students were supporting the line, along with members from the UE, the International Association of Machinists, and the United Steelworkers of America. On that Saturday morning, strikebreakers were being escorted to work by twenty-one police officers, literally a quarter of the Peterborough police force.[15] The morning was initially peaceful, but when a strikebreaker attempted to enter, the forty picketers gathered around the door to the *Examiner* facility, and had to be forcibly removed by police.[16] "Fists flew as a wedge of a dozen policemen tried to break through a shoulder to shoulder formation of picketers jammed into the narrow rear doorway," the *Toronto Star* reported; a picketer was injured and evacuated by ambulance.[17]

The first mass pickets were organized in late November, when CUP approached students for support. It was an easy sell, says Brian Switzman: "The guild was more than receptive, because there was a small group of people there. And it was a Thomson newspaper. You can't get more beautiful than that, taking on the Thomson empire!"[18] Some 120 supporters, primarily from the University of Toronto and the University of Western Ontario, joined the strikers on the morning of 29 November. The guild began actively soliciting aid on campuses, and offered to pay transportation and food costs.[19] Student journalists from the *Varsity,* York's *Excalibur,* and the University of Waterloo's *Chevron* arrived to show support (the Canadian University Press, consisting of two hundred student editors, later voted its support for the *Examiner* workers).[20] With arrests, coverage increased in student newspapers, publicizing the issues of media concentration and monopoly capitalism.

By 6 December, 250 supporters – a shocking number – had joined the picket lines, bussed in and billeted (often on basement floors) at the Peterborough Labour Centre.[21] The numbers led to violence, and several supporters were arrested during a melee that occurred when a large group of police escorted managers and strikebreakers into the *Examiner* building.[22] By the end of the day, fourteen students and one printer had been arrested in a seemingly "random method of harassment," as International Typographical Union members began fighting their way through the lines.[23]

For many students, this was their first time on a picket line. Many were shocked by the physical demands and the early hours. One wrote of "soggy coffee, frozen feet" on the line, recounting an early-morning December shift.

He described how "cold and tired and miserable" they were, how they simply could not stand anymore, and how at the end of a shift "all we wanted was that bus, to sit down and be warm, to be students again instead of workers who spend weeks on the line."[24] This was hard, slogging work, but a feeling of respect toward the strikers emerged. There was excitement too, as something new was happening. This was *action*.

By early December, the tenor of the strike had changed as students took a more prominent role. Warrian began phoning universities in Toronto, Ottawa, and Kingston for reinforcements and publicly declared that the strike was "the first of a move towards 'more total involvement' by students in the labour movement."[25] In a front-page *Globe and Mail* article, Wilfred List observed that students appeared to assume "command" of the picket line from the striking workers.[26] The RCMP echoed this, noting that the militant students "took over control" of the line.[27] Supporters brought militancy to the line, not only in their ideology and expectations of what a picket line should be but also in their unfamiliarity with industrial legality. The union, Penney says, had "mixed feelings."[28] These New Leftists were often perceived as unruly and hard to control.

January saw a second push by the supporters, planned for the 15th to the 17th.[29] The ad hoc Peterborough Strike Committee, established by student journalists and other supporters, sent a public appeal in early January to "the people" of Toronto. The University of Toronto student council voted to support the strike.[30] Waterloo's student paper, the *Chevron*, hoped for a mass picket of five hundred students.[31] Warrian publicly stated that "every student in Ontario should be on these lines." A Waterloo student council member suggested that students "have the choice of hiding in their rooms and pretending that they can learn about people without ever meeting real conditions or of getting up here and finding out what is really happening in their world."[32] Buses were continuously organized from Toronto for those who could not go for the entire time, arriving each night so students could learn protocols for the next morning.

This critical mass resulted in a large educational gathering that explored the very nature of workers, students, capitalism, labour, and other themes that had been discussed at CUS congresses and that would now be practically enacted. For those three days, New Leftists came to join picket lines but also to attend seminars and lectures, to watch such labour films as *Salt of the Earth*, and to meet workers. Penney, now writing for the strike committee, saw this "as a real breakthrough in student-labour alliances and also in the much-needed organizing practice and understanding that we hope will evolve."[33] A mass picket occurred, demonstrating some of its limitations. Penney was shocked at being arrested when New Leftists decided to "simply form a line" in front of the *Examiner* building and were quickly arrested and hauled off to jail.[34]

Despite the pickets, the *Examiner* continued to publish. Thomson was a determined, tough employer. It would come to light after the strike that "volunteers" had been brought in from other newspapers, including the *Orillia Packet and Times*.[35] New Leftists, however, did not chalk up the defeat simply to Thomson and the state. Watching the lack of other external support on the picket line, which forced guild members to allow International Typographical Union members through their lines – going so far as to wave them through their picket lines after the first few made their way through – an unnamed student concluded to a Hamilton reporter, "That's a hell of a way to run a strike."[36] The last day of support was 17 January, when the remaining 150 students walked off the line after four short hours. The union had made it clear that students were not to "engage in any militant action, and they were required to step out of line every time someone wanted to enter the Examiner building."[37] The students left, realizing that "little or nothing was being accomplished by their presence on the lines."[38] The strike failed. By late April, only fourteen of the picketers remained, the numbers having dwindled since the end of the external involvement. The picket lines disappeared and ten of the remaining picketers elected to re-apply for their jobs; the others found other work.[39]

New Leftists had learned about the possibility of making a worker-student alliance a reality. For Warrian and other New Leftist leaders, the *Examiner* strike was significant.[40] The *Varsity* claimed that the strike was a short-term loss but a long-term gain: the "unfavourable student image" had been dispelled, and workers could "now feel that students do have something in common with them. All students are not at school to learn the ins of being big corporation president and exploiting the workers." The *Varsity* saw the next step as choosing the right strikes to engage in. They needed to look to blue-collar workers, as blue-collar workers might be more "co-operative, or at least less cynical, in dealing with student-labour alliances."[41] Many New Leftists also felt that they should stick to their own community, where students would be more familiar, rather than travelling. Not everybody had a formative experience there, but for some, such as Wernick and Warrian, lessons were learned which they carried forward. Wernick highlights the significance such events had for people who had never been on a picket line or even experienced the labour environment, so that the *Examiner* strike served as a "very quick education into the history of Canadian labour."[42]

Ed Finn of the *Toronto Star* was explicitly dismissive of the students. He traced how New Leftists were now looking toward labour after abandoning the dispossessed, and saw Peterborough as an example of how a true alliance could never form. Unionists may be generally tolerant, Finn remarked, but the youthful "combination of political extremism, long hair, unconventional attire, sexual promiscuity and drug addiction" would "disgust" even the most open-minded unionist. He highlighted student rhetoric around being "picket fodder" and stated that the striking workers were "visibly relieved to see them leave."[43] The *Chevron* rebutted that nobody was happy the relationship had broken down, and that the failed strikers could hardly be celebrating. It further lambasted Finn for failing "to recognize a growingly dissident group among young labour," ignorant of his writing on the topic elsewhere.[44]

In Peterborough, New Leftists realized how complicated strikes were. It had been a messy situation, especially for those first encountering labour. The *Examiner* was an introduction, and New Leftists had made the strike into something far more important than the strikers could have on their own. Yet it would be two more years before another opportunity presented itself to New Leftists in Ontario.

"American Bastards Who Don't Give a Shit": The Left Rallies to Texpack[45]

On 16 July 1971, two hundred employees at the Texpack plant in Brantford, Ontario, went on strike against the American Hospital Supply Corporation. It became a flashpoint, bringing together several issues and garnering support from students, Wafflers, and other activists from across the province. Thanks to work by historian Joan Sangster, the story of this strike is fairly well known in academic circles and even beyond. Sangster expertly recounts the narrative and meanings of the strike, but her promise to explore the "emerging connections between labour, [and] the New Left" is largely left unkept, the discussion confined to the Waffle's high-profile contribution to the strike.[46] The Waffle did certainly rise to prominence during the strike, and throughout, its members were the ones commonly thanked, reported on, and discussed. Given the Waffle's nationalist approach toward labour, the strike fit well with it and represented an opportunity for meaningful work with labour. Although the role of New Leftists was largely subsumed by the better-organized Waffle movement, Texpack played an important formative role for much of the broader New Left and helped bring involved individuals closer to labour. For our story here, Texpack played an incubatory role for a new generation of New Leftist labour supporters.

Indeed, it was the eye-opening effects of the Texpack strike that brought many student radicals into the fold, leading to larger conflagrations at Dare Cookies and Artistic Woodwork. The support of students and academics was given top billing by the union.[47] It is important to also remember that the Waffle had many New Leftist members, even if the leadership might not have self-identified as New Leftists.[48] The group was not a New Left organization per se, but it had been influenced by many of its ideas, and several New Leftists had moved into the group – most notably co-founder James Laxer, formerly of SUPA. Explicitly breaking with New Leftists, faulting them for adhering too strongly to American issues (be it civil rights, Vietnam, or aping the experience of the American New Left), Laxer and co-founder Mel Watkins attempted to create a brand-new social movement under the aegis of the New Democratic Party.[49] Given that they shared many of the same personal and political influences, however, it is unsurprising that the Waffle was swept up into the same general turn toward labour and the working class as the broader New Left.

Texpack was founded in 1935 as a family-run business, made public in 1964, and bought by the American Hospital Supply Corporation in 1965.[50] The company manufactured mostly medical supplies and industrial filters. It was unionized in 1958 by the Canadian Textile and Chemical Union (CTCU), a member of the Council of Canadian Unions (CCU), led by Kent Rowley and Madeleine Parent. They had been militant union leaders in Quebec, organizing with the United Textile Workers of America before breaking with international unionism and founding the independent CTCU in 1954.[51] Rowley and Parent were able to rally supporters around them because of their charismatic personalities and because of what they represented. Unlike the mainstream, American-dominated labour movement, the independent labour movement represented an appealing alternative to New Leftists. Supporters could look to the CTCU not only as more democratic and less bureaucratic but also as an anti-imperialist force standing up to the international labour movement in particular and thus the broader American Empire.

Texpack was fought primarily over wages, though exploitative working conditions characterized by a paternalistic management were also an issue. However, the strike quickly became defined by a fight over strikebreaking and injunctions. Armoured school buses were brought in daily and strikers were invited back to work, leading to conflict on the picket line as picketers sought to stop strikebreakers from entering the plant.[52] Large pickets, brimming with large numbers of New Leftists, Wafflers, and especially rank-and-file unionists disobeying their union's directions to have nothing to do with the CCU, came to fight alongside the strikers. Two injunctions were issued, restricting picketing and leading to arrests of picketers who disobeyed. Eventually, a collective agreement was negotiated by mid-October 1971.

This was a violent strike. Many of the picketers and supporters refused to obey the injunction, realizing that the strike would be lost if the plant continued to produce unimpeded. On 27 August alone, twenty-six arrests were made as police dispersed the line and destroyed personal effects at strike headquarters with nightsticks, leading one observer to quip that "if it had been anybody other than the police they would have been arrested."[53] Policing was stepped up, and the strikebreakers were assembled in Hamilton to board school buses for their trips to the Texpack facility, escorted by police the entire way.[54]

Texpack crystallized the problems within the labour movement for observers, especially when Texpack reopened a disused secondary plant in the Rexdale neighbourhood of Etobicoke to avoid the picketers disrupting its Brantford activities. Two days after the announcement, the rival internationalist Textile Workers Union of America (TWUA) revealed that it had unionized these strikebreakers. This led to widespread outrage about the TWUA's complicity. Sangster explains that this was ideologically motivated, situating it within the long-standing tension between the two unions.[55] The CTCU and Waffle claimed that the TWUA was scabbing for Texpack.[56] The lack of support from mainstream labour made supporters all the more important, and the CTCU consciously adopted a strategy to draw them in. As Rick Salutin says:

> They immediately politicized [the Texpack strike] by saying this is the issue
> of the takeover of the Canadian economy, and they're exploiting Canadian
> workers, and they're putting out shoddy bandages that are going to hurt
> patients in Canadian hospitals because they're American bastards who don't
> give a shit.[57]

This tactic was effective, and involved various issues beyond simple bread-and-butter demands of collective bargaining for garnering support. The CTCU was reacting to an implicit understanding that the monetary demands of unions would not be well received by many supporters.

The Rexdale location also facilitated support on the picket lines, as it brought the picket lines closer to the large community of Toronto New Leftists. It is hard to know exactly who was coming to the lines. Sometimes the supporters were explicitly referred to in reporting as Waffle members, but often it seemed to be a broader New Left and student mix. Students at York and the University of Toronto were especially singled out for participation in the strike, aided by the popularizing efforts of Mel Watkins and James Laxer.[58] The York Federation of Students kept tabs on the strike, leading a boycott campaign at York and beyond.[59] Indeed, the CTCU thanked the federation for its efforts in a victory letter: "The Texpack strike caught the imagination of organized Labour and many other sections of our society, including especially many academics and students in our universities, because it epitomized certain urgent ills of our society."[60]

The Waffle helps explain the general absence of New Leftists as a distinct group, however. When the University of Toronto's student government coordinated a meeting to discuss the Texpack strike, the meeting was cosponsored by it and the Waffle.[61] The support of the York Federation of Students was only financial, and its president responded to "suggestions that student impact might be greater through individual letter writing, work on the picket lines and boycott of Texpack products" by stating that groceries were far more important for strikers.[62] This approach led to working under Waffle leadership, as other entities did not take leadership roles in the struggle. Elsewhere, in CTCU bulletins, the Waffle was given top billing.[63]

Most of the supporters became involved through the aegis of the Ontario Waffle, such as John Lang, a course director at York.[64] At Texpack, he became involved in one of the most recounted stories as he attempted to stop a bus that was loading strikebreakers at a suburban Hamilton shopping mall. Eighty to one hundred supporters – Wafflers from Toronto and Steelworkers from Hamilton – were demonstrating. Suddenly, as the RCMP reported, Lang "jumped on the front of a bus, opened the hood and attempted to pull wires from the engine to prevent it from moving."[65] When the bus driver gunned the engine, Lang was thrown to the ground.

Texpack was an important struggle in many respects, but it was not an attempt at a worker-student alliance. New Leftists did not try to change the parameters of the struggle, leaving that to the Waffle and the CTCU. The Waffle brought an organizational role to the strike, and recast it in a distinctive way. The angle of the strike was that of anti-Americanism and helping Canadian workers. For example, when the TWUA became involved, it was framed as an American-based union not caring at all for the struggles of Canadian workers. New Leftists were there on the picket line, without doubt, but in a different capacity than they had been in Peterborough and would be later. The organizing role of the Waffle played a part in this.[66] Perhaps for this reason, Texpack did not reach the heights of popularity that the other struggles did within the student newspapers such as the *Varsity* and *Chevron,* or even attain national CUP coverage in the *Dalhousie Gazette* or *Carillon.* This was a Waffle show, and it called the shots. Things would be different two years later at another strike in Kitchener, Ontario.

"Don't Buy Dare Cookies!" Testing Endurance and Fighting for Gender Equality at the Dare Cookie Strike, 1972

The 1972 Dare Cookie strike was one of the most significant strikes for testing the endurance of New Leftists. Local 173 of the International Union of United Brewery, Flour, Cereal, Soft Drink and Distillery Workers represented workers at the Dare Cookie plant in Kitchener, Ontario, three-quarters of whom were female.[67] Greater attention within many New Leftist groups toward gender, as well as the overwhelming demographic imbalance within the plant, finally brought gender front and centre in this fight. Negotiations stretched beyond the expiry of their earlier collective agreement, which had been reached after a short thirteen-day strike in 1970.[68] This earlier event had seen Waterloo students flock to the picket line, photos of which were featured on the front page of the *Chevron*, and a committee had been formed to "bridge the gulf between students and workers and develop some common understanding."[69] However, the strike promptly ended without confrontation. Things were different two years later. This strike again animated significant numbers of Waterloo students. Jim Harding, then at the University of Waterloo as an instructor, identifies the strike as significant "because it brought the students ... back into a labour struggle where they felt that they could actually forge ... relationships with the working class."[70]

The strike began on 26 May 1972 when 380 production workers, 281 female, went on strike.[71] The issues that precipitated the strike were gender pay equity, as well as better working conditions and more respect from managers. Management was offering a raise of 55 cents an hour over two years for men, and 45 cents an hour for women, whereas the union was seeking an equal raise of 40 cents per year – along with maternal benefits, a forty-hour workweek, lower temperatures in the often sweltering cookie plant, a less abusive paternalistic atmosphere in the plant, and better relief protocols to allow workers breaks.[72] As a union press release put it, the workers wanted "stronger union authority to fight miserable working conditions leading to female employees fainting and vomiting on the production belts."[73] These conditions attracted New Leftists from nearby Waterloo.

The strike was quiet for the first few days but quickly turned bitter when the company decided to hire the Canadian Driver Pool (CDP). This decision prompted student involvement. The CDP consisted of professional strikebreakers known for aggressive tactics. Hiring them spurred supporters to action. Picket lines were quiet and organized until 1 June, when strikebreaking began. The lines turned ugly when the CDP arrived to remove stockpiles from the plant for shipment.[74] An action on 6 June saw two hundred workers and supporters assembled, watched by another five hundred members of the community. In a dangerous turn of events, fifty "young people entered the plant, helped themselves to candy and threw some out of the windows," fleeing only when the police went in.[75] Strikers and management alike blamed local teenagers for causing the devastation.[76] As reported on the front page of the *Globe and Mail,* violence erupted: "Strikers threw stones and beer bottles, broke windows, tossed Molotov cocktails and scuffled with police."[77] New Leftists remember the extreme violence used by strikebreakers, and their strategy of unpredictably showing up at different times in the night or the day. Supporters at the University of Waterloo set up a telephone tree, enabling news of imminent strikebreaking to be quickly disseminated.[78]

In light of the violence, the company got an injunction restricting active picketing at the plant. The timing of this injunction could not have been worse, as the picket-line solidarity had worked. After 6 June, Dare had announced that the company would halt all strikebreaking.[79] The CDP had not arrived the next morning, but Dare had quietly applied to the Ontario Supreme Court for an injunction. Claiming that the strike had already cost it $25,000, and that its stockpile was now contaminated, given the broken glass scattered on the factory floor, Dare obtained an injunction on 13 June, effective the next day.[80] Union officials complied with the ruling, which held that the union could not "harass any vehicles or persons entering or leaving Dare."[81]

After a peaceful interval where managers ran the plant without strikebreakers, in early July striking employees were asked to return without a union.[82] Managers pledged wage increases as well as police protection entering and exiting the plant. This move preyed on workers feeling the financial pinch of comparatively lower strike pay. Replacement workers began entering the plant on 6 July, and the CDP was back to make sure that they could pass the line. Predictably, the CDP's return was accompanied by its violent techniques. The cycle continued: an even more punitive injunction was granted, restricting pickets to four members at each of the four entrances and further stipulating that half of the picketers had to be female.[83] The injunction led to despair, as one striker complained to the *Chevron:* "If we do nothing violent, we're beat; if we do anything violent, the laws are against us."[84] Despite condemnation, the injunction was largely respected. Cookies continued to be made and shipped.

With the injunction, support had to take other forms. *Chevron* coverage shifted away from the pickets and toward a consumer boycott, a boycott that would be fairly successful. The Ontario Committee on the Status of Women backed it and picketed stores that carried Dare products. It produced posters that publicized the plight of the female workers inside the plant and explained what the issues were, blaming violence on the CDP, and encouraged people to post them at stores not honouring the boycott.[85] Brochures were prepared that explained issues in detail and said that the strike was the next step in demonstrating how serious feminists were; they also provided templates for protest letters to grocery store managers.[86] The boycott soon won over large national grocery chains such as Loblaws, IGA, A&P, and Steinberg's.[87] The chant "Don't buy Dare cookies" became a dominant message of the strikers, repeated at mass rallies and in Joyce Wieland's memorable 1973 film, *Solidarity*.

The Dare strike had become significant for four separate yet connected reasons: women's rights, violence, its proximity to the University of Waterloo, and the use of professional replacement workers. Women's rights emerged as a significant reason, thanks to the demographic makeup of the factory and to the attention given to women's rights in the workplace. Women were paid dramatically less than their male counterparts, because of wage differentials and gender-specific job categories. All females, irrespective of their tasks, were put into the job category of packer.[88] Dare management could thus falsely claim that women were paid less than men because they did a different job, not just because they were female. The consciousness-raising efforts of activists helped the mainstream media see through this ruse.[89]

Beyond poor compensation, work conditions were dreadful. There was only one washroom for the seventy women who made up each shift, whereas there were three washrooms for thirty men. Women had to wear dress-type uniforms yet had "no time to swat flies when they [were] on the line – but a supervisor [came] around periodically to spray their legs with chemicals."[90] Strikers publicized these demeaning and sexist conditions. Yet they also used prevailing notions of femininity to portray themselves sympathetically, as when a striker declared to Kitchener City Council that they needed help: "We're only women; we have to protect ourselves."[91]

The involvement of the women's movement also demonstrates that before the famous 1978 Fleck strike, tentative feelers were being cast toward both the working class and toward the labour movement from the feminist movement.[92] These links confirm Meg Luxton's argument about a working-class orientation in the women's movement, and help to refute the common trope of second-wave feminism as being solely focused on middle-class issues.[93]

Local feminists from the University of Waterloo were involved as well, either as supportive individuals or under the auspices of the local student movement. External feminist involvement was spearheaded by the Ontario Committee on the Status of Women, which focused on raising publicity, fundraising, the boycott, and a short-lived attempt to mediate between the union and management during the strike.[94] There were two interconnected campaigns: the mainstream feminist one and the more direct, action-oriented New Leftist approach. On-campus feminists played a prominent role in "encouraging the relationship" between New Leftists and strikers, making the campaign what it was.[95]

As noted, another reason for the strike's high profile was its proximity to the University of Waterloo, which itself was one of the hotbeds of the Ontario New Left. Indeed, the name of the elected student government was the Radical Student Movement. Given this spirit of radicalism, when the Dare strike occurred in 1972, it gave Waterloo student activists a place "to do [their] thing ... Kitchener was down the road."[96] Whereas the *Examiner* strike had tested New Left leaders, Dare tested the strategic implications of a worker-student alliance.[97] Student interest in the strike was palpable from the outset. The University of Waterloo's student newspaper, the *Chevron,* dedicated its entire 9 June issue to Dare, claiming that media coverage has been "extensive, yet incomplete ... the *Chevron* felt a need to provide a more cogent interpretation. The implications of this strike are broad, for the effects are felt not only by the workers of Dare, but also by those of unions across Canada."[98] Support was also essential, Waterloo student activist Terry Moore says, because the workers had such minimal strike pay, and "they were out there largely on their own, fighting this company that had untold resources."[99] The lines of confrontation were clear: they were between good guys and bad guys.

A working relationship formed between the Strike Support Committee and New Leftists, many from the Radical Student Movement. Much of this collaboration took the form of promotion through the *Chevron* but also through picketing, coordinating reinforcements, and working with the community to help in whatever way possible. A respectful relationship emerged. "We do what they want us to do," Moore recalls the attitude as being. "They're leading this. This is their struggle and not ours." To Moore, the distinction between New Leftists and Old Leftists became clear. The Canadian Party of Labour and the Communist Party of Canada (Marxist-Leninists) adopted an aggressive stance, telling "the workers what they should be doing ... We basically tried to marginalize those guys in the sense that they were always trying to escalate things." At the end of the day, and especially with the injunction to restrict picketing, the reasoning was "We've got some resources that [the strikers] don't have, so we'll put those resources at their disposal."[100]

The extensive *Chevron* coverage demonstrates the extent to which New Leftists publicized the strike for supporters. The strike began in the summer and, uniquely among student papers, the *Chevron* was delivered to students at their summer addresses. Supportive letters came in from the OFL secretary-treasurer, two letters from Dare strikers (both of whom emphasized that the "truth" had now been told), and the Labour Council of Metro Toronto, which lauded the coverage:

> I particularly appreciate the fact that you did not, as is usually the case, suggest how issues such as this can be resolved. Normally the academic community, when they deal with matters of this kind, "advises" the labour movement of how wrong we act in such situations.[101]

The coverage was supportive and respectful. The *Varsity*, at nearby University of Toronto, also ran several supportive articles.

One last action took place in early 1973. Thirty-five Dare strikers joined another 115 picketers at the York Region Canadian National Express terminal to picket trucks that had been transporting cookies there from Kitchener. The *Varsity* prominently advertised the event, and buses were arranged. Toronto New Leftists protested that unionized CN workers, represented by the CBRT, had to cross the picket lines. They also tried to link up with a rumoured "militant caucus" in the CBRT.[102] On arrival, they were cautioned by the Dare picket captains to not cause trouble. Only about half of the pickets went out onto the road to obstruct traffic. Drivers proceeded slowly, but continued through the lines.[103] The protest was broken up by police and condemned by CBRT workers, who said that the supporters should return to Kitchener.[104]

The Dare strike was long. Publicity waned and it continued quietly. A tentative settlement was reached in May 1973 but broke down as 57 strikers were found to be on a Dare blacklist and would not be rehired. Their places had been taken by strikebreakers.[105] The strike drew to an end in September and October when the Dare strikebreakers waged a decertification campaign. By that point, 100 employees had returned to work and 125 were still on strike.[106] The union-busting campaign was successful, and the strike ended on 31 January 1974.[107]

Despite the union's defeat, the issue of strikebreaking was again showcased, as was the ongoing fight for pay equity. The issue had received a fair amount of publicity in the press, much of it supportive of the strikers. This sympathetic attention was made possible by the picket support, which elevated the strike from a small local affair to a national issue. The strike cast a spotlight on many issues, as Moore remarks:

> I think it played a role in moving the yardsticks on some things, putting some issues on the agenda, the strikebreaking issue on the agenda, equal

pay for equal work on the agenda. For a lot of folks, it put on the agenda how we actually engage with community politics, how we deal with labour – the labour bureaucracy, the officials. We learned a lot about how to talk to staff reps, international reps. How not to just heap abuse on them for being porkchoppers or hacks.[108]

As Warrian notes, New Left support at Dare was also a test of more general strategy, that of "testing out the notions in the debate at the time of the student-worker alliance."[109]

This was the story of Ontario New Leftists and labour as it had played out on picket lines. A very different story emerged on the previously quiet east coast, where labour played a key role in the emergence of a New Left. Out of a 1970 fishermen's strike in Nova Scotia came a unique example of New Leftist activity being driven by working-class struggle.

A New Left from Labour: The Canso Strike and the Formation of the East Coast Socialist Movement, 1970-73

The East Coast Socialist Movement (ECSM) was the most significant worker-oriented left formation in Atlantic Canada, though almost nothing has been written about it. Uniquely, the ECSM grew *out* of a labour struggle, the 1970 Canso fishermen's strike. It saw the local New Democratic Youth (NDY) transition into a worker-oriented leftist group while maintaining key elements of the mainstream New Left. Accordingly, the ECSM was influenced by debates about the role of the working class but was also shaped by the Canso strike. Canso was a bitter, long strike that saw poor fishermen with little job and income security facing down a recalcitrant employer, an abetting government, and a collaborating international union hierarchy.

Halifax formed the heart of the regional New Leftist movement. One of the most significant early community organizing projects occurred in the city, when Burnley "Rocky" Jones was sponsored by SUPA to return to his home province of Nova Scotia. Targeting community members, rather than working simply through leaders, Jones began to advocate direct action. He remained to help found the Black United Front, with the achieved aim of gaining black participation in political, economic, social, and cultural spheres of the cities and province.[110] This was a successful movement with enduring impact, but it largely occurred within the black community.

Beyond Jones, the Black United Front, and the increasingly active black community, universities did not develop significant New Leftist hubs of activity.

Dalhousie University had a small student movement, mostly responding to an authoritarian administration. The lack of activism was noted by several observers, as well as by the official university history.[111] Local student leader and NDY founder Kim Cameron decried the lack of engagement in the *SUPA Newsletter*. It is impossible to precisely explain this low level of activism, though Cameron speculated that students might have been hoping to succeed and "escape" the east coast.[112]

With a negligible SUPA presence, the student-based Halifax New Left emerged from King's College (a small university associated with and co-located with Dalhousie) and the NDY. As student Ken Clare says, "It was then small enough that everybody knew everybody, so that two or three people could have a real influence on the whole milieu."[113] These networks formed at the *Dalhousie Gazette*, traditionally edited by King's students. The first campus sit-in occurred over Sydney Steel, which was being closed (the subsequent public outcry led to nationalization under Pearson). For Steve Hart, who would go on to become active in the NDY and the ECSM, this was a significant moment for him: "It was a huge, big, big event ... it really awakened people to this sense of a large group of people gathering to deal with an issue that almost always was just the realm of the official politicians."[114]

These students at the *Dalhousie Gazette* decided in 1967 to form the Nova Scotia NDY. This would become the hub of Atlantic New Leftist activity, though the Dalhousie Graduate Students Union, led by Larry Katz, also emerged as a politicized group, perhaps because of the preponderance of foreign radicalized graduate students at the university.[115] The NDY would become more significant, as members had the opportunity to establish a youth wing from scratch, set policy, and enact it. Their ages ranged from sixteen to twenty-four, according to member Barbara Harris.[116]

The early stirrings of a working-class perspective were seen in the NDY's strike support activities at a Truro car dealership named Goodspeed's. Members went to support a mechanics strike there by picketing.[117] At one point, one of the supporters sneaked over to a police car that had proudly cruised through the picket line to gas up, tied the hose that rang the bell for service to the handle of the police car, and watched as the police car drove away and took the hose – "We thought that was just about the best thing we'd ever done!" says Clare.[118] Such shenanigans notwithstanding, they had made a first contact with workers: both those on strike and those who came to support the picketers. As Hart notes, "It really felt like workers' solidarity, because you weren't watching it on TV, or hearing some resolution – you know, 'Send twenty people to this site and demonstrate' – it was people you got to talk to, and so on."[119] The young supporters also realized that these workers did not have an overly negative view of them.

The NDY did other solidarity work, including leafleting supermarkets to boycott California grapes in support of the United Farm Workers' strike there.[120] This work brought them attention, most notably from Homer Stevens, whose SFU contacts had already made him aware of the New Left's transformative potential. He thus looked to the NDY when he arrived in Nova Scotia to organize Cape Breton fishermen.

Stevens was the Communist leader of the BC-based United Fishermen and Allied Workers Union (UFAWU), which was outside the Canadian Labour Congress (CLC). The congress had backed the Canadian Food and Allied Workers Union (CFAWU) as the organizer of choice in the field. Despite its name, the CFAWU was the Canadian wing of the Chicago-based Amalgamated Meat Cutters and Butcher Workmen.[121] In 1966, however, UFAWU representatives approached the Nova Scotia Federation of Labour (NSFL) and local labour councils to see if any organizing of fishermen was planned, learned that there was none, and received the NSFL's blessing to organize.[122] Mainstream labour had given up on organizing Nova Scotian fishermen after a failed 1947 campaign: an affiliate of the Canadian Seamen's Union had secured representative rights in Lunenburg, but the Supreme Court disallowed representation on the grounds that fishermen were "co-adventurers" rather than employees, sharing with management the risks and profits of fishing trips.[123]

After securing the NSFL's blessings, the UFAWU set out to unionize the fishermen of Acadia Fisheries in Canso and Mulgrave, as well as Booth Fisheries in Petit-de-Grat. The three communities lie along the Strait of Canso, which divides mainland Nova Scotia from Cape Breton Island. In his evocative book *The Education of Everett Richardson,* Silver Donald Cameron describes Canso as a tough, shrinking community of 1,190 people, with limited opportunity. Young people, exposed to the outside world through television, were leaving in droves. Residents had no fresh vegetables, no local dentist, and poor medical care:

> In 1972, Everett Richardson's family didn't have a flush toilet ... You *know* you work hard and live thriftily, and yet somehow you can't be permitted a flush toilet ... not because you're lazy, but because there's something out of joint in your world. It doesn't matter how hard you work; you never get ahead.[124]

On 30 March 1970, the Canso fishermen came ashore, tied up their boats, and rejected their "co-adventurer" label. This act launched a bitter strike against

Acadia Fisheries. The cannery workers, represented by the Canadian Seafood Workers, were also now out of work and, initially, without unemployment benefits. Yet they still supported the strike.[125]

The strike moved to the next level when an injunction was issued by the Nova Scotia Supreme Court forbidding all picketing at onshore plants. Forty-five fishermen faced contempt of court proceedings for ignoring injunctions. Thirteen men were imprisoned for violating the injunction, and one fisherman, Everett Richardson, faced a shocking nine months of imprisonment. Nova Scotia "exploded" over the sentence. A campaign to write in Richardson's name in the provincial election began.[126] The NSFL and the provincial NDP became actively involved in the defence of the imprisoned fishermen.[127] A wave of sympathy strikes exploded across the province, now on the brink of a general strike for the first time since the 1920s Workers' Revolt.

Even before the strike, Stevens had realized that he needed to reach out to other groups in the province. The NDY's pro-labour approach made it a potentially appealing group to work with. In 1969, Stevens approached Kim Cameron. Stevens had discovered the group as he had been "looking for any left-wing organization other than the NDP, because he knew the NDP wouldn't have anything to do with him because of his Communist union ... [he came] asking us to provide support."[128] The NDY would play a significant role in the Canso strike. During the walkout, some NDY members solicited support. Barbara Harris and two or three other people went down to a construction site in Halifax, telling the unionized employees there that their fellow workers in Cape Breton were walking off the job. "And these guys walked off," Hart recounts. "And that happened in, I don't know how many places – I don't want to blow it out of proportion. But that one, at least one incident, happened."[129] The cumulative effect of these walkouts and strikes across the province was the release of the imprisoned fishermen. Here, at least, was an issue that could unite all unionists and concerned citizens in the province.

The NDY began its true transformation during the Canso strike. The activities themselves were humble, modest contributions that respected the role of Stevens and of the fishermen. Silver Donald Cameron realized that something special was happening:

> A couple of lithe kids, their long hair rippling in the little breeze up from
> the harbour, display signs indicating their solidarity with the working-class
> movement around the world. They have never worked a day in their lives,
> and it is easy to make fun of them as the guilt-ridden children of the middle
> class ... But don't knock these kids. All over the continent student leaders

are calling for a "worker-student alliance," only to find that workers don't like them, don't trust them, view their hand of fellowship with suspicion. These kids in eastern Nova Scotia have actually forged such an alliance; they are walking picket lines, selling fish, babysitting, writing leaflets and press releases, putting the education of privilege to work against the very institution of privilege. Some of them are naïve, some of them are doctrinaire, some of them will turn out to be bond salesmen after all, perhaps. Some will turn out to be sinewy lifelong leftists. But right now they are in full flush of their youth and conviction. They are devoted, and they are beautiful.[130]

Their activities were simple. Youth, mostly from Halifax, went to Canso, Mulgrave, and Petit-de-Grat. They slept on the floor of the union hall, ran fish-sale fundraisers in Halifax and Dartmouth, "trying to be supportive in any way we could," as Larry Katz recalls.[131] At one point they organized a demonstration that blocked the Canso Causeway, the sole connection between Cape Breton and the mainland. These events showed the fishermen that outsiders cared.[132]

What made it possible? The world of Cape Breton fishing communities could not have been further from the relatively privileged life of university students, or even of most Halifax residents, who had both running water and opportunities. These disparities certainly helped bring New Leftists on side, as the fishermen could not be accused of being members of a co-opted, affluent, and complacent working class. The struggle harkened back to earlier, romanti-cized struggles. Barbara Harris, who had been radicalized through studying Industrial Workers of the World songs at McGill, remembers that "it was like being in the days of that union, it was so black and white. There [were] the good guys and the bad guys."[133] Once the school year picked up again in the fall of 1970, the *Dalhousie Gazette* seized on these themes and made the case that this was a representative struggle – that basic rights and freedoms were at stake in the battle over injunctions.[134]

In my interviews, Homer Stevens emerged as the single driving force behind the Canso strike and the resulting ECSM. "Homer set that tone," Harris says. "He was not at all superior, and I don't think he would have put up with too much shit from students who thought they were better than fishermen, I'm pretty sure he wouldn't have." Herb Gamberg, a New Leftist and Dalhousie sociology professor involved in the strike, believes Stevens made the confluence possible. Katz is succinct: "Homer rather uniquely welcomed students and people involved in political activity in Halifax into the fishing communities to try and help."[135] In return, youth "did good work ... [and] supported in a way that was helpful for the strike."[136]

The injunctions did not have the desired calming effect. The provincial government announced an inquiry into the strike, which subsequently issued a report calling for the fishermen to return to work without an agreement, to safeguard the "economic welfare" of Canso, Mulgrave, and Petit-de-Grat.[137] The union rejected this. In August, a labour delegation including CLC, NSFL, and UFAWU officials met with the minister of labour. Hart represented the NDY at Stevens's explicit request. A subsequent meeting saw the NSFL president expel Hart on the grounds that they were "discussing union matters, not political ones."[138]

Mainstream labour had been cool throughout the strike, with the NSFL providing tepid support and the CLC making it known that the UFAWU was "not entitled to the services of the Congress,"[139] but what followed would solidify the ECSM's perception of the mainstream labour movement. On 31 October 1970, the strike came to an end – a signed collective agreement.[140] For the agreement to be finalized, however, the provincial government needed to pass legislation to legalize collective bargaining among fishermen. The 1970 election saw the Liberals take power under Premier Gerald Regan, who announced that they would do so.[141]

On the eve of the legislation, however, the unthinkable happened: a union raid, carried out while details were still being finalized. The CLC did not regard it as such, as technically the union had not yet been fully recognized. The CFAWU swept into Petit-de-Grat and concluded a voluntary recognition agreement with Booth Fisheries, claiming the majority support of the fishermen without a meeting or vote.[142] Acadia Fisheries in Canso and Mulgrave quickly followed suit. Closed-shop agreements were negotiated, requiring fishermen to be members of the CFAWU as a condition of their employment. At Acadia Fisheries, 75 of the 107 fishermen were fired for refusing to join.[143] Outrage mounted and pressure grew for a free vote, coordinated by leading Nova Scotian activists, including Larry Katz and journalist June Callwood.[144]

The vote itself was carried out in early May 1971, and the results were decisive: of the sixty-nine fishermen who voted, representing 60.5 percent of those who had been employed by Acadia in March 1971, sixty-six of them voted to be represented by the UFAWU.[145] Yet the CLC regional representative publicly denounced the vote as a "farce," and CLC president Donald MacDonald warned that if the UFAWU was certified, it would "usher in a decade of violence and destruction."[146] The CFAWU denounced Stevens and the UFAWU, calling the Canso strike "disastrous" – despite the strike having resulted in the very representation the CFAWU sought to obtain – and extolling its own virtues as an upstanding citizen.[147] Acadia Fisheries closed for good in July 1971, claiming continued labour strife as a reason.[148]

The ECSM would thus owe its foundational ethos to the Canso strike. Katz says:

> I think it provided a form of grounding that perhaps other people on the New Left, or not all people on the New Left, were able to obtain because we were involved very directly in a very practical organizing campaign. It was a great school of learning ... I cut my teeth in terms of trade unionism.[149]

Others echo this. Working alongside the progressive UFAWU led them to realize the possibilities of the labour movement, and led the young supporters to want to do further pro–working-class activities.[150] Hart is clear: the ECSM "absolutely" came out of Canso.[151]

As the 1970 school year began, many of the supporters returned to the Halifax area to resume studies. There the push finally came to leave the NDY to form a new organization. Katz and Alan Storey provided the impetus for this move. The new group had a clear membership: "Those who wanted to engage in working-class politics should join." The name itself, the East Coast Socialist Movement, was consciously chosen by member Steve Strople to highlight the regional focus.[152]

An NDY organizing meeting was held in the fall of 1970 to decide the organization's future. Twelve people attended. People who could not make the initial meeting for whatever reason were not included in the new group. Indeed, until the very waning days of the group, these initial members were unable to decide on membership criteria. ECSM member Jane Hart remembers to this day a man who could not make the meeting because he was at work, and others who could not make it for legitimate reasons, who were left outside the decision-making structures.[153]

Politically, however, the ECSM had an ideology that grew directly out of Canso. Stevens himself spoke of the group in his 1992 autobiography: "These weren't people I'd consider to be loonies or phonies."[154] It was a revolutionary group, solidly on the side of the working class and seeing it as the agent of social change. They considered themselves part of the "broader New Left ... definitely part of that New Left that was more oriented towards working with working-class people, but sure, we were part of the New Left."[155] The group was aware that there was a broader tendency toward working-class involvement throughout the global New Left, which was being demonstrated in Ontario and Saskatchewan at the time. The ECSM explained itself in the first issue of the

East Coast Worker, the group's newspaper, which came to become its dominant focus. This was as close as it came to defining what it was, in language that echoed the Industrial Workers of the World and the "ashes of the old," of "Solidarity Forever":

> Who and what is the East Coast Socialist Movement? We are a revolution-
> ary socialist movement established in Halifax in the fall of 1970. We believe
> that only through disciplined, militant and long-term action by working
> people and socialist intellectuals can fundamental change be made in Canada
> and a socialist society built from the ashes of the old.[156]

The *Worker* occupied the majority of their time. A monthly eight-page news-paper was a time commitment for the small group, responsible for its writing, production, and distribution. The group also engaged in strike support activities. During a Halifax municipal workers' dispute, the ECSM formed a citizens' committee and ran a "really boisterous" rally, according to Hart. "It was one of the best things that we ever did. And I think that it actually did support them."[157]

The group was also instrumental in distributing the *People's History of Cape Breton,* authored by David Frank on a federal Opportunity for Youth grant.[158] The *People's History* recounted Cape Breton history, from J.B. McLachlan and the coal strikes to the Canso strike, situating the contemporary struggle in a broader continuity of labour history.[159] The first run, a few thousand copies, quickly sold out in the summer of 1971, leading to a second printing. Katz distributed the book in Cape Breton and was constantly solicited for it.[160]

Explicitly influenced by Gorz's theories of workers' control, the *East Coast Worker's* biggest target was mainstream labour.[161] That is not to say that it wasn't opposed to the labour policies of Regan's government, or big business, which was steadily reinforcing the regional underdevelopment of the Maritimes, but with the labour movement it had a target it could sway through rank-and-file education. Canso had demonstrated labour's antipathy toward political radical-ism, from the NSFL to the CLC. The publishers of the *East Coast Worker* believed that the labour movement was dominated by the right wing, and that "workers have been forced to toe the company-government line ever since."[162] This was fleshed out by the ECSM, which penned a program before the NSFL's Sep-tember 1971 convention. They stressed the business unionism aspect of modern unions, with its focus on investing union dues and paying salaries to full-time executives. It also urged for true rank-and-file control of unions. Yet it left its greatest scorn for the "labour fakirs," the mis-leaders of unions who thought that they could "individually defend the working class without fundamentally altering the relationship between those who own and those who work and produce for the owners."[163] The ECSM's major conflicts were with labour leaders. This was unsurprising as the *Worker* was being handed out at plant gates, from the Halifax Shipyard to Cape Breton's General Instruments and Sydney Steel.[164]

Cape Breton was significant in that it had a large working-class population and threatened industries. There had been some limited connection between the ECSM and radical rank-and-file workers, particularly at Sydney Steel, who were represented by USWA Local 1064.[165] On 6-7 November 1971, the movement made its first attempt at an educational meeting with these rank-and-file workers, as Katz and Storey went to address fifty committeemen at the union hall. They had been invited to address the men, as had four high-ranking members of the labour bureaucracy: assistant national director George Eamon Park, Gower Markle and Ken Valentine of the USWA education department, and New Brunswick Federation of Labour president Paul LePage. Katz and Storey later wrote: "The national office of the Steelworkers sent down its heaviest political artillery to turn the session into an assault on the *East Coast Worker* and progressive trade unionists."[166] This confrontation is significant in that it represented a direct attack on New Leftists and also demonstrated that leaders were not only aware of the group but also anxious enough about the group's influence to come down in person. That local members had set up this meeting must have been distressing, a direct challenge to national hierarchies in favour of rank-and-file leadership.

The animosity between Park, former NDP president (1965-69), and those at the *East Coast Worker* was personal, as seen in the vitriol with which the two sides attacked each other. The *Worker* denounced Park for his role in the Canso strike – he had supported the CFAWU's raid – and for his later role in forcing a contract on Local 1231 in Trenton at Hawker Siddeley. That case had seen the Steelworkers pressuring the employees to take a tentative agreement, and the *Worker* had contended that the international union had become a third opponent facing the workers. As one worker described the situation, it was "like you're in a tough scrap with two bullies and then your supposed friend jumps on your back."[167]

The editorial cartoon entitled "Now We Know What Happens When the Lights Go Out!" and which accompanied the article perhaps best encapsulates the personal attack made on Park, and provides a succinct summary of the ECSM's indictment of labour leaders. In the illustration, Park lay in a post-coital position next to a Hawker Siddeley "boss" as they clink wine glasses and gaze into each other's eyes in mutual lust and admiration. If anyone was unclear who Park was, his briefcase carried the caption "Yep, I'm a Union Man." Looking in through the window were two picketing workers, obviously alarmed. Not only was the international union in bed with the employer, but it seemed to be enjoying itself.

This cartoon was brought to Park's attention. When Katz and Storey came to the hall, he had a chance to respond to the allegations. Beyond the political connotations, there was an attack on his personal dignity. Along with sub-district officer LePage, Park denounced the *East Coast Worker* as a "rag," told the Steelworkers that it was full of "lies," and compared the ECSM to the UFAWU, as both aimed to "divide the labour movement." The executives then attacked specific stories. Park took particular umbrage at a story denouncing his role in the Canso strike, explaining that he had been helping fishermen on behalf of the minister of labour, and downplaying his criticism of the UFAWU. Katz and Storey did not reply, as they felt that "if anyone was to challenge [the] lies, it should be the steelworkers. To some extent this was done. For example, Gordon (Gramps) Kiley, executive member of 1064[,] told Paul LePage, 'You say the *East Coast Worker* is printing a lot of tripe, well I think you have been talking tripe all weekend.'"[168]

The *Worker* dealt with other issues also. Regional underdevelopment was a staple: corporations were moving into the area to take advantage of cheap wages but were simply exporting the profits and reinvesting nothing.[169] Steve Strople carefully explained the concept of economic underdevelopment in his series on "socialism vs. capitalism," which explained basic underlying concepts, connecting the broader theory with concrete examples such as Hawker Siddeley.[170] Critically, in light of debates that had sundered much of the earlier New Left apart, women's issues were explored. This reflected a growing awareness among the group of feminism and gender equality. For example, differential pay between waitresses and waiters was exposed.[171] The *Worker* covered strikes, lockouts, plant closures, working conditions, and a host of other issues for its readership. In a region where the leading papers did not cover many of these issues, it filled a significant niche.

Was the ECSM successful in reaching out to the rank and file of the labour movement, its intended audience? It is hard to tell. Its mail subscription base was around one hundred, but the prime distribution method was plant-gate sales.[172] Some issues hit hot buttons. For example, an edition about the Halifax Shipyard spurred massive sales for the following edition – "People were grabbing the thing," Hart says. For the most part, however, paper sales at plant gates were a hard slog; many people just walked by. But some members were more talented salespeople than others: Storey, for example, sold many through charisma and quick-talking alone.[173]

The ECSM was sensitive to the *East Coast Worker*'s reception. After eight months, it surveyed readers about their opinions of the paper and on a host of political and social questions.[174] In hindsight, Clare sees the questionnaire as significant: "One of the things this speaks to ... was how unsure we were of the effect of what we were writing. The degree to which we were uncertain about the level of language, whether or not the things we wrote about were topical and interesting."[175] Records of the feedback are now lost, but Clare recalls that it spurred the group to run a few more "popular" stories, such as one on hockey.

The ECSM nonetheless collapsed in an acute, sudden manner that demonstrated the organization's structural problems. As a closed organization, it was slow to expand and incorporate new members – and the existing members were putting in long, exhausting days. Plant-gate distributions meant that members had to be at the gates early in the morning to catch shift changes; political discussions, however, went late into the night.[176] "I think part of it was that it had literally run its course ... twelve people just can't keep on doing this in this context," Hart says.[177] The small group demanded a huge proportion of people's time, dominating their lives at a high personal cost.[178]

In the context of these structural pressures, the ECSM fell apart in the wake of the circulation of a manifesto. One account of this came from Herb Gamberg. His wife, Ruth, a recent addition to the group allowed in when the restrictive policy changed near the end of the ECSM's existence, took umbrage at a plan to bring a black high school student into the organization. His admission, according to her, was being advanced on the grounds that "you can't have an organization without blacks because there are blacks in Nova Scotia."[179] She penned a formal criticism of the decision on the basis of tokenism and distributed it to the group. "It was a blast that came seemingly out of nowhere," Hart says, consciously not naming in our interview who penned the document, and noting that the letter (whether it was Gamberg's or another one) destroyed the group in about a week's time.[180] News of the split reached Stevens, who stayed in touch with members of the group over the next few years, corresponding with Katz about career options and with Ruth Gamberg and her husband about the continuing factional splits in Halifax.[181] That these members stayed in touch with Stevens so long speaks to the enduring link created, as well as to the personal importance of such a supportive role. Stevens wistfully wrote that the ECSM was "dealing in their own way with what has been referred to as the 'cult of personality' ... because none of them would abide by any form of discipline or agreement whereby if they had differences amongst themselves they would continue to thrash them out without splitting up."[182] Hart points out, "The fact that it would split like that over one epistle says something about the organization anyway."[183] The ECSM had moved rapidly, and without an established procedure to grow the organization, pressures grew.

So why did the group matter in light of its short-lived existence? It was more important than its small size might indicate, mostly through the remarkable dedication of its members and their production and distribution efforts for the *East Coast Worker*. First, it is the sole formation of the period that came *out* of labour struggle, and reflected a distinct character forged in the Canso fishermen's strike. It had a strong emphasis on rank-and-file activities, but also – while part of the NDY – made a meaningful contribution to the lives of the striking fishermen. Members continued to work on this theme, thanks to the education received along the Strait of Canso. It also represented the most meaningful New Left–inspired activity in Nova Scotia. The ECSM presents a cautionary tale, however. Succession problems and issues of expanding the group led to structural problems that left the group vulnerable to an ideological break. All this in a province often regarded as peripheral to the history of the 1960s. Despite the dominant folk identity of Nova Scotia, these young men and women were able to draw on an earlier tradition of radicalism and revitalize it.

Conclusion

At picket lines and strikes in Peterborough, Brantford, Kitchener, and Cape Breton, New Leftists and labour encountered each other. An often awkward relationship emerged, but lessons were also learned. The tension that was felt by some at the end of the *Examiner* strike gave way to a longer-lasting, community-based relationship with those involved in the Dare Cookies strike. In Canso, an embryonic New Left rose to see the importance of organized labour in effecting social change. It was through these interactions that many New Leftists began their slow moves into the labour movement. These baby steps toward a link between a New Left and labour would be brought to fuller fruition in the 1973 Artistic Woodwork strike.

One strike stands apart from the others and deserves brief further mention. In Fort William, Ontario (now Thunder Bay), between 3 October and 9 December 1968, retail clerks at the downtown Chapples department store struck over union security.[184] Lakehead University students joined picket lines after a *Port Arthur News-Chronicle* article singled out the union president and published her home address; she then invited students to join the picket line.[185] This early November demonstration was driven by students who felt they "should actively support groups of people in the non-university community who are consciously struggling to improve their working and/or living conditions."[186] Groups of up to fifty students at a time engaged in demonstrations, attempting to prevent strikebreakers from entering or leaving the store. This eventually led to an injunction on 15 November – ignored by some students, who instead went into the store to raise consciousness inside.[187] Russ Rothney, then a New Leftist at Lakehead, remembers the circus-like atmosphere, but the situation culminated with a favourable settlement. In the strike's aftermath, a short-lived student-labour committee was set up, reflecting the "recent show of student support."[188]

There was a crucial difference between this strike and the others. Apart from an occasional Canadian University Press article, little news made it out of Lakehead, and it failed to generate substantial interest beyond those directly involved. As Rothney explains: "News coverage appeared to have been systematically blocked on all of the major national media," though the local newspaper *Argus* attempted to rectify this with a special strike support edition.[189] It thus stood outside the narrative established at Peterborough, Kitchener, Brantford, and Cape Breton. At these places, New Leftists rapidly developed and thought out their ideological preconceptions, refining their beliefs about class and gender, and their tactics for effecting meaningful change.

The *Peterborough Examiner*, Dare Cookies, and Canso struggles all represented connections between a grassroots New Left and unions that were struggling for a variety of reasons. The *Examiner* strike represented a first approach to labour, Dare Cookies the first sustained contribution, and Canso the limits of out-and-out militancy. Yet these strikes are also a story of missed opportunities. Although some student New Leftists looked to Paris, May 1968, for inspiration, there was no substantial development of a worker-student alliance that ever threatened liberal capitalism, let alone the elected governments, for even an instant.

The strikes discussed here mattered. Each was significant on its own merits. For instance, the *Examiner* demonstrated the intransigence of a large media empire determined to cut costs, as well as the future possibilities inherent in a worker-student alliance. At Dare, partially through the efforts of the Ontario Committee on the Status of Women, many learned of deplorable working conditions and unequal pay for equal work. These were important issues that spurred discussion and change. Yet these issues would not have reached the public eye without an influx of young people on the picket lines.

Strikebreaking was revealed to be a serious problem, garnering substantial attention in the mainstream and student presses alike, and the continuing issue of labour injunctions was highlighted. Left feminists learned of the issues that working-class females faced, and were able to do something about it at the Dare strike – through joining the picket line and later supporting the cookie boycott. Labour unions learned that they needed to reach beyond their labour community for support on picket lines, and that New Leftists were not ignorant of their problems. These stories also put to rest claims that New Leftists were ignorant of problems facing their broader community and the working class more specifically. Some quickly learned the basics of the labour movement and its history, and forged a relationship with these groups. The presence of New Leftists on these picket lines was important. Supporters offered a helping hand to the workers and forged a distinctively New Leftist way of working with labour. These themes would all come together in one high-profile conflagration in Toronto: the Artistic Woodwork strike of 1973.

6

A Relationship Culminates: The 1973 Artistic Woodwork Strike

Now the force of all our numbers and our actions on the line
Won a victory for the workers, and a contract they could sign.
But while workers are exploited, then our struggle won't decline
So the lines go marching on.

– Excerpt from the Artistic picket-line song[1]

The daily ritual of violence began at dawn. In a desolate industrial park in Metropolitan Toronto's North York, men and women gathered to protest their working conditions. Some of them were older immigrants, with weathered yet determined faces. Most, however, were students, social workers, and teachers representing a wide milieu of the Toronto New Left and who came out to stand with these few workers. Here they could put their theory into action, in the culmination of nearly a decade of debate and thought on the question of social change, the state, and exploitation. The Canadian Textile and Chemical Union (CTCU) was on a first-contract strike against Artistic Woodwork, a picture-frame manufacturer, in one of the nastiest and most significant strikes in Toronto's history. The strike had begun in the summer warmth of late August 1973, but it was now cold mid-November and no end was in sight.

Around 7 a.m., the police arrived en masse, assembling across the street from the Artistic plant and the line of picketers. The chanting began: "Cops are tops, the bosses say ... cops are thugs, the workers say." One picketer, who had known police only from friendly school visits and neighbourhood settings, realized that "these police look a lot different, menacing and contemptuous."[2] A car arrived, rounding the bend of Densley Avenue, its headlights flickering. Suddenly, havoc. Police charged toward the line, attempting to open Artistic's driveways for cars carrying strikebreakers. Stopping these cars was essential if the union was to win the strike. Picketers who reacted slowly were quickly grabbed and thrust out of the way by uniformed men; picketers and police alike descended on the cars, the picketers trying to stop them and the police trying to facilitate their entry. In the ensuing melee, confusion reigned. An arrest was made, and policemen carried away a protester. It was hard to determine why they targeted one person over another, though the picketers did notice a special animus toward both the long-haired and the young. Within ten minutes, Densley Avenue was calm again. Another morning of now-ritualized violence was complete; the cycle would repeat itself almost every day between 21 August and 5 December 1973.

The Artistic strike captured the attention of not only the left-wing milieu of Toronto – from students, to rank-and-file militants, to activists from a plethora of political groups – but also the entire city. Although New Leftists had been previously active on picket lines, at Artistic they were among the true leaders of picket lines and of organizing campaigns. Women were by now rising to leadership positions, at least in comparison with earlier events. They were also critical as picket-line supporters. For many strike supporters, this was about more than just one struggle for a first collective agreement. These young men and women woke well before dawn, on chilly fall mornings, to put their rhetoric into action; here was an opportunity to fight the evils of capitalism – in the guise of the manager or the police officer – head on. Artistic became an opportunity to fight the system and act out the Marxist sociology of the time. The largely unstudied story of Artistic demonstrates the confluence of a variety of forces at the end of the 1960s: the widespread turn toward Marxism and the working class as a necessary component of social change; the importance of nationalism as a unifying factor; and the continuing social responsibility of the student and the intellectual. As a story, it helps crystallize the complicated ideologies, beliefs, and actors at the end of English Canada's long sixties.

This chapter focuses on the supporters, their reasons for taking to the picket lines at the Artistic strike, and what it meant for the evolving story of the New Left and labour. It is not a history of the strike per se.[3] The working conditions in the plant were deplorable, and the story of the strike itself rightfully belongs to the workers. Supporters, however, allowed the strike to continue for a long period, led it to dominate news coverage, and considerably shaped the ongoing picket-line confrontations essential to the strike. The picketing workers quickly dwindled to a handful, and the strike's narrative was then dominated by the role of supporters.

Organizing Artistic Woodwork

The CTCU stumbled on Artistic by accident. By 1971, the union was organizing female immigrant workers in knitting mills throughout the city. Some of their husbands manufactured picture frames for Artistic, and they brought their workplace concerns to the union's attention. Artistic was a small plant of 115 mostly male immigrant workers, with four plants in Metro Toronto and smaller branches in Montreal, Vancouver, and Cleveland.[4] Six Estonian immigrants had founded Artistic, and the firm's management style was characterized as "anti-communist, anti-union, conservative, and authoritarian." This conservatism was epitomized by Artistic's spokesperson during the strike, assistant general manager Sorel Van Zyl, who embodied "a mix of manipulative paternalism and an army style barracks discipline."[5] Two onlookers from a nearby Canadian Brotherhood of Railway, Transport and General Workers Union local would later characterize it as a "medieval fiefdom."[6]

Artistic was representative of small manufacturing firms that were largely unorganized, given the difficulties of organizing a small number of employees.[7] Fairly large industrial parks dotted Toronto's suburbs, many home to small firms with specialized products and smaller production runs, such as Artistic Woodwork. These expanses of short, nondescript brick buildings on winding roads hosted various industrial activities, largely hidden from the main arterial streets. Throughout the 1960s, southern Europeans (Greeks, Italians, and Portuguese) were entering the labour market in great numbers and finding waged employment in poorly paid manufacturing and service sectors; non-British immigrants made far less than the average Canadian, many hovering around the poverty line.[8] They often found employment with these small, exploitative firms that had no history of unionization.

Organizing Artistic was difficult because of the diverse languages spoken in the predominately immigrant workplace. Artistic was a "United Nations" of ethnicities that generally stuck within their own linguistic groups, and the CTCU relied on a few English-speaking workers to translate for others. Most of the men were eager for a union.[9] One worker in particular, Joe Sinagoga ("Synagogue"), an Italian veteran of the Second Italo-Abyssinian War, emerged as a central figure in the union drive. He had a position that allowed movement around the plant, and he carried messages between plant workers and organizers outside. This, combined with his charisma and good English, allowed union supporters to sign enough cards – 85 of the 115 – to see a union certified.[10] The immigrant nature of the plant lent an additional dimension to the campaign. Artistic's ethnic diversity could be seen in the organizing flyers, translated into English, Greek, Italian, and Portuguese.[11] In this, we see aspects of the relationship between the immigrant experience and radicalism – some immigrants were politicized by virtue of Old World radicalism, but the different languages could also inhibit solidarity. In particular, strike organizer Daniel Drache notes that workers from Latin America and Greece had a tradition of resistance, whereas those from the Caribbean and the outports of Newfoundland had little.[12] This is the view of one of the organizers on the ground and must be balanced against the tradition of black Caribbean activism, vividly witnessed during the events of the Sir George Williams Computer Centre riot and the ensuing politics of the Montreal black community (which spread to and helped radicalize parts of the Caribbean).[13] In any event, the union certification drive was successful and secured on 19 April. Bargaining would now begin.

The usual sticking issue of wages and benefits was quickly resolved. By early August, all indications were that a contract would be reached.[14] A wage increase of $0.65 per hour had been agreed on; given pre-strike wages of $2 to $2.95 per hour, a sizable wage increase had been granted even in the context of inflation.[15] The strike would be fought over non-monetary issues: seniority, security, and management rights.

The management rights clause was especially insidious, as it gave management the right to change rules at any time and to dismiss workers without any recourse to a grievance procedure. Although the fundamental issue of management rights was unsurprising, the discipline clause gave managers the ability to unilaterally terminate workers for any breach. The clause would mean a union in name only. Managers did (and do) typically dictate the rules in a workplace, but what was startling here was the demand to enforce them all through unilateral dismissal. Grievances were to be limited to determining whether the employee broke the rule, regardless of the severity of said rule. Madeleine Parent described this clause as one of "the most pernicious clauses I've seen in thirty years of union bargaining. If the negotiators had agreed to it, they would have sold out the workers. The rest of the contract would be worthless."[16] If they wanted to continue as a genuine union, no option was left but to strike. The strike was called on 20 August 1973.

The strike quickly drew attention – significant in light of the facility's relatively invisible suburban location, small immigrant workforce, and niche service of producing picture frames. Despite this, the strike became a cause. Union organizer John Lang remembers returning home from his vacation on the

Sunday after the strike began and calling around to his friends. Nobody was home – they were out on the picket lines. It was only late that night, when people had returned home, that he learned of the strike.[17] This speaks to the power of New Leftist networks in Toronto, as the picket lines were invisible, tucked away in a suburban industrial park. Word had spread quickly about the strike, facilitated by the press coverage that had appeared right from the outset, but especially by a web of contacts.

New Leftists Meet the Confederation of Canadian Unions

Whereas the previous interactions between New Leftists and labour had seen the former providing critical support and resources, Artistic saw supporters adopting leading roles of organizing, recruiting, leading, and eventually sustaining the picket line. These organizers are important for several reasons. First, they each had links to various sixties currents, from New Left activism to counterculture to educational reform. Second, the organizers were the glue that made the strike edifice possible, as many picketers came because of their presence. They were able to tap into broader Toronto New Leftist social networks.[18]

Many of the organizers and high-profile picket-line leaders, notably Laurell Ritchie, John Lang, Daniel Drache, and Rick Salutin, found their way into the Council of Canadian Unions (CCU) through a fortuitous meeting with Parent and Rowley. These future organizers met Parent and Rowley when, at some point in 1970 or 1971, the two dropped by the Anti-Imperialist Squad, a small reading group that included Lang, Salutin, Drache, and Ritchie, among others, and which met weekly to discuss left and labour topics. Salutin remembers the day they came by: "They looked like an elderly couple ... on their way back from church. But they had this incredible history, and at the end of the talk, they said, did any of us want to work with them?"[19]

Each organizer had New Leftist links and would form the backbone of the CTCU before, during, and after Artistic. Ritchie had taken a circuitous route into the union, having been involved with the York University student government, though her time there was cut short by a lack of money. Living in a housing project at Jane and Finch, in north Toronto, Ritchie was identified "as somebody who could talk about poverty issues."[20] She went from there to Ontario Welfare Council, the Toronto Social Planning Council, and Rochdale College, and was an activist with various leftist social justice groups, such as Just Society and the Poor People's Conference. She was also involved with the first Women's Press collective. The range of groups Ritchie engaged with demonstrates an enduring commitment to social justice, but also how intertwined these groups were, forming a progressive network in Toronto. Along with Lang, Ritchie would become a full-time CTCU organizer and employee.

Lang, then a York University contract professor, had come from working-class Sudbury, where his father had been a Mine Mill organizer. Doing well in school, Lang spent two years as a seminarian at the University of Toronto's St. Michael's College. Here, his politicization began in the context of the Catholic debates brought on by the Second Vatican Council. Graduating from the University of Toronto in 1967, he took his master's degree at Guelph, writing a thesis on the history of Mine Mill in Sudbury before continuing on to a doctorate at the University of Toronto. Dropping out of the program after realizing that he was spending "more time in the union hall than in the classroom," Lang became involved with the Waffle. He came into contact with Parent and Rowley through his work fighting the Americanization of the university and the labour movement. He had been a York course director during the first four or five weeks of the Artistic strike, though its demands would force him to subsequently step down.[21]

Drache was a student activist and political scientist who came out of the disarmament movement and who had worked with SUPA before subsequently co-founding the Canadian Liberation Movement. He had also written the Drache Report, part of the Commission on University Government at the University of Toronto, which addressed student participation, authority, and decision making in the university. At Texpack, he was among those who were arrested.[22] Coming out of the Marxist and nationalist traditions of the Canadian left, Drache was an organizer during the Artistic strike and was often cited in the press, particularly the student press.

Salutin had recently returned to Toronto after spending the sixties in New York City (and a year in Israel), doing his doctorate at the New School for Social Research. He was a veteran of protests at Columbia University and the New School. Running out of money, and finding himself barred because of his activism from further work at the C.W. Post College of Long Island University, where he had been teaching for a year, he returned to Toronto to write. After meeting Parent and Rowley, Salutin went to work as a CTCU volunteer, assisting in organizing – on top of his day job as a freelance writer, writing satires and radio documentaries for the CBC, as well as his own highly successful plays.[23]

Two others, Sarah Spinks and Bob Davis, partners with a young child, came into the Artistic strike after first encountering labour at Texpack, where they met the other organizers. Spinks, one of the organizers and the person responsible for liaising with the police and arranging legal counsel during Artistic, had her roots in the nuclear disarmament movement and subsequently SUPA's

Kingston Community Project, in the summer after her last year at high school. An active New Leftist, she then moved into the women's liberation movement. In 1969, Spinks was involved in starting the University of Toronto's daycare centre and became a leader in the sit-ins over the issue. She later became involved in the Texpack strike, along with Davis and several other friends, and then moved to the CCU.[24]

Davis made a transition in the strike from educational reformer to picket captain. He had been involved in the Everdale alternative school in Guelph. A teacher and founder of *This Magazine Is about Schools,* Davis had become quite taken by the CCU after Texpack; it fit well with his politics of being a "revolutionary hippie." After several of the leaders at Artistic were arrested and prevented from taking active roles on the picket lines, Davis became a picket captain there.[25] During the important early-morning shift – 6 a.m. until 11 a.m. – Davis not only helped run the picket line but also reached out to supporters.[26] His presence inspired others to join. As D'Arcy Martin says, "It was certainly Bob Davis who got me there. Bob and Sarah [Spinks]."[27]

These people each drew on their personal networks and New Leftist legacies when they came to organize Artistic. They drew on various parts of the broader New Left milieu: the free educational movement, student power, Canadian nationalism, and left nationalist unions. The organizers helped make Artistic what it was, which speaks to the continuing involvement of the New Left into the early 1970s. It was the broader Marxist ideology of the New Left, however, that attracted supporters. These organizers had interpreted the struggle in a way that cast it as an important fight against a brutal capitalist system, in the guise of management and police, rather than simply a bread-and-butter union struggle.

The CTCU needed supporters on the picket line. With the strikers isolated from mainstream labour, having small numbers, and facing an employer determined to keep the plant open through strikebreakers, a picket line was essential to pressure the employer. "Without the supporters we wouldn't have won," concluded one unnamed Artistic worker. A second agreed, noting that "when the support started to come in big and we had a big picket line, the workers started to believe again that we had a chance to win."[28] Yet the supporters became the dominant story of this strike, both their presence and their role in the ensuing violence.

The number of actual workers on strike was small for several reasons. Many of the workers who either did not go on strike or returned to work fairly quickly were Newfoundlanders from outports with little history of resistance or unionization.[29] Others may simply have returned for the security of paid employment. Life on the line was tough. Yet some who left the picket line did so under more desirable circumstances. The pay at Artistic was so low that workers could find better jobs elsewhere, even in the economic climate of 1973. "People realized that they could get better jobs than this," says John Lang. One young Italian man picketed for about three weeks. Artistic was his first Canadian job. Realizing that it would be a long strike, he found a new job as a unionized forklift operator, making twice what he had been making at Artistic. For some, the strike became an opportunity to re-enter the labour market and gain confidence.[30] Finally, the violent police actions frightened some foreign workers, especially those from police states.[31] Those without Canadian citizenship must also have feared retaliation.

Given this, the union had to reach out for external support – it could not sustain a picket line itself, and it was clear that the picket line was key to winning the strike, because of continued production.[32] In early September, Andreas Papandreou, a former Greek cabinet minister who would later become prime minister of Greece, Toronto politician John Sewell, and Waffle leader James Laxer came to the picket line to demonstrate their solidarity.[33] Sewell and Laxer would emerge as important in drumming up New Left support – the former in successfully convincing the Toronto City Council that police actions and strikebreaking were out of hand at Artistic, the latter in using Artistic as a vivid example of the necessity of Canadian nationalism.

The issues were also comparatively simple: "A small plant, with immigrant workers, trying to get a first contract, being paid minimum wage most of the time, and a vicious management. And the fact is that in Canada, workers do have the right to a union contract. I think it was as plain as that," Sarah Spinks says.[34] The immigrant workers could be used to make a sweeping argument about the rights of all workers to unionization and bargaining. Beyond this, their specific struggle was marshalled to a larger cause. Workers' rights were being trampled by the capitalist system, as exemplified by management and backed by a violent police force. Supporters may not have been fully versed in the collective bargaining issues, but they saw the capitalist system in action – and an opportunity to contest it.

The CTCU employed a deliberate strategy of distilling a strike down to a simple message that could be rallied around, in this case, the rights of workers to unionize. Whereas the earlier Texpack strike had been fought around the Americanization of the economy and the exploitation of Canadians by an American corporation, and the later Puretex strike was framed around the issue of worker surveillance, the Artistic organizers conveyed a simple message about the "exploitation of new immigrants."[35] Parent and Rowley had wonderful skills at interpreting labour strife to a general audience,[36] as seen in their ability to isolate a sympathetic non-wage issue for supporters to capitalize on.[37] When nineteen-year-old supporter Peter Dorfman was violently arrested on the Artistic picket lines and beaten in a paddy wagon by a police officer who claimed Dorfman had kicked his "crown jewels," Parent arranged a media interview immediately after Dorfman was bailed out later that morning. "But I [Dorfman] was so wired that instead of sounding reasonable, I think I sounded, I was lashing out, so I think I blew the interview ... I remember Madeleine was mad at me. Because it was an opportunity to kind of be a poor boy who was harmed by the police, and instead I was a militant."[38] Throughout the strike, on the other hand, Parent maintained a focused narrative.

Supporters became increasingly important to the strike, and more and more could come, thanks to its accessibility by Toronto's public transit system. The initial number of employees in the CTCU bargaining unit was 115, though management claimed only 68 actually went on strike.[39] In mid-October, union and management agreed that there were about 60 employees on strike, with the rest either crossing the line or working elsewhere.[40] By the end of the strike in December, the number had dropped to 47 workers.[41] Picket numbers averaged about 175 by November and sometimes reached as high as 400; thus, workers were far outnumbered by supporters.

A conscious attempt was made to attract supporters, with union organizers such as Sarah Spinks going to universities throughout the area, as well as to large supportive union locals such as that at Hamilton's Stelco.[42] A large conference was held downtown at the Ontario Institute for Studies in Education in late September, with two hundred people showing up to discuss the then-young strike and opportunities for further involvement. Students came, as well as a smaller number of rank-and-file workers from other unions. Rick Salutin remembers militant rank and files reflecting a militant Old World unionism as they spoke in their thick Scottish brogues: "I know these people are supposed to be outside the house of labour," commented one, "but a strike is a strike, and a scab is a scab."[43] Throughout the strike, a concerted effort was made to reach out to the community, tapping into the civic spirit that had been mobilized to stop the Spadina expressway in the early 1970s, linking the struggle to the top-down process that had characterized that earlier conflict: "An overriding issue that we are all involved in is regaining control over our lives and the decisions that directly affect us. This is what is at stake for the strikers at Artistic."[44]

The strike was about bigger issues, for the labour movement and for immigrants in Toronto: "Many people believed far more was at stake than the future of just one union local in one small company."[45] As Bob Spencer, student council president at the University of Toronto, declared when his group took an explicit supportive stance of the Artistic strikers in November: "This strike affects every worker, not just those at Artistic Woodwork."[46] This struggle resonated with the people of the city in a way that other strikes did not. It was about power and poverty-level wages. Some unions did come out. As the president of UAW Local 439 (Massey Ferguson) stated, "We have ideological differences [with the CTCU]. We're defending the rights of the immigrant workers."[47]

Gasoline on the Fire: Violence at Artistic Woodwork

Yet the real attention came with the violence, the arrests, and the escalating political rhetoric from all sides. Violence began almost immediately – picketers trying to stop strikebreakers, and police trying to stop the picketers from stopping the strikebreakers, leading to rough arrests. Such violence lost the support of the mainstream media, including the liberal *Toronto Star,* which denounced city council when it urged police – as early as 4 September 1973 – to refrain from violence on picket lines: "Police have to protect the rights of strikers, but they also must uphold the right of non-striking workers and other authorized persons to enter the plant."[48] The *Globe and Mail* took a similar line.[49]

Police violence was widespread at the Artistic Woodwork plant. Photographs show the mass picketing, the arrests, and the constant surveillance of those who came out to the picket line. Artistic was determined to continue producing, and the Metropolitan Toronto police force was determined to help it exercise its legal right to do so. As the lines grew, the Toronto police believed, in Drache's words, that "they had an imperative from God to keep the factory open."[50] All agreed that there was violence on the picket line, though whether one blamed it on the police themselves, their mandate to keep the plant open, or the supporters was generally up to each person's pre-existing bias. Given the picket line's suburban location, unless they actually saw vivid proof of police violence, most onlookers did not believe what was happening. This may have emboldened the police. This was not the Eaton's strike, waged in full view of passersby, streetcars, and cars; this was a hidden picket line. The point of the picket line was to stop strikebreakers, rather than solicit public support.

The law was certainly being enforced zealously, as the arrest figures demonstrate. Thirty-seven had been arrested by 25 September, most of whom had been charged with mischief as a result of blocking the entry driveway to the struck plant.[51] By mid-October, the number had risen to 60,[52] by late November to 111.[53] Only 9 of them were striking workers.[54] This point was made by the title of a *Toronto Star* article: "Arrests Outnumber Workers on Strike."[55] Given the imbalance between the number of supporters and the number of strikers, the workers themselves were becoming emblematic of the broader struggle of immigrant workers. Parent and other strike organizers continually attempted to make sure that the struggle did not become entirely symbolic to supporters – workers continued to be on strike at great personal risk.[56]

The daily arrest rolls read as lists of twenty-somethings, most living in the downtown Annex neighbourhood near the University of Toronto, a favourite residential area of students. For instance, on 26 September, of the seven arraigned, two were York community members (one 25-year-old professor and one 22-year-old student), and six lived in or near the Annex. Except for one 41-year-old man, all seven were also in their twenties. Similarly, on 16 October, four were arrested: two 29-year-olds, a 22-year-old, and a 21-year-old, all of downtown addresses.[57] These young people made the very-early-morning trip north from downtown. The physical and cultural differences between the leafy environs near the University of Toronto and the comparatively desolate industrial parks of North York cannot have been lost on them.

Debate spanned the municipal, metro, and provincial levels. Some Toronto municipal politicians were victims of police violence, and one, Dan Heap, was arrested on 15 October for allegedly assaulting a police officer. City councillors John Sewell (later mayor of Toronto from 1978 to 1980), William Kilbourn, and Dorothy Thomas were also on the picket line.[58] Toronto City Council was supportive and sympathetic of the strikers. They implored the provincial labour minister, Fern Guindon, to use his powers to settle the strike quickly and heard testimony from Sewell about police violence on the picket line.[59] They faced the wrath of the police chief, Harold Adamson, who had to apologize for his "steamed up" behaviour toward city council when he had refused to release police videotapes taken at the line to a council questioning him over police violence.[60]

Other Supporters

The CTCU's position on outside supporters was that they were welcome to "come out and get their heads cracked by the cops ... but they have no say, because the union is run by the workers."[61] As Spinks recalls, Parent was quite firm on this position, making it perfectly clear that the local "was making the decisions, and the other people were supporters."[62] The union attempted to delineate these roles. This led to disagreement, especially among several groups that demanded meetings with the union leadership on strategy. Salutin remembers

Parent phoning him at home and asking him to come to the CTCU office: a group of "revolutionaries" had gathered in there, and she was afraid that files would be stolen. The office was full of people when Salutin arrived. He gathered with CCU-affiliated Bricklayers to simply stand, arms crossed, to let the intruders know that a fight would ensue should they try to move on the files.[63] They stood down. The incident is indicative of the tensions that emerged during the strike, and the attitude of strike leadership toward some supporters.

We can see this demonstrated elsewhere, as organized groups such as the Revolutionary Marxist Group, the Canadian Party of Labour, the League for Socialist Action/Young Socialists, and the Communist Party of Canada (Marxist-Leninist) – CPC(ML) – attempted to play roles in the strike but were rebuffed by the CTCU for being divisive.[64] Despite this, the CPC(ML) issued pamphlets calling for armed revolutionary struggle; it commended the "unity amongst the workers in Toronto and amongst the students and democratic people in support of the Artistic strike," seeing the Artistic strike as part of a broader class war against monopoly capitalism.[65] The Trotskyist Revolutionary Marxist Group saw Artistic as an opportunity to support the working class and gain experience doing so, as well as an opportunity to intervene "politically in the dispersed left milieu" of students and youth. The group's views on the strike were that the union needed to begin an "off-picket-line" strategy, with picketing at City Hall and at Labour Council/Ontario Federation of Labour offices, and to pursue a more militant, possibly illegal strategy.[66]

Other unionists did bolster the picket lines on occasion. The mainstream leadership of the CLC and the OFL were largely unsupportive of the strike, a legacy of the long-standing tension between the mainstream labour movement and nationalist unions. In particular, the CTCU and the OFL had a history of sparring. As recently as 1971 during Texpack, the CTCU had accused the OFL of allowing the Textile Workers Union of America to organize strikebreakers at a suburban satellite location.[67] Although there could be limited cooperation of issues of shared significance – such as strikebreakers and violence on the picket lines – the reaction of mainstream labour was generally restrained. Support instead came from local unions themselves. Two notable locals were the United Electrical Workers (UE) at Toronto's Northern Telecom plant, and the United Auto Workers Local 1967 at McDonnell-Douglas.[68]

UE was particularly important, as it had been at the earlier *Peterborough Examiner* strike. As both the CTCU and UE were outside the mainstream labour movement, there was sympathy between them, despite the obvious difference of the former being nationalist and the latter being an international union. David Monie, a UE leader at Northern Telecom, came to the picket line to offer "financial and moral assistance." He was arrested for common assault on two police officers during a mass picket on 14 November 1973; despite the testimonies of two police officers, his charges were dropped after it became apparent he had been singled out for arrest by aggressive police officers who had provoked him by yelling "Let's get this fucking bastard."[69]

Members of United Auto Workers (UAW) Local 1967, which represented the workers at Douglas Aircraft, came to the line as well. Bargaining chairman Archie Wilson and two other members, including one of the local's vice-presidents, came out to the morning picket lines in early October, arriving late for their scheduled shifts at Douglas because of heavy traffic. This led to the company alleging that they were picketing during company time. The three men were suspended. The next day, members of UAW 1967 responded by calling in sick, an action seen by the company as an illegal work stoppage.[70] Five union leaders, including Wilson, were dismissed for either encouraging the walkout or failing to stop it. This dismissal was seen by the Strike Support Committee as proof that "bosses stand together," a slogan used as a rallying cry in Artistic strike propaganda.[71] This would be the last straw for Wilson, who had been suspended three times since an earlier 1971 strike that had been carried out contrary to the international union's wishes. Salutin has suggested that the UAW international headquarters rejoiced, as its internal problem was solved.[72]

Other unions contributed through correspondence. The minister of labour, Fern Guindon, received voluminous amounts of correspondence from labour unions regarding the Artistic strike. Many took the opportunity to use Artistic as a way to push for the wholesale revision of labour legislation in the province, especially laws allowing strikebreakers to work at struck plants. UAW Local 673, representing technical, office, and professional workers in Etobicoke, wrote to protest legislation, demanding an end to police attacks.[73] Similar arguments came from other unions.[74] The Municipal Committee of the Labour Council of Metro Toronto unanimously passed a resolution calling on Metro Toronto Council to protest the police actions and do anything possible to impede the company.[75]

Just as many unions used Artistic as an opportunity to argue for bigger causes than the strike itself, the Canadian Manufacturers Association wrote to Guindon to counterbalance the public attacks being made on him for his inaction in the labour dispute. They denounced the "interlopers" on the picket lines. Its manager of industrial relations was quick to support the police officers' actions and to express disdain for the union: "I will resist the temptation to comment on the union leadership and their past history or on some of the personalities who have chosen to involve themselves."[76] Similar sentiments came from the vice-president of corporate relations at Toronto's head office of Noranda Mines.[77] These representatives of capital hoped that the public would learn about the rights of struck enterprises.

Endgame

With the revelations of a video, taped on 12 November by Laura Sky from the National Film Board's Challenge for Change program, and released to city council the next day, the debate became increasingly charged. The video showed the daily morning violence. In one scene, a police officer could be seen beating up a picketer; in a second, a group of three officers seized another picketer, dragging him to a door, and roughly knocking his head around while making the arrest. Police officers were seen removing their hats, which had their badge numbers on them. Law student Vicki Trerise, a supporter, was seen on camera being dragged by her hair.[78] That day was the most violent of the strike yet; twelve strikers had been arrested, and several sent to the hospital with injuries. William Temple, a 76-year-old former CCF MPP and long-time temperance crusader who had been arrested on the picket line, was interviewed and described the events of the day as "a disgrace to civilized society ... I've never been so disgusted and sickened in my life ... and I've been in two world wars."[79] Temple had been arrested on charges of drunkenness and attacking a police officer. That a long-time temperance crusader and 76-year-old man was accused of such acts stretched credibility, perhaps contributing to a wider sense that the police were out of control. Indeed, Dorothy Thomas quoted Temple in a letter sent out to the members of Metro Toronto Council, imploring them to watch Laura Sky's video. She booked the members' lounge and invited councillors to see the video for themselves.[80]

It was this video that made the situation clear to those who were not near the lines. The video's release polarized and shocked the city. Many "middle-class people couldn't believe what they were seeing," says John Lang.[81] The politicians who had been active in the strike were outraged, whereas conservative politicians saw the police as doing a "fantastic job," as Scarborough controller Brian Harrison declared.[82] A group of Toronto city councillors, led by Arthur "Art" Eggleton (mayor of Toronto from 1980 to 1991 and Liberal federal MP from 1993 to 2004), called for the police to be withdrawn from the picket lines; this was predictably denounced as "insanity."[83] Eggleton later clarified his views in a long letter to city council, describing his visit to the lines on 16 November. He described seeing arrests and police rushing the picket lines, and how disturbed he was that the police were clearly abetting management and the strikebreakers. Eggleton wanted the police removed so they could no longer break the lines.[84] In response, the North York Council voted to *commend* the Metro Police and asked Metro Toronto Council to "stop 'its political interference' in a borough matter."[85]

The video of 12 November also set in motion a week that Lang and Drache, as well as others, would later consider the turning point.[86] The OFL convention had begun in downtown Toronto. Leaflets circulated at the convention, calling for support on the picket lines. By 14 November, OFL delegates joined to create a mass picket. This, combined with the video, led to growing pressure on Guindon, who agreed to the city council's recommendation that the labour ministry become more involved. Guindon and William H. Dickie, the assistant labour minister for industrial relations, became personally involved in late November and met with Artistic and CTCU representatives. By this time, union hierarchies had to act in light of growing rank-and-file pressure.[87]

The RCMP Security Service also took an interest in the events of November. An unnamed agent submitted an extensive report during the week, noting the larger-than-normal picket lines, the approximately four hundred supporters on the next Monday, and the large lines on the following Wednesday and Friday as well. Violence was described: large rocks were being thrown indiscriminately into the mob of pickets and police. The agent also claimed that many of the injuries reported by picketers were wholly fabricated, as he observed "a few pickets with faces covered with a blood-like substance and hollering police brutality and talking to the news media ... [An] examination of this blood-like substance[,] by the centre of forensic science, revealed it to be a type of theatrical makeup."[88] It is impossible to verify or disprove this claim, but its truth is unlikely. Mention of fabricated injuries did not appear in any of the relatively exhaustive post-strike trial proceedings.[89]

The combined pressures of media coverage, mass picketing, the minister of labour, and Metro Toronto Council finally forced Artistic to cave on several key bargaining issues. An initial agreement was reached in late November, though this quickly collapsed when it became clear that the issue of rehiring arrested workers was unresolved, prompting banner headlines in the *Toronto Star*.[90] Although the terms of the collective agreement had been settled, the two sides fought over the back-to-work protocol for several more days. Such a protocol is never part of the formal collective agreement, yet it would be necessary for the two parties to reach agreement in order to end the strike.[91] Wrangling over these issues seemed to lose the attention of the many supporters, and pickets dwindled to a hundred or fewer.[92]

Artistic's management was quite firm on the protocol. Eight workers had been charged during the strike. Artistic framed the issue as being that of worker safety, raising the spectre of law-abiding workers who exercised their rights to work in the struck plant being forced to work alongside arrested and convicted picketers. It did, however, offer to submit the issue of rehiring convicted workers to binding arbitration. The union eventually conceded. Two weeks later, the union relented on union security clauses, won the crucial issue of management rights, and agreed to send the issue of rehiring workers to arbitration.[93] A triumphant Fern Guindon rose in the provincial legislature to address the strike. He blamed the lengthy strike on "outsiders" who "contributed nothing ... although many had the best of intentions." He continued, "Outsiders may well have found it personally satisfying to raise the Artistic dispute to the symbolic level, where they could find their own meanings in the struggles of others."[94]

The strike was over, with the union having made substantial material gains. It had stood up to Artistic's desire to have a union in name only, and the discipline clause originally proposed was entirely removed. This, coupled with the wage gains, represented a very real change in the daily lives of Artistic workers. The paternalistic authority of management had been dispersed and effectively shown to be vulnerable. The union was legally entrenched in the plant. It had been a long and brutal strike. Many of the workers had found work elsewhere and would not return to Artistic, and several core members of the union found themselves unable to return to work because of their arrests on the picket lines and the back-to-work clause. At the end of the struggle, it may have been a pyrrhic victory.

The Aftermath

The supporters did not cohere around the Artistic strike for long, perhaps reflecting the ad hoc nature of much of the support as opposed to that of more formally organized political groupings. Although individuals continued their journey into the labour movement, there was no sustained activity on the scale of the mass pickets. One activity that continued out of the strike was the Right to Strike Committee, which published a series of booklets on important strikes – beginning with Artistic – and stressed the need to continually fight for the right to strike.[95] This organization continued for at least another year beyond the Artistic strike, highlighting province-wide strikebreaking and attempting to cement links between left-wing strike supporters and trade unionists.[96] After Artistic, the Revolutionary Marxist Group had a sustained discussion about the future direction of picket-line involvements: Had Artistic been a success? How should revolutionary groups work with institutions such as the CTCU? A current emerged in the responses that the group had to decisively move in front of more reformist groups such as unions, and post-strike analysis focused on the Revolutionary Marxist Group's betrayal and ostracism from the mainstream CTCU.[97] Artistic may not have been as central to the personal trajectories of members on the Marxist-Leninist left, but it played an important role in their thinking vis-à-vis the state, unions, and the broader left.

Although the strike was certainly declared a clear victory, with Joe Sinagoga and Parent writing their supporters that the victory was "especially significant because it concerns mostly immigrant workers, typical of hundreds of thousands in unorganized plants in Metro Toronto, where exploitation is rampant and insecurity is the rule," the workers were not rehired after the grievance procedure broke down.[98] Arbitration broke down when the process took too long, as was to be expected with a complicated legal procedure. Workers were suspended without pay during the proceedings, and after six months with no end in sight, the union representatives walked out of the proceedings.[99] During the first five months of the Board of Arbitration's existence, only four meetings could be scheduled and held.[100] The union was especially incensed that these workers had no means of support, while Artistic continued to produce completely unhindered. It was also unhappy with the suspect testimony of numerous police officers. After the union walked out, the suspensions became terminations.[101] Indeed, even when the criminal charges against one man were dismissed, Artistic management alleged that this was because of technicalities and upheld his termination.[102] Because the militant members were not rehired, the Artistic strikers who returned to the plant were "outnumbered by the scabs," both those who stayed inside during the strike and those who were hired as strikebreakers (and had been kept on by management).[103] Two years later, 84 signatures out of a workforce of 110 were presented to the Ontario Labour Relations Board in a request for decertification.[104]

The decertification campaign against the CTCU drew heavily on the experience of the strike. Letters were distributed throughout the plant, drawing on anti-Communist themes, questioning what the strike was fought for. Posters consisting of sensational headlines that highlighted the violence of the strike were distributed. They highlighted the role of outside supporters – of students, politicians, and so on – accusing them of opportunistically using the strike. All the posters included headlines that highlighted the violent history of the Artistic strike, and several included photos of picket-line scuffles. The past was presented to the membership, along with stark invitations to help prevent it all from happening again.[105] In the face of both the campaign and the employee makeup of the plant – many of the strikebreakers as well as those who had not found alternative employment – the eventual vote was sixty-two to thirty-six in favour of decertification.[106] The workers may have voted their hard-fought union out of existence, but appeals continued through the system for those arrested on the picket lines; a shocking thirty people awaited their appeals of summary convictions five years after the strike ended.[107] The campaign to defend the "Artistic 108," as the group was called after 3 of the 111 original charges were dropped, continued vigorously for a few months but slowly ran out of steam as court dates dragged on and on into the future.

In light of the union's decertification, one reaction was to characterize the Artistic strike as a defeat. On one level, it was: the union was decertified, fears marshalled to lead the majority of workers to vote against collective representation. It also certainly did not set in motion widespread organizing throughout the city; if anything, the high costs of organizing small facilities were revealed to be even higher in the face of intransigent employers. For some, Artistic had been conceived as a "jump off for a general organizing strategy," but a decisive victory was needed to create a dynamic; this never occurred. It was a missed opportunity in that respect.[108] Yet others continued to organize small operations, leading to subsequent conflagrations such as the Fleck and Radio Shack strikes, in 1978.[109] Artistic had not been a decisive victory, but nor had it been an entirely decisive defeat. That said, for many there had been severe personal hardship – arrests and sheer effort for supporters, loss of pay and termination for many picketers – and on a strict material basis, the means did not justify the end.

Positive developments came from the strike, however. First, as Lang later argued, it had shown that Canadians *could* run a viable strike without the support of the mainstream labour leadership.[110] Salutin agrees, holding that the Artistic strike showed the possibilities of idealistic, Canadian unionism.[111] Even without many picketers and without wider labour-movement support, the strikers held on for 109 days and made significant gains against an intransigent employer. Labour learned other lessons also. Labour activist and educator D'Arcy Martin holds that Artistic "showed the potential for social networking ... it showed the path that was later picked up by these other [work]places that were not CCU."[112] Indeed, Drache and labour-law professor Harry Glasbeek later wrote that the strike helped make clear the need for "invoking the support of popular groups."[113]

The strike influenced the realm of public policy and opinion. Using strike-breakers presented a stark example to the public of what legalized strike-breaking could lead to. Although picket violence on this scale has not been seen in Toronto since – there were far more arrests than workers on strike – Artistic was a vivid example of the threat to public order when strikebreakers were allowed to threaten the livelihood of workers exercising their right to bargain collectively and withhold their labour. It thus contributed to a realization that anti-scab legislation at least needed consideration. Currently, British Columbia and Quebec are the only two provinces to have such legislation on their books – Ontario's short-lived legislation under the Rae government having been re-voked by the neo-conservative Mike Harris government.[114]

Strikebreaking, as we have seen, had risen to be an issue in the 1960s and early 1970s amid labour unrest. Yet strikebreaking continues to be a pertinent public policy issue, especially as it is legal in all Canadian jurisdictions except Quebec and British Columbia. Standing in the federal Parliament in April 2005, federal NDP leader Jack Layton – who had been an active picketer at Artistic and first-hand witness to police brutality – evoked the spirit of the Artistic strike when he urged for the Canada Labour Code to be amended to outlaw strike-breakers in strikes under federal jurisdiction:

> When replacement workers are brought in and they cross the picket lines
> and striking workers see busload after busload of these workers taking their
> jobs, as I witnessed myself in the early 1970s at the famous Artistic Wood-
> work strike, undercutting their very ability to bargain a fair deal, it does not
> bode well for a future of harmonious labour relations.[115]

At the municipal level, many of the Toronto councillors had been arrested or shocked by what they had seen on the Artistic line – Arthur Eggleton, David Crombie, Dorothy Thomas, Dan Heap, among others – and it reinforced a new concern about unions and the working class for a city that had not thought much about these issues until the strike.[116]

Further lessons can be gleaned from the Artistic strike: the need for first-contract binding arbitration, which would be introduced in Ontario with Bill 65 in 1986 but which continues to be a political issue today. It also demon-strates the caution police must take in their activities on the picket lines, as strict enforcement of the law results in aiding management – not that the police strictly enforced the law at Artistic, as picketers' right of communication was not honoured.

Finally, and perhaps most importantly, there was the strong personal impact that the strike had on supporters. Certainly, Artistic was a strong lesson that you "had to stand up and fight for what you believe in."[117] For Davis, who went on to play a large role in the 1975 Metro teachers' strike and lead a life of educational activism and leadership, the Artistic strike was a great influence in his own teaching.[118] Yet for many more, this was an opportunity to put politics into action:

> There was this whole network of progressive people ... who really helped people to see the connection between this broader vision of social justice where the left intellectuals were and a tangible moment in our community in which you could do something about it.[119]

After all of the discussion, which had stretched from the early 1960s onward, about how to effect social change – and debates over the role of the working class – a decisive opportunity was opened to those in Toronto's progressive milieu to play a role. And they did. The connection between theory and concrete action was demonstrated, just as it had been hinted at to growing degrees at *Peterborough Examiner*, Dare, and Texpack. For the immigrant workers too, this strike was significant. Their concerns were publicized, as Parent noted in 1979, which helped highlight the specific issue of immigrant exploitation in the Toronto area.[120] Ritchie contends that Artistic continues to be a "touchstone for a lot of people. People will say, 'Were you at Artistic?' 'Did I first meet you at Artistic?' 'Do I remember you from Artistic?' 'Was that guy at Artistic?'"[121] It helped bring immigrant society a little further into the mainstream and under the spotlight. Spinks concurs: "It was one of the first times that immigrant workers' struggles had been publicly revealed, and how difficult their working conditions could be. So a lot more people came to know about this."[122] Dorfman agrees:

> It certainly raised issues of working conditions, of immigrants in Toronto, and raised the profile of immigrants in Toronto in a way that was very significant ... That was kind of the beginning. I mean, if you trace the trajectory back to Toronto, [a] diverse [city] dominated by people from other places, this was the first significant strike of those people who were doing something to defend themselves at work.[123]

As far away as the University of Regina campus, press releases for a 1975 speech by Parent advertised how the strike "brought wide attention to exploitation of immigrant workers in Canada and the oppression they [met] when attempting to organize a union."[124]

The lessons learned at Artistic would later be put to use at two afore-mentioned 1978 strikes: the Fleck strike in Huron Park, Ontario – a touchstone in the feminist movement, involving 120 workers also trying to get a first collective agreement – and the Collingwood Radio Shack (Tandy) strike.[125] Artistic was also significant enough in that it arguably drew several activists off the campus. Warrian suggests that Artistic "burned up a lot of people who either went off into their own political activism stuff, or decided to get involved directly from the bottom up in the labour movement as union members and [thus] disengaged people from the campus struggle."[126] Many supporters did come to be involved in the labour movement out of these struggles, and were on the picket line at Artistic: Judy Darcy, who subsequently rose to prominence in the library workers' union at the University of Toronto and later became national president of CUPE; Martin, a labour educator and activist; Warrian, later research director with the United Steelworkers of America. The opportunities were there, and they seized them. For some, this first encounter opened up the labour movement as a career option: "It certainly contrasted with going to school," Dorfman says, "as an inspiration and a sort of direction in my life, it was huge, and made school just seem totally irrelevant."[127]

Conclusion

The Artistic strike is a compelling study of how several currents within the Toronto New Leftist milieu – from the intellectual turn toward Marxism to the rise of nationalism and the continuing emphasis put on social responsibility – converged near the end of the long sixties. The opportunity for change and improvement demonstrated at Artistic was in some ways representative of a period that was about to end. For as the seventies progressed, the labour movement found itself on increasingly unsettled ground as it faced increasingly repressive policies. A new chapter of labour history would begin.

Although the political and economic context today is far removed from that of the early seventies, we can still derive meaningful direction from an event like Artistic. Artistic presents a valuable lesson for policy makers considering anti-strikebreaking legislation. In addition, the power and importance of social networking was avidly demonstrated, as groups of friends were urged to take action and join each other on early-morning picket lines. New Leftist organizers were able to do this by framing the narrative as an opportunity to fight the system and act out the increasingly pervasive Marxist sociology of the time, connecting Artistic with ongoing social issues and concerns. Supporters were not there for the critically important bread-and-butter matters of a new collective agreement but for more abstract ideals of justice and rights. In 1973, the Artistic organizers were able to capitalize on these various trends, presenting supporters with an opportunity to put theory into action, leading many to wake up early on dark, cold mornings, stand against oppression, and put their bodies on the line for what they felt was right and just. For three months, New Leftists were able to put their principles into action – principles crafted by a decade of debate, writing, and political action – and they did so.

Conclusion

New Leftists, unions, and young workers were all intimately connected to the youth explosion throughout the late 1950s and 1960s. In growing numbers throughout the period, youth turned toward a new culture of anti-authoritarianism and self-expression, which gave rise to the New Left but also to oppositional movements within labour unions. This demographic bulge came of age in the sixties and moved through a variety of institutions, leading to a generalized perception of a youth crisis. This was a pan-Canadian phenomenon, touching university campuses, large industrial operations, and even seemingly remote picket lines across the country. Youth had power. In the labour market, their numbers gave them bargaining power; they could move between jobs, and they often found themselves clustered together in low-seniority positions. It was not a coincidence that Stelco hit its employment peak on the eve of the 1966 wildcat strike, which stemmed from a concentration of rebel youth. The rapidly growing universities also saw youth unrest, as students challenged *in loco parentis,* fighting for greater control over their daily lives and involvement in the institution's ruling structures. Some formed New Leftist organizations, seeking fundamental social change and fighting for participatory democracy, civil rights, university issues, and peace. Although there were certainly distinctions between young workers, students, and New Leftists, they were all active expressions of a broad anti-authoritarian youth culture. It would be in the 1970s and beyond, discussed briefly here, that these various currents would finally come together to various extents.

What did this all mean? What impact can youth, a transitory category by nature, have? As this book demonstrates, these young men and women brought material and cultural changes to labour unions, universities, and even municipal and higher-order governments. The shared cry for greater democracy and anti-authoritarianism found itself directed at both the foreman and the university dean, leading to workplace and curricular changes alike. Reaching a crescendo with the 1965-66 wildcat wave, this youthful labour militancy led to significant procedural changes, recriminations, and eventually a dramatic readjustment in labour's view of youth. New Leftists turned their attention toward questions of social change and the role of the working class, and in some places, such as Regina and Vancouver, forged meaningful coalitions with working people. Elsewhere, they put their bodies on picket lines, garnering significant political and media attention at an array of strikes, from the Strait of Canso to the industrial heartland of southern Ontario. This current culminated in the 1973 Artistic strike, a high-profile event that would not have been possible without the preceding years of debate, development, and outreach. By this time, however, New Leftists were increasingly graduating, and the demographic bulge of anti-authoritarian youth was working itself out of the system. In a way, many had to graduate into "regular" jobs. This was a process of continuity, however, rather than a profound detachment or "selling out."

Artistic represents the culmination of a definite historical process, bringing together several representative themes. Steelworkers national director Larry Sefton had been right. His daughter, Laurel Sefton MacDowell, remembers him declaring that allying with students would be problematic because of their transitory nature – that they were "not workers in the sense that you're going to stay ... [students] were then going to move on."[1] From this, we can see a broader point about the fleeting nature of students as a force for social change. Indeed, the student and New Leftist movements can be accurately seen as several successive generations of students. Some of the leadership came from longer-term graduate students, like Jim Harding and John Cleveland, but most undergraduates spent only four short years in university. There was often little inter-generational transfer of memory, and university for many would be a period of experimentation (politically, sexually, culturally), without many perceived consequences. One cannot be a student forever, at least not in a formal, full-time context. Young workers, though, were earning a living in a profoundly long-term way. Their continuing militancy would thus take a different shape in the wake of Artistic. As noted earlier, youth is an intrinsically instable category. At some level, people do grow up.

Beyond the reality of graduating and aging, there was now a new political, economic, and cultural context for young people to operate in. As 1973 came to a close, it became clear that New Leftists, young workers, and labour unions were on new terrain. The mid-1970s would bring a different narrative. The "sixties" as an idea and periodization were over. University campuses, far from being sites of active resistance, were now "hotbeds of quietism," as we saw with SFU. Radical political groups still existed, but to some with considerable and even growing numbers, such as the Revolutionary Marxist Group or *In Struggle/ En Lutte,* the idea of a New Left now seemed a quaint relic of years past. For political inspiration, many of this new generation of activists now looked explicitly to Old Leftist ideology. Many leftists increasingly saw the future of revolutionary change in the industrial working class rather than in a Marcusian dispossessed, community organizing, or middle-class professionals.

While New Leftists continued their valuable activities as individuals or in smaller groups, working with community members, and eventually moving into established institutions such as labour unions (which many had maligned only a few years previously as porkchoppers or power elites), a moment had passed. New Leftists failed to regenerate themselves. A new generation of students and young workers found themselves preoccupied with their own dismal job futures. Many of the routes that took young men and women down the road to radicalism, as discussed in Chapter 1, were now blocked off. American involvement in the Vietnam War tapered off with Nixon's Vietnamization policy, and the January 1973 Paris Peace Accords saw the withdrawal of most American military personnel. This had been critically important for the inculcation of a radical consciousness, forming a backdrop to much of the decade's upheaval, even in Canada. In the United States, the most egregious civil rights violations saw legislation, and although socio-economic structures of discrimination continued, these were harder to directly rally around for some. The most visceral examples had been at least superficially dealt with, leaving pervasive yet somewhat hidden structures of discrimination and repression.

In Canada, overt suppression or repression touched some (be it the War Measures Act or narcotics arrests), but programs like the Opportunity for Youth and the Local Initiatives Programme, and a system of youth hostels, among other initiatives, served to co-opt many young activists.[2] There were still involved, active youth, but the mood had shifted. The new generation would arguably look elsewhere – to the individualism of disco, which helped them make do in an extremely harsh economic context, or toward the increasingly powerful and significant feminist movement.[3] For many, the belief that a revolution was around the corner disappeared. Change could still come, but it would be a tough slog. Yet most did not falter, instead continuing to demonstrate a sustained commitment to their earlier ideals.

Unions also found themselves entering a new period of militancy, albeit on different political and economic ground. Through the 1960s, the mood could be summed up as one of hope, even if some leaders vehemently disagreed with the particular tactics: hope that young workers would fight for better working conditions, hope and a firm belief that higher real wages were on the horizon, even hope that some of the excesses of capitalism might be trampled down. There was a different mood in the increasingly angry demonstrations and strikes of the mid-1970s. It was now a defensive battle: holding onto the gains that had been made during and since the Second World War, and fighting an increasingly repressive state marked by a growing number of back-to-work legislation bills and draconian wage controls. Over a million Canadian workers protested in 1976 at the pan–Canadian Day of Protest, an impressive demonstration of solidarity. Yet ultimately, 1976 can be seen as defensive defiance. With a slacker labour market, there was less chance taking, and with unions under attack, many young workers did not take them for granted, as they had only years before.[4]

Significant exceptions existed, of course, demonstrating a continuity of 1960s activism. The most notable was the continuance of a militant youthful spirit at Inco in Sudbury. Youth had made themselves known in the 1966 and 1969 strikes, a trend that continued into the next decade. A short strike in 1975 was run by "all young guys," says David Patterson, who was subsequently elected as Steelworkers Local 6500 president in 1976 (after a first election was tossed out for being rigged).[5] Patterson, remembered by Norris Valiquette as a "long-haired hippie," brought a new questioning energy to the local, advocating nationalization and aggressive bargaining tactics, and emphasizing his own roots as a miner as opposed to the union bureaucracy.[6] When Local 6500 struck Inco in 1978, it was an inspiring pan-Canadian event: small plastic shovels became a staple of union solidarity across Canada, local leaders fought off attempts by the international to see them take a deal they deemed substandard, and the union eventually won its "thirty-and-out" demand (after thirty years, one was eligible for retirement). They hoped and fought for ambitious goals, and unequivocally won. Cathy Mulroy remembers the "thirst for knowledge" that permeated the local through the Patterson years, inspiring workers to question "their places in the hierarchy: Why are some people called this [title or that title]? How are the banks involved?"[7] Solidarity held between younger workers, older workers, and the women's committee, and the 1979 settlement was seen as a victory for rank-and-file workers. But even within Local 6500, hope could not last forever.

Patterson was elected as the Canadian national director (at the Steelworkers' District 6) but was stymied by bureaucratic resistance and, after a messy "civil war," was defeated after one term.[8] At Local 6500, the fun and energy were gone, and the hopeful spirit of Patterson – a legacy of earlier activities during the sixties – was snuffed out.

Working women also brought tremendous energy to the labour movement, in high-profile strikes like Fleck and through groups such as Organized Working Women (Ontario) and the International Women's Day Committee (which was marked by considerable cooperation with labour).[9] Organizations like the National Action Committee on the Status of Women also developed a strong socialist-feminist approach, looking toward working women.[10] Groups like SORWUC continued to organize working women to varying degrees of success. Beyond that, a large grassroots array of Status of Women committees brought a New Leftist approach to feminist organizing, representing continuity. That the feminist movement increasingly looked toward and cooperated with labour was a partial legacy of intellectual developments that had taken place throughout the sixties.

Hope would eventually be found in the breaking down of the dichotomy between New Leftist and worker. For the sixties' zeitgeist, this hope for a new world to emerge lived on in the actions of individuals who continued to make meaningful contributions to social movements and community activism. These individuals had experienced many personal and political defeats: the splintering of early New Leftist formations, the defeat of the SFU 114 and the PSA Department in British Columbia, and picket-line interventions that may have been personally fruitful but often resulted in overall failure. In spite of all this, most continued to strive for a fairer and more equitable world in their career choices, personal political decisions, and overall trajectories. These activities stemmed from the intellectual and cultural context in which these young men and women had come of age: they were wartime babies or baby boomers, with upbringings full of promise, drawn toward a questioning or radical political stance, forged through intellectual debates and action, on picket lines, in protests, demonstrations, or elsewhere, within the New Left or labour movements. Many had to compromise some of their earlier intransigent positions to make a living, raise children, own property, or engage in some other relationship with mainstream society. Yet this is not synonymous with selling out, as pop culture stereotypes hold. Their continuing actions demonstrate a noteworthy continuity as they grew older and graduated into jobs with unions, social movements, universities, and other institutions. The New Left as a movement had declined, yet its ideas lived on with its former participants.

After years of hesitant steps and attempts to reach out and understand each other, it was here that New Leftists and labour converged in the end. University-trained and -based activists found their way into the labour movement, and not simply through the newly unionizing public service. As noted in Chapter 2, union officials had come to the realization that they were facing a youth crisis within their organizations. After the events of the wildcat wave, especially the strikes at Inco and Stelco, young workers were now explicitly part of the union world. Leaders would have to figure out their new members, and hosting conferences and gatherings did not suffice. With the generation of labour leaders who had piloted the movement through the 1930s and the Second World War coming to the end of their careers, new energy and blood was needed in national offices. In 1974, when Sam Gindin was hired as national research director by the Canadian office of the UAW, National Director Bob White observed that Gindin did not look like a typical economist – jeans, work boots, windbreaker – but "he asked more questions of me than I asked of him." "He's bright," White thought, "and besides, we've got nothing to lose. He wants to work for the union so I think we ought to try him."[11] Gindin was not alone in wanting to work for a union.

Thanks to timing, many New Leftists were then beginning to cast about for new careers. Many moved into the labour movement, representing a profound continuity. This made sense for them as well, given the intellectual development of New Leftist thought, especially as participants began seeing the working class as an agent of social change and moving into sites of active resistance such as picket lines. As seen in the experiences of Peter Dorfman, their eyes had been opened to a new career path. This stood in stark contrast to Ed Finn's declaration as late as 1971 that "today's idealistic college graduate does not gravitate to the labor movement."[12] Such long-term career choices demonstrate a sustained commitment to these ideals. Many former New Leftists in the labour movement found a way to further their earlier political interests, ideals, and concrete activism.

The list of people who continued their activism in this institutional milieu is impressive, and my list here is only a sample. Several people went on to high-level research and education positions. As mentioned, Peter Warrian, D'Arcy Martin, and several others became directly involved in the labour movement in the wake of the Artistic Woodwork strike. Joining the USWA during a period of growth and reorganization, Martin introduced and championed the "back to the locals" model of union education. He prioritized the training of local activists as grassroots educators, which led to a profound increase in rank-and-file participation; this can be seen as a quintessentially New Leftist approach.[13]

This had a tremendous influence on union education. Larry Katz of the East Coast Socialist Movement became CUPE research director, and Judy Darcy rose to become CUPE national president from 1991 to 2003. Others became arbitrators, staff members, or local activists, including Brian Switzman, Guy Pocklington, Karen Naylor, Marcy Toms, Terry Moore, Peter Dorfman, and Sharon Yandle. Still others carried on with independent working-class or labour activism. Stan Gray, named the Greatest Canadian Shit-Disturber by *Canadian Dimension* in 2004, became heavily involved in workers' health and safety, eventually becoming an independent legal advocate for workers in Hamilton. Through his work in health and safety, Gray encountered Jim Brophy, who became a tireless activist in the field, as well as Homer Seguin, who continued to be a voice for workers' safety before succumbing to lung cancer and chronic obstructive pulmonary disease – due to his own occupational health issues – in 2013. Joan Kuyek, Jennifer Penney, and Dorothy Wigmore (who had been head of Canadian University Press) continue to do valiant work in the environmental and safety movements. Indeed, I was often surprised to encounter people whom I knew from my research as living in different parts of the country, involved in different activities, working together more than forty years later – a testament to an enduring New Leftist and labour network. The number of people who chose labour as a career path should not be understated. More work remains to be done on how those who moved into the labour milieu had an impact on it: Did they change its cultural values, or did they find themselves changed by their institutional encounters?

Many of the lessons of the 1960s and early 1970s would prove significant for labour over the following decades. From Artistic Woodwork and other picket lines throughout Ontario, to British Columbia's Lower Mainland, to southern Saskatchewan, to Nova Scotia's Strait of Canso, a generation of engaged activists came into contact with labour. Beyond opening up this world as a career path and thus preserving individual hopes for social transformation, these events provided tangible political lessons. Far from seeing labour and workers in monolithic forms, many New Leftists quickly learned that things were far more complicated: unions were different from each other, workers were divided along many lines, and a battle continued to be waged over the shape of the labour movement to come. Rick Salutin says that at places like Artistic, people "saw that a more idealistic, militant unionism seemed possible under even a miniscule Canadian union," compared with the much larger internationals.[14] Indeed, from that strike grew the careers of several union activists who rose to staff positions within the Canadian Auto Workers, which merged with the CTCU in 1992. These included Laurell Ritchie, a national representative and frequent opinion maker, and John Lang, eventually a lawyer with the union. Hundreds of young men and women came out in the morning to stand up for what they thought was right, on picket lines or at pro-labour demonstrations across English Canada. This must have had a profound impact on the larger body of rank-and-file picket supporters, many of whom are now lost to anonymity. As the Canadian labour movement rose, with the high-profile formation of the Canadian Auto Workers out of the United Auto Workers in 1985 and the semi-successful movements toward more national autonomy within the Steelworkers, former New Leftists could see the possibilities of independent action. They had seen a preview more than a decade earlier.

Labour was not an end point for all, of course, and many continued important work in various other ways, such as community or environmental activism. Dimitri Roussopoulos, for example, has been an enduring civic force in Montreal, and Jim Harding has worked in the anti-nuclear movement, while Debbie Field has run Toronto's major food-security organization Foodshare. Those that moved into the professional sphere often brought activist agendas, from members of the Law Union of Ontario (which received renewed vitality from Artistic) to educators like Bob Davis in Ontario and Marcy Toms in British Columbia, who brought their energy to provincial teachers' federations.[15] Many others moved into academia, where they continue to inculcate a questioning consciousness in a new generation of students and with their research agendas. Labour history, as one pertinent example, largely owes its early vitality to this generation. Without moving into an exhaustive list of their achievements, it is clear that these men and women did not adhere to the tired "stockbroker" narrative. They largely do not eschew their earlier radicalism but instead see it as key to their subsequent intellectual and political development. Although some may now disagree with elements of their youthful agenda and particular actions, most continue to generally see themselves today as having similar political outlooks. The period lives on with those who were shaped by it. Many continue to hope profoundly for a fairer, more equitable world. They may disagree on how to achieve it or what it would entail, but that does not necessitate a nihilistic perspective on the period. Continuity is key.

Youth radicalism was not simply the province of the New Left or university students, as I have argued emphatically here. Defiant anti-authoritarianism and self-expression marked young New Leftists in the universities, but this spirit also animated workplace-bound youth. These were the majority of the generation, as only a minority of the baby boom generation – about 10 to 12 percent – went to college or university. Historians have generally neglected this important aspect of the period, a significant omission given the overall project of social history. We need to incorporate this majority of youth into our narrative of Canada's sixties. For these young men and women were not removed from the overall cultural spirit and social trends that animated the period, demonstrating the enduring significance of these shifts. Indeed, the decade saw young workers challenge their aging union leaders, most notably by leading wildcat strikes at large industrial operations. These young workers brought a questioning spirit to internal labour union operations and politics, which subsequently led to cultural changes within labour.

Significant material and cultural differences existed between these two streams of youth culture, particularly around lived experiences (the tyranny of the foreman was a different type than that of the college dean), social mobility, and cultural expectations, yet this must be balanced against the existence of a shared youth culture. As students faced *in loco parentis* on campus, and young workers faced autocratic leaders in their jobs, a common reaction to culturally comparable circumstances can be seen. Youth across class lines demanded more control over their lives, rejecting the authoritarian status quo. It is not surprising that New Leftists would aim to cooperate and sympathize with progressive unionists around issues of industrial democracy, as such a project spoke to youth concerns across class lines. Indeed, observers from academia, labour, and government noted the existence of a shared youth culture – the wildcat wave that swept the labour movement in 1965 and 1966 must be seen as part of a broader youth upheaval that included the student and New Left movements. This point, which seemed clear to the Woods Task Force on Industrial Relations, the Centre for Industrial Relations, and union officials at the time, needs to be moved once more to the forefront of our understanding of the 1960s.

Despite this shared cultural backdrop, no political alliance formed between these two streams of youth culture. This was most striking in the years 1965 and 1966. For just as young workers actively challenged their conditions of employment, leading wildcat strikes, gathering together on streets, and aggressively making themselves heard, their counterparts in the New Left were explicitly looking away from rank-and-file workers and labour unions. New Leftists instead looked to the American experience of community organizing with African Americans and the working poor in places like Newark, New Jersey; they looked overseas to Europeans such as Herbert Marcuse and André Gorz; they read of labour elites and the co-opted working class of C. Wright Mills and John Porter. In light of this intellectual world, it is unsurprising that many saw their idea in the dispossessed – the working poor in Kingston or the Aboriginals in northern Saskatchewan, for example, rather than the seemingly affluent and complacent working class.

By the time New Leftists began looking explicitly back toward the working class, following the perception of unsuccessful community organizing efforts, demographics, and a global intellectual shift to Marxism, young workers had been largely quelled as a force within their unions. The period would begin to see the rise of Red Power, itself inspired by Black Power in the United States and responding to some general currents of global youth unrest, but that movement was led by young militant Aboriginals themselves; they did not need the efforts of New Leftist projects such as the Neestow Partnership.[16] In Halifax, black activism rose with the Black United Front and the activism of Rocky Jones, but this happened largely off the radar of much of the central Canadian or even Maritime university-based activist communities. With these points in mind, as well as the further realization that, unlike in the United States, there was not a large African American community to organize around, New Leftists returned to an older line on the working class.

Although New Leftists moved out to picket lines and formed meaningful coalitions with the community, a truly transformative moment that might have seen the combination of youth across class lines had passed. Without engaging in counterfactual history, it is at least a compelling thought. A domestic analysis might see a very different story, but many understandably looked south of the border or overseas for the means to make sense of their reality. These narratives initially excluded workers.

The story played out in different ways across Canada, demonstrating political, cultural, and historical differences in disparate regions. In Quebec, a shared anti-colonial ethos dominated the province's political and intellectual world, enabling New Leftists to find places of cooperation with labour, community activists, and others. The crucial role of nationalism, the ever-present issue of language (heightened by the final report of the Royal Commission on Bilingualism and Biculturalism in 1969), and the impact of the Quiet Revolution gave that province a distinctive experience.

The story elsewhere in English Canada needs to be understood as local reactions that can be stitched together into a national narrative. Ontario, the industrial heartland of English Canada and home to a large number of New Leftists by virtue of its number of universities and sheer size, saw a hesitant and faltering relationship between New Leftists and labour organizations. Fears about Communism and radicalism especially defined labour there. When these official entireties failed, Ontario New Leftists took to picket lines in support of the *Peterborough Examiner* strike, the Dare Cookies strike, and the Artistic Woodwork strike. In Nova Scotia, a previously dormant New Left emerged out of the fishermen's strike along the Strait of Canso, as progressive union leader

Homer Stevens reached out to it to do the work that mainstream provincial labour federations and unions would not do. Through that experience, New Leftists there developed a different attitude toward mainstream labour, an understanding of intra-union complexities, and a special emphasis on the rank and file. It was a different story in British Columbia and Saskatchewan. In those locales, New Leftists and labour reactivated old coalitions and networks of a shared left history, attempting to forge a coalition that saw varying degrees of success. Indeed, the entire narrative of Simon Fraser University's unrest during the sixties needs to be reconceptualized as one of community outreach. This left a substantial legacy, as New Leftists came off the mountain and established meaningful links with the community and the working class. They staked out a claim that the university was for all people, a significant clarion call.

Through these various strands, from young workers, to intellectual debates between New Leftists over the agent of social change, to the various coalition and outreach efforts between the left and labour, we can see that the Canadian sixties were defined by labour. This was the major narrative that propelled almost all aspects of the period, from the earliest stirrings of SUPA, to the feminist movement, and especially to the widespread cross-country turn toward Marxism. As a new generation of progressive activists came to grips with a changing economy and labour market, they forged their own political awareness. Yet they were often removed from broader continuities of their own histories: there was barely an accessible left history, nor a labour history, and these youngsters instead relied on oral traditions and smatterings of knowledge about past resistance. In places with very recent left events, such as Saskatchewan with the 1962 doctors' strike, the story was very different. New Leftists and workers there could reactivate palpable left traditions, which they did between 1968 and 1971.

As our economy again demonstrates its vulnerability to business cycles and continues the shift away from a manufacturing economy to an ever-expanding service sector, future activists will need to have a firm grasp on how a previous generation grappled with these changes. The nature of work is always changing, yet this should not mean a wholesale repudiation of what has come before. Despite the pronouncements of some New Leftists and theoreticians, unions were not obsolete nor as ensconced in power structures as they argued in the 1960s. This remains true in the early twenty-first century, where – especially in Canada – labour unions remain one of the critical institutions to counter the growing power nexus between capital and government. We must learn from the past and heed the ironic missed opportunities of this generation, especially as contemporary activists and politicians come to grips with a new narrative to understand our circumstances. Through this, meaningful social change can again become a feasible goal.

A further word of caution is in order as sixties scholarship continues to develop. As this field grows within the Canadian academy and historiography – as witnessed by the recent proliferation of workshops, conferences, and journal theme issues, and an explosion of dissertations – we will increasingly need to resist the urge to become insular. Incorporating labour history into the existing sixties scholarship makes it more relevant, in terms of contemporary political, economic, and social issues, and critically so that historians can recognize narratives of the decade that previously eluded them. It also helps build connections between the sixties and the rest of the historical field, a crucial development for a maturing historical field. By doing so, we can expose the recurrent theme of labour and the working class that cuts through many layers of this history. We gain a deeper understanding of the labour movement, at both the hierarchical and the rank-and-file levels, and can thus get at the overall project of writing social and cultural history. Through these insights, we can arrive at a synthetic labour history of the period. The decade was obviously about more than just middle-class students and New Leftists rebelling against alienation and liberalism, and we can establish the period's true significance by showing how it touched youth of *all* classes as well as interacted with previous social movements such as labour.

The Canadian sixties were a decade of labour as much as any other theme. The central question of the working-class and labour unrest provides a significant lens through which to view the major intellectual developments, debates, and events that shook the nation through this period. Labour formed the backdrop for the experiences of the vast majority of young Canadians at the time, as nearly 90 percent moved into the paid labour market rather than the post-secondary milieu. Yet they were fundamentally animated by the same anti-authoritarian culture and spirit, a cross-class youth phenomenon. Although ultimately bisected by lines of gender and class, this group of young men and women posed a substantial challenge to both institutions and the state. As they grew up, they carried this orientation toward labour into their future activities, forming a new professionalized stratum within many labour unions. The resulting legacy of these events was a permanent change in Canadian society. The collision between these two spheres of youth culture – middle class and working class – altered the Canadian labour movement. The sixties need to be understood through the prism of labour, and our contemporary labour movement is in many ways a child of that period.

Notes

Introduction

1 The global sixties are provocatively dealt with in Karen Dubinsky, Catherine Krull, Susan Lord, Sean Mills, and Scott Rutherford, eds., *New World Coming: The Sixties and the Shaping of Global Consciousness* (Toronto: Between the Lines, 2009).

2 The most significant of these studies is Roberta Sharon Lexier, "The Canadian Student Movement in the Sixties: Three Case Studies" (PhD diss., University of Alberta, 2009). See also Douglas Nesbitt, "The 'Radical Trip' of the Canadian Union of Students, 1963-69" (MA thesis, Trent University, 2010); Robert Frederick Clift, "The Fullest Development of Human Potential: The Canadian Union of Students, 1963-1969" (MA thesis, University of British Columbia, 2002); James Pitsula, *New World Dawning: The Sixties at Regina Campus* (Regina: Canadian Plains Research Center, 2008); Hugh Johnston, *Radical Campus: Making Simon Fraser University* (Vancouver: Douglas and McIntyre, 2005); and Dionysios Rossi, "Mountaintop Mayhem: Simon Fraser University, 1965-1971" (MA thesis, Simon Fraser University, 2003). For the Québécois context, see Jean-Philippe Warren, *Une Douce Anarchie: Les Années 68 au Québec* (Montreal: Boréal, 2008). We have also had our understanding of Canadian youth considerably enhanced by a recent local study on Yorkville. For this, see Stuart Henderson, *Making the Scene: Yorkville and Hip Toronto in the 1960s* (Toronto: University of Toronto Press, 2011).

3 Bryan D. Palmer, *Canada's 1960s: The Ironies of Identity in a Rebellious Era* (Toronto: University of Toronto Press, 2009).

4 Sean Mills, *The Empire Within: Postcolonial Thought and Political Activism in Sixties Montreal* (Montreal and Kingston: McGill-Queen's University Press, 2010).

5 Ibid. For a more focused account on the student movement, see Warren, *Une Douce Anarchie*.

6 M. Athena Palaeologu, "Introduction," in *The Sixties in Canada: A Turbulent and Creative Decade*, ed. M. Athena Palaeologu (Montreal: Black Rose Books, 2009), xii.

7 Especially when contrasted with earlier periods of student unrest, as discussed in Paula S. Fass, *The Damned and the Beautiful: American Youth in the 1920s* (New York: Oxford University Press, 1977); A.B. McKillop, *Matters of Mind: The University in Ontario, 1791-1951* (Toronto:

University of Toronto Press, 1994). A good overall descriptive treatment can be found in Mark Edelman Boren, *Student Resistance: A History of the Unruly Subject* (London: Routledge, 2001), and the earlier Seymour Martin Lipset, *Rebellion in the University* (Chicago: University of Chicago Press, 1971).

8 Cyril Levitt, *Children of Privilege: Student Revolt in the Sixties* (Toronto: University of Toronto Press, 1984), 176. He writes that "the retreat to the campus had been completed by 1967."

9 Craig Heron, *The Canadian Labour Movement: A Short History*, 2nd ed. (Toronto: James Lorimer, 1996), esp. 92-94 and 100-3; Bryan D. Palmer, *Working-Class Experience: Rethinking the History of Canadian Labour, 1800-1991*, 2nd ed. (Toronto: McClelland and Stewart, 1992), 315-20; Peter B. Levy, *The New Left and Labour in the 1960s* (Chicago: University of Illinois Press, 1994). Some American scholarship has explored the connections and barriers between New Leftists, students, and labour unions. See Frank Koscielski, *Divided Loyalties: American Unions and the Vietnam War* (London: Garland, 1999). Koscielski studies the group Concerned Unionists, which sought to oppose the "racist, imperialist Vietnam War" and transform the union movement into a movement that would "truly represent and fight for the interests of the working class" (Walter P. Reuther Library of Labor and Urban Affairs, Wayne State University [hereafter WRL], Concerned Unionists Collection, box 1, file 1-1, Letter from Irving B. Canter, Secretary of Concerned Unionists to Fellow Unionists, 14 January 1970).

10 Palmer, *Canada's 1960s*, chap. 7; Peter McInnis, "Hothead Troubles: 1960s-Era Wildcat Strike Culture in Canada," in *Debating Dissent: Canada and the Sixties*, ed. Lara Campbell, Dominique Clément, and Gregory S. Kealey (Toronto: University of Toronto Press, 2012), 155-70.

11 See Judy Rebick, *Ten Thousand Roses: The Making of a Feminist Revolution* (Toronto: Penguin, 2005).

12 Daniel James, *Doña María's Story: Life History, Memory, and Political Identity* (Durham, NC: Duke University Press, 2000), esp. 121-25. Steven High's work on this point is especially illuminating, particularly his focus on the life stories and narratives of the people he and his team interviews. His work around deindustrialization is particularly useful in that he incorporates crucial discussions of class. See Steven High and David W. Lewis, *Corporate Wasteland: The Landscape and Memory of Deindustrialization* (Toronto: Between the Lines, 2007); Steven High, "Placing the Displaced Worker: Narrating Place in Deindustrializing Sturgeon Falls, Ontario," in *Placing Memory and Remembering Place in Canada*, ed. James Opp and John C. Walsh (Vancouver: UBC Press, 2010); and, for the fruitful product of 137 "life story" oral history interviews, see Steven High, *Industrial Sunset: The Making of North America's Rust Belt, 1969-1984* (Toronto: University of Toronto Press, 2003). See also his forthcoming *Oral History at the Crossroads: Sharing Life Stories of Survival and Displacement* (Vancouver: UBC Press, 2014), which expands on the "shared authority" conception for the entirety of the Montreal Life Stories project. There are interesting cautionary notes in Leon Fink, "When Community Comes Home to Roost: The Southern Milltown as Lost Cause," *Journal of Social History* 40 (Fall 2006): 119-45.

13 A growing literature discusses oral history and provides valuable suggestions on this current. In particular, Alessandro Portelli has provided useful cautionary notes on oral history when dealing with the sixties, noting the particular states of flux that youngsters were in throughout the period, as constant change made it difficult to stabilize memory. See Alessandro Portelli, *The Battle of Valle Giulia: Oral History and the Art of Dialogue* (Madison: University of Wisconsin Press, 1997), 191-92.

14 For more on authority, see Michael Frisch, *A Shared Authority: Essays on the Craft and Meaning of Oral and Public History* (Albany: State University of New York Press, 1990), as well as the special issue of the *Journal of Canadian Studies* 43, 1 (Winter 2009), especially Steven High's "Sharing Authority: An Introduction," 12-34.

Chapter 1: The Challenge of Rebel Youth

1 Evelyn Dumas, "Union Structures Under Scrutiny," *Montreal Star,* 19 June 1968, 11.

2 A point also raised in Palmer, *Canada's 1960s,* 217.

3 Committee on Youth, *It's Your Turn ... A Report to the Secretary of State by the Committee on Youth* (Ottawa: Information Canada, 1971), 7.

4 Peter Braunstein, "Forever Young: Insurgent Youth and the Sixties Culture of Rejuvenation," in *Imagine Nation,* ed. Peter Braunstein (New York: Routledge, 2002), 243.

5 Henderson, *Making the Scene,* 20.

6 Archives of Ontario (hereafter AO), Ontario Federation of Labour fonds (hereafter OFL), box 4 (barcode B399517), file "Speeches, Articles, and Press Releases – 1968," Address by David B. Archer, President of the OFL, to the 13th Annual Convention, London, ON, 3 November 1969.

7 For an American overview of postwar youth experiences, particularly useful for a discussion of immigrant children, see Steven Mintz, *Huck's Raft: A History of American Childhood* (Cambridge, MA: Harvard University Press, 2004). An interesting Canadian discussion of postwar (albeit a bit later) immigrant youth is the primary document by Dionne Brand and Kristantha Sri Bhaggiyadatta, "Rivers Have Sources, Trees Have Roots," in *Histories of Canadian Children and Youth,* ed. Nancy Janovicek and Joy Parr (Toronto: Oxford University Press Canada, 2003): 277-84.

8 This paragraph draws on Doug Owram, *Born at the Right Time: A History of the Baby Boom Generation* (Toronto: University of Toronto Press, 1996), esp. chaps. 2 and 3.

9 Kenneth Norrie, Douglas Owram, and J.C. Herbert Emory, *A History of the Canadian Economy,* 4th ed. (Toronto: Thomson Nelson, 2007), 371-73.

10 As seen in Owram, *Born at the Right Time,* and Levitt, *Children of Privilege.*

11 "Unions Gain 9.3% in Membership to Canada Record," *Globe and Mail,* 21 October 1966, B3.

12 Mona Gleason, *Normalizing the Ideal: Psychology, Schooling, and the Family in Postwar Ontario* (Toronto: University of Toronto Press, 1999), 9. See also Mary Louise Adams, *The Trouble with Normal: Postwar Youth and the Making of Heterosexuality* (Toronto: University of Toronto Press, 1997).

13 Owram, *Born at the Right Time,* 112-13.

14 Robert M. Stamp, *The Schools of Ontario, 1876-1976* (Toronto: Ontario Historical Studies Series for the Government of Ontario, 1982), 194-95.

15 Ibid., 134-35. See Mona Gleason, "Disciplining the Student Body: Schooling and the Construction of Canadian Children's Bodies, 1930-1960," *History of Education Quarterly* 41, 2 (Summer 2001): 196.

16 Michael Zweig, *The Working Class Majority: America's Best Kept Secret* (Ithaca, NY: Cornell University Press, 2001), 48.

17 E.P. Thompson, *Making of the English Working Class,* 1980 ed. (London: Victor Gollancz, 1963; London: Penguin Books, 1991), 8-9.

18 Nancy Pottisham Weiss, "Mother, the Invention of Necessity: Dr. Benjamin Spock's Baby and Child Care," *American Quarterly* 29, 5 (Winter 1977): 540.

19 James Lorimer and Myfanwy Phillips, *Working People: Life in a Downtown City Neighbourhood* (Toronto: James Lorimer, 1971), 40-41.

20 Jon Stratton, "On the Importance of Subcultural Origins," in *The Subcultures Reader,* ed. Ken Gelder and Sarah Thornton (New York: Routledge, 1997), 185-86.

21 William Graebner, *Coming of Age in Buffalo: Youth and Authority in the Postwar Era* (Princeton, NJ: Princeton University Press, 1990), 39. See also Amy L. Best, *Prom Night: Youth, Schools, and Popular Culture* (New York: Routledge, 2000), 7.

22 Owram, *Born at the Right Time,* 140, 150-51.
23 The role of music is discussed in ibid., 154-57.
24 *Blackboard Jungle,* directed by Richard Brooks (1955, Burbank, CA: Time Warner, 2005), DVD.
25 Glenn C. Altschuler, *All Shook Up: How Rock 'n' Roll Changed America* (Oxford: Oxford University Press, 2003), 32-33. See also Owram, *Born at the Right Time,* 151.
26 Paul Friedlander, *Rock and Roll: A Social History* (Boulder, CO: Westview Press, 1996), 32.
27 Economic Council of Canada, *Canadian Economy From the 1960's to the 1970's – Fourth Annual Review of the Economic Council of Canada* (Ottawa: Queen's Printer, 1967), 69. See also Wolfgang M. Illing and Zoltan E. Zsigmond, *Enrolment in Schools and Universities, 1951-52 to 1975-76* (Ottawa: Queen's Printer, 1967).
28 McMaster University William Ready Division of Archives (hereafter MUA), Ontario Union of Students fonds (hereafter OUS), box 39, Robert Rabinovitch, "An Analysis of the Canadian Post Secondary Student Population, Part 1: A Report on Canadian Undergraduate Students," February 1966. Published booklet.
29 MUA, Canadian Union of Students fonds (hereafter CUS), box 21, file "Communications – General," CUS brochure, December 1966. Emphasis in original.
30 MUA, CUS, box 39, file "Universal Accessibility – General Correspondence," Daphne Kelgard, "University Accessibility: A Background Paper for This Is CUS," undated but ca. 1968.
31 MUA, OUS, box 39, Rabinovitch, "An Analysis."
32 Ibid.
33 Pat Armstrong, interview.
34 Charles M. Johnson and John C. Weaver, *Student Days: Student Life at McMaster University from the 1890s to the 1980s* (Hamilton, ON: D.G. Seldon Printing, 1986), 93.
35 Mitchell, interview.
36 Yandle, interview.
37 Committee on Youth, *It's Your Turn,* 17.
38 Owram, *Born at the Right Time,* 178. See also Lexier, "Canadian Student Movement," 70-74.
39 WRL, United Auto Workers Region 7 Collection (hereafter UAW 7), box 54, file 5, Text of Remarks Made by Dennis McDermott, Labour Day Speech, Jackson Park, Windsor, 2 September 1968.
40 AO, OFL, box 4 (barcode B399517), file "Speeches, Articles, and Press Releases – 1968," Address by David B. Archer, President of the OFL, to the 13th Annual Convention, London, ON, 3 November 1969.
41 John Crispo and Harry Arthurs, "Industrial Unrest in Canada: A Diagnosis of Recent Experience," *Relations industrielles/Industrial Relations* 23, 2 (1968): 254.
42 Fred Tabachnick, "Student Revolts Not Comparable to Union Unrest," *Canadian Transport,* 15 December 1969, 3.
43 WRL, UAW 7, box 14, file 8, Conference on Industrial Democracy flyer, 13-14 March 1970.
44 *Our Generation* 8, 3.
45 Conway, interview.
46 Gray, interview.
47 Patterson, interview.
48 Hersh, interview; Brophy, interview; Hall, interview.
49 Reginald G. Smart and David Jackson, *The Yorkville Subculture: A Study of the Life Styles and Interactions of Hippies and Non-Hippies* (Toronto: Addiction Research Foundation, 1969), 25.
50 Ibid., 27-28.
51 See Palmer, *Canada's 1960s,* chap. 10, for an overview of Aboriginal conditions and activism during the period.
52 James St. G. Walker, "Black Confrontation in Sixties Halifax," in Campbell, Clément, and

Kealey, *Debating Dissent*, 173-91. The broader significance of black power in Canada is discussed in David Austin, "All Roads Led to Montreal: Black Power, the Caribbean, and the Black Radical Tradition in Canada," *Journal of African American History* 92, 4 (Autumn 2007): 516-39.

53 Shepherd, interview.

54 Clare, interview.

55 WRL, UAW 7, box 54, file 5, Text of Remarks Made by Dennis McDermott, Labour Day Speech, Jackson Park, Windsor, 2 September 1968.

56 AO, OFL, box 4 (barcode B399517), file "Speeches, Articles, and Press Releases – 1968," Address by David B. Archer, President of the OFL, to the 13th Annual Convention, London, ON, 3 November 1969.

57 AO, OFL, box 4 (barcode B399517), file "Speeches, Articles, and Press Releases – 1968," Labour Day Message 1969 by David Archer.

58 WRL, UAW 7, box 14, file 8, "Conference on Industrial Democracy, 1970," Chris Trower, "Industrial Democracy: An Ideal Dream or the Stairway to Freedom?" January 1970; Library and Archives Canada (hereafter LAC), Harry D. Woods fonds, vol. 1, file "General Correspondence 'M,' 1965-1983," S. Muthuchidambaram, "Trade Union Movement and Student Movement on the North American Continent: A Comparison."

59 This idea appeared in many of his writings, notably Ed Finn, "The New Militancy of Canadian Labour," *Canadian Dimension* 3, 1 (November-December 1965): 16-17, 28.

60 Louis Greenspan, "Wages and Wildcats," *Canadian Forum,* February 1967, 244-45.

61 Stuart Marshall Jamieson, *Times of Trouble: Labour Unrest and Industrial Conflict in Canada, 1900-66* (Ottawa: Task Force on Labour Relations, 1968), 483.

62 Crispo and Arthurs, "Industrial Unrest in Canada," 249.

63 "How Young Workers Look at Labor," *Globe and Mail,* 27 September 1972.

64 Brophy, interview.

65 Ian McKay, "Sarnia in the Sixties (Or the Peculiarities of the Canadians)," in Dubinsky et al., *New World Coming,* 25.

66 Hart, interview.

67 Harding, interview; Hyde, interview; anonymous former University of Waterloo student, interview; among others.

68 Armstrong, interview.

69 Levy, *The New Left,* 1-2.

70 Koscielski, *Divided Loyalties.*

71 University of British Columbia Special Collections, Vancouver and District Labour Council fonds, box 21, Minutes of Meeting, 15 September 1970.

72 Heron, *Canadian Labour Movement,* 102.

73 AO, OFL, box 82 (barcode B394999), OFL 9th Annual Conference, Report of Proceedings, 1965, Windsor, ON, 9-11 November 1965.

74 Crispo and Arthurs, "Industrial Unrest in Canada," 255.

75 Maxwell Flood, *Wildcat Strike in Lake City* (Ottawa: Task Force on Labour Relations, 1968), 75.

76 This is discussed in Myrna Kostash, *Long Way from Home: The Story of the Sixties Generation in Canada* (Toronto: James Lorimer, 1980), 6.

77 Gray, interview; Conway, interview; James Laxer, *Red Diaper Baby: A Boyhood in the Age of McCarthyism* (Vancouver: Douglas and McIntyre, 2004).

78 Pocock, interview.

79 Hyde, interview.

80 Ester Reiter, "Camp Naivelt and the Daughters of the Jewish Left," in *Sisters or Strangers? Immigrant, Ethnic, and Racialized Women in Canadian History,* ed. Marlene Epp, Franca Iacovetta, and Frances Swyripa (Toronto: University of Toronto Press, 2004), 365.

81 J. Laxer, *Red Diaper Baby*, 128.
82 See Catherine Gidney, "Poisoning the Student Mind? The Student Christian Movement at the University of Toronto, 1920-1965," *Journal of the Canadian Historical Association* 8, 1 (1997): 147-63.
83 Bruce Michael Douville, "The Uncomfortable Pew: Christianity, the New Left, and the Hip Counterculture in Toronto, 1965-1975" (PhD diss., York University, 2011).
84 Lang, interview; Ward, interview.
85 McAninch, interview.
86 Hardy, interview.
87 Lexier, "Canadian Student Movement," 70-74.
88 Kenneth Westhues, "Inter-Generational Conflict in the Sixties," in *Prophecy and Protest: Social Movements in Twentieth-Century Canada*, ed. S. Clark, J. Grayson, and L. Grayson (Toronto: Gage, 1975), 401.
89 See Heron, *Canadian Labour Movement*, chap. 2.
90 Judy Fudge and Eric Tucker, *Labour before the Law: The Regulation of Workers' Collective Action in Canada, 1900-1948* (Toronto: University of Toronto Press, 1994), 3.
91 Donald M. Wells, "Origins of Canada's Wagner Model of Industrial Relations: The United Auto Workers in Canada and the Suppression of 'Rank and File' Unionism, 1936-1953," *Canadian Journal of Sociology* 20, 2 (Spring 1995): 193-225.
92 Gil Levine, "CLC's Reformers: Victorious or Co-Opted?" *Canadian Dimension* 7, 1-2 (June-July 1970), 12.
93 Andre Beckerman, "An Organizer's Guide to Workers' Control," *Canadian Dimension* 8, 7 (June 1972), 16.
94 A process described in Johnston, *Radical Campus*, 184-217.
95 Gordon Hardy, e-mail message to author, 23 April 2010.
96 Ibid.
97 Such as Yandle, interview, and Pocklington, interview.
98 Sharon Yandle, e-mail message to author, 15 September 2010.
99 Thomas N. Trenton, "Left-Wing Radicalism at a Canadian University: The Inapplicability of an American Model," *Interchange* 14, 2 (1983), 55.
100 Jim Harding, Review of *Children of Privilege: Student Revolt in the Sixties*, by Cyril Levitt, *Canadian Review of Sociology and Anthropology* 24, 4 (1987): 601.
101 Trenton, "Left-Wing Radicalism," 60.
102 Ibid., 62.
103 Warrian, interview; Gray, interview.
104 Conway, interview; Kossick, interview; Mitchell, interview. Martin Loney, who was elected president of the Canadian Union of Students in 1968, credits his election to the Moose Jaw Caucus (Loney, interview).
105 Yandle, interview.
106 Lizabeth Cohen, *A Consumers' Republic: The Politics of Mass Consumption in Postwar America* (New York: Alfred A. Knopf, 2003), 113-14.
107 Graham, interview.

Chapter 2: Punching In, Walking Out

1 Flood, *Wildcat Strike*, 8-9.
2 "Rail Expressmen in Wildcat Strike," *Toronto Star*, 3 August 1966, 1, and "Rail Peace Here but Montreal Holds Out," *Toronto Telegram*, 4 August 1966.
3 Palmer, *Canada's 1960s*, 223.

4 Cy Gonick, "The Trusteeship and the Decline of Canadian Trade-Unionism," *Canadian Dimension* 1, 3 (December-January 1963/64): 7.

5 Canada Labour Data Branch, *Strikes and Lockouts in Canada/Grèves et lockouts au Canada* (Ottawa: Queen's Printer, 1963).

6 LAC, Harry D. Woods fonds, Manuscript Group (hereafter MG) 31-D169, vol. 2, file "OFL," "Labour and the Future," 16 February 1963.

7 Fudge and Tucker, *Labour before the Law,* 154, 197-98.

8 WRL, UAW 7, box 12, file 1, Stuart Jamieson, "The Third Wave – Labour Unrest and Industrial Conflict in Canada: 1900-1967," 18-19 June 1969.

9 Ben B. Seligman, *Most Notorious Victory: Man in an Age of Automation* (New York: Free Press, 1966), 227.

10 "Automation," *Labour Gazette,* 28 February 1964, 99.

11 David Steigerwald, "Walter Reuther, the UAW, and the Dilemmas of Automation," *Labor History* 51, 3 (2010): 429-53.

12 David Archer, "Management's Rights," *Information* (USWA magazine) 12, 5 (December 1964). Indeed, Canadian concerns over automation were exposed in 1964 when a wave of illegal strikes broke out along the railways. Workers were responding to "run-throughs," or the transiting of trains through customary rest stops because of technological advances. The subsequent Royal Commission argued that employers had the right to implement technological changes while the collective agreement was in effect, and also unsuccessfully recommended that the Industrial Disputes Investigation Act be amended to make major changes an unfair practice. See Justice Samuel Freedman, *Report of the Industrial Inquiry Commission on Canadian National Railways "Run-Throughs"* (Ottawa: Queen's Printer, 1965).

13 Ed Finn, "Labour – The Rand Report," *Canadian Dimension* 5, 6 (September-October 1968), 8.

14 Patterson, interview.

15 AO, Record Group (hereafter RG) 18-152, Royal Commission Inquiry into Labour Disputes, box 3, Rand Inquiry Transcript, Toronto, 11 January 1967.

16 Crispo and Arthurs, "Industrial Unrest in Canada," 243.

17 WRL, UAW 7, box 23, file 1, Letter from George Burt to Bryan M. Downie, 25 November 1965.

18 Crispo and Arthurs, "Industrial Unrest in Canada," 254. The point was also raised in Arthur Krueger, "Strike Wave – 1966," *Canadian Forum* 48, 545 (July 1966), 74.

19 WRL, UAW 7, box 12, file 1, Stuart Jamieson, "The Third Wave – Labour Unrest and Industrial Conflict in Canada: 1900-1967," 18-19 June 1969.

20 D'Arcy Martin, *Thinking Union: Activism and Education in Canada's Labour Movement* (Toronto: Between the Lines, 1995), 39-40.

21 LAC, RCMP/CSIS fonds, RG 146-3, vol. 84, file 1027-98-A-114, pt. 1, Report on International Union of Mine Mill and Smelter Workers, Local 598, Sudbury, ON, 27 July 1966.

22 Lovely, interview.

23 Patterson, interview.

24 Historical Statistics of Canada, Table D223-235 "Unemployment Rates, by Age and Sex, Annual Averages, 1946 to 1975," Statistics Canada, http://www.statcan.gc.ca/.

25 Hall, interview; Seguin, interview; Patterson, interview.

26 Jamieson, *Times of Trouble,* 417.

27 Hall, interview; Conway, interview.

28 "Wildcat Strike Poser: Are Leaders Out of Touch with Members?" *Globe and Mail,* 19 November 1965, B01.

29 Christopher Dummitt, *The Manly Modern: Masculinity in Postwar Canada* (Vancouver: UBC Press, 2007), 142.

30 WRL, UAW 7, box 12, box 201, "Fact: 95% of All Union-Management Agreements Are Settled Peacefully," undated. This is also mentioned in Palmer, *Canada's 1960s,* 223.
31 As discussed in LAC, Department of Labour fonds, Strikes and Lockouts files, RG 27 D 2 (hereafter S&L), vol. 3106, file 16, newspaper clippings and reports.
32 LAC, S&L, vol. 3116, file 65, Report on Industrial Dispute Commencement, 24 March 1966.
33 LAC, S&L, vol. 3116, file 415, Report on Industrial Dispute Commencement, 4 April 1966; LAC, S&L, reel T-3421, vol. 3122, file 447, Report on Industrial Dispute Commencement, 23 September 1966. These events are described by Peter McInnis, "Hothead Troubles," in Campbell, Clément, and Kealey, *Debating Dissent,* 260.
34 WRL, UAW 7, box 96, file 7, "United International UAW Supporters Blue and White Bulletin," November or December 1966.
35 WRL, UAW 7, box 96, file 7, Letter from Clarence Williams to George Burt, 7 December 1966.
36 WRL, UAW 7, box 96, file 7, Telegram from Charles Brooks to George Burt, 16 December 1966.
37 WRL, UAW 7, box 96, file 8, Statement to Local 444 UAW News by George Burt, early 1967.
38 Brophy, interview.
39 WRL, UAW 7, box 96, file 8, Statement to Local 444 UAW News by George Burt, early 1967.
40 See, for example, Meg Luxton and June Shirley Corman, *Getting By in Hard Times: Gendered Labour at Home and on the Job* (Toronto: University of Toronto Press, 2001).
41 Craig Heron, *Working in Steel: The Early Years in Canada* (Toronto: McClelland and Stewart, 1988), 18-19, 27.
42 Bill Freeman, *1005: Political Life in a Union Local* (Toronto: James Lorimer, 1982), 15-43.
43 Heron, *Working in Steel,* 174-75; Freeman, *1005,* 44-69.
44 Extensively discussed in Freeman, *1005,* chap. 3.
45 Flood, *Wildcat Strike,* 50-54.
46 Ibid., 54.
47 MUA, USWA 1005 fonds, box 5, file 11, handwritten documents, undated and unsigned.
48 Flood, *Wildcat Strike,* 75.
49 Ibid., 70.
50 Ibid. Flood noted that the "average age of all employees ... is not known, but observations made as men changed shifts seemed to indicate that the company had the normal age-spread that a large company would have in terms of its total labour force. This would suggest that younger members of the workforce were disproportionately involved."
51 MUA, USWA 1005 fonds, box 13, file "Recording Secretary Correspondence, 1967," Letter from Harry Greenwood to Murray Cotterill, 19 December 1967.
52 Flood, *Wildcat Strike,* 8-9.
53 LAC, S&L, RG 27, reel T-3421, vol. 3121, file 358, Report on Industrial Dispute Commencement at Stelco, 10 August 1966.
54 Gray Smith, "Stelco Strike Idles 11,000," *Hamilton Spectator,* 4 August 1966, 1.
55 LAC, S&L, RG 27, reel T-3421, vol. 3121, file 358, Special Report Regarding Industrial Dispute – Wildcat Strike, 4 August 1966.
56 "Norman Simon, "Stelco Strikers in Vicious Clash," *Toronto Telegram,* 5 August 1966.
57 Rudy Platiel, "Vote to End Stelco Strike," *Globe and Mail,* 8 August 1966.
58 Flood, *Wildcat Strike,* 76-82.
59 LAC, S&L, RG 27, reel T-3421, vol. 3121, file 358, Special Report Regarding Industrial Dispute – Wildcat Strike, 5 August 1966.
60 Paul Murphy, "Tearful Union Head Turned Away by Jeers," *Hamilton Spectator,* 4 August 1966, 7.
61 "Stelco: Yacht Club Picketed," *Toronto Telegram,* 4 August 1966, as well as in Flood, *Wildcat Strike,* 12.

62 "Violence Hits Peak at Stelco," *Hamilton Spectator,* 6 August 1966, 1, and "33 Stelco Strikers Arrested," *Ottawa Citizen,* 6 August 1966.

63 "It's Back to Work at Stelco, Inco," *Toronto Star,* 8 August 1966.

64 "Wives Bring Lunches, Stick with Their Men," *Hamilton Spectator,* 6 August 1966, 7.

65 Flood, *Wildcat Strike,* 28.

66 LAC, S&L, RG 27, reel T-3421, vol. 3121, file 358, Report on Industrial Dispute Commencement at Stelco, 10 August 1966.

67 Flood, *Wildcat Strike,* 31, and "Firings Stir Stelco Unrest," *Hamilton Spectator,* 8 August 1966, 1.

68 Garry Smith, "Stelco Pensions to Top All," *Hamilton Spectator,* 18 August 1966, 1.

69 Flood, *Wildcat Strike,* 46; Garry Smith, "Men Say Yes in Record Stelco Vote," *Hamilton Spectator,* 31 August 1966, 1; and MUA, USWA 1005 fonds, box 8, form letters to dismissed workers, 29 November 1966.

70 Freeman, *1005,* 108-9.

71 Jamie Swift and the Development Education Centre (hereafter DEC), *The Big Nickel: Inco at Home and Abroad* (Toronto: Between the Lines, 1977), 34-43.

72 Homer Seguin, *Fighting for Justice and Dignity: The Homer Seguin Story; An Autobiography* (Sudbury, ON: Self-published, 2008), 31-35.

73 Mercedes Steedman, Peter Suschnigg, and Dieter K. Buse, eds., "Introduction," in *Hard Lessons: The Mine Mill Union in the Canadian Labour Movement* (Toronto: Dundurn, 1995), 7.

74 Swift and DEC, *The Big Nickel,* 59.

75 Seguin, interview, and Seguin, *Fighting for Justice,* 45.

76 Maxwell Flood, "The Wildcat Strike: Non-Institutional Response in the Industrial Sector" (PhD diss., Michigan State University, 1971), 200-1, 206-7.

77 LAC, RCMP/CSIS fonds, RG 146-3, vol. 84, file 1027-98-A-114, pt. 1, Report on International Union of Mine Mill and Smelter Workers, Local 598, Sudbury, ON, 27 July 1966.

78 Lovely, interview.

79 Seguin, interview.

80 Seguin, *Fighting for Justice,* 65.

81 Flood, "The Wildcat Strike," 263.

82 Lovely, interview.

83 "More Than 100 Walk off Job at Levack Mine This Morning," *Sudbury Star,* 14 July 1966.

84 Flood, "The Wildcat Strike," 211-12.

85 Seguin, interview.

86 "More Than 100 Walk off Job at Levack Mine This Morning," *Sudbury Star,* 14 July 1966.

87 Lovely, interview; Valiquette, interview; Flood, "The Wildcat Strike," 215.

88 LAC, RCMP/CSIS fonds, RG 146-3, vol. 84, file 1027-98-A-114, pt. 1, Report on International Union of Mine Mill and Smelter Workers, Local 598, Sudbury, ON, 27 July 1966.

89 Seguin, interview.

90 Flood, "The Wildcat Strike," 235, 238-39, 253.

91 Seguin, interview.

92 "Man Is Stabbed in Wildcat Walkout," *Port Arthur News-Chronicle,* 15 July 1966.

93 Valiquette, interview.

94 Flood, "The Wildcat Strike," 232.

95 LAC, RCMP/CSIS fonds, RG 146-3, vol. 84, file 1027-98-A-114, pt. 1, Report on International Union of Mine Mill and Smelter Workers, Local 598, Sudbury, ON, 27 July 1966.

96 Seguin, interview.

97 Hans Brasch, *A Miner's Chronicle: Inco Ltd. and the Unions, 1944-1997* (Sudbury, ON: Self-published, 1997), 64-71.

98 Norman Simon, "Picketers Veto Union Passes," *Toronto Telegram,* 22 July 1966.

99 Lovely, interview.

100 "Negotiators Given Majority Backing as 6,000 at Arena," *Sudbury Star,* 6 August 1966.
101 Seguin, interview.
102 LAC, S&L, RG 27, reel T-3420, vol. 3120, file 314, Report on Industrial Dispute Termination, 10 August 1966.
103 LAC, S&L, RG 27, reel T-3421, vol. 3122, file 437, Report on Industrial Dispute Commencement, 22 September 1966.
104 Swift and DEC, *The Big Nickel,* 60.
105 Patterson, interview.
106 "Strike Spreads at CN Express," *Globe and Mail,* 4 June 1965.
107 LAC, S&L, RG 27, reel T-3415, vol. 3108, file 152, various reports on industrial dispute commencement, all dated 3 June 1965.
108 LAC, S&L, RG 27, reel T-3415, vol. 3108, file 152, Report on Industrial Dispute Termination, 8 June 1965.
109 LAC, RCMP/CSIS fonds, RG 146-3, vol. 111, file AH-2000/00278, file on Associated Non-Operating Railway Unions, 13 July 1966.
110 LAC, S&L, RG 27, reel T-3416, vol. 3120, file 353, Report on Industrial Dispute Commencement, 9 August 1966.
111 "Rail Expressmen in Wildcat Strike," *Toronto Star,* 3 August 1966, 1.
112 "Rail Peace Here but Montreal Holds Out," *Toronto Telegram,* 4 August 1966.
113 Ibid., and "CN Men in New Walkout," *Toronto Telegram,* 5 August 1966.
114 "Wildcat Freight Strike Over; Another Looms," *Montreal Gazette,* 8 August 1966.
115 "CN Yards Hardest Hit," *Montreal Gazette,* 19 August 1966; "Railway Wildcats Spread in Ontario," *Toronto Star,* 18 August 1966. This strike is described in A.W.R. Carruthers, *Report of a Study on the Labour Injunction in Toronto* (Toronto: Department of Labour, 1966), Book 2, 402.
116 LAC, S&L, RG 27, reel T-3416, vol. 3121, file 405, Report on Industrial Dispute Termination, 9 September 1966.
117 Canada Labour Data Branch, *Strikes and Lockouts in Canada/Grèves et lockouts au Canada* (Ottawa: Queen's Printer, various dates).
118 Kuyek, interview.
119 Committee on Youth, *It's Your Turn,* 17.
120 Ed Finn, "Bureaucratic Conservatism in the Trade Unions & the Growing Rank and File Threat," *Canadian Dimension* 8 (June 1971), 32.
121 MUA, USWA 1005 fonds, box 13, file "Recording Secretary Correspondence, 1967," Letter from Harry Greenwood to Murray Cotterill, 19 December 1967.
122 Robert Laxer, *Canada's Unions* (Toronto: James Lorimer, 1976), 210-15.
123 "Trouble on the Line," *Canadian Dimension* 9, 7-8 (December 1973), 10.
124 R. Laxer, *Canada's Unions,* 211.
125 "Trouble on the Line," 10-11.
126 Ibid.
127 Ibid.
128 Naylor, interview.
129 Cy Gonick, "Wildcats, Prices and Profits," *Canadian Dimension* 10, 2 (July 1974), 7.
130 MUA, Harry J. Waisglass fonds, box 2, file 1, Address by A.W.R. Carrothers to the Economic Council's National Conference on Labour-Management Relations, Mont-Gabriel, Quebec, 23-24 June 1969.
131 Jamieson, *Times of Trouble,* 5.
132 Ibid., 401-2.
133 Ibid., 470.
134 Ibid., 478.

135 Ibid., 480, 481, 482. Emphasis in original.
136 H.C. Pentland, "A Study of the Changing Social, Economic, and Political Background of the Canadian System of Industrial Relations," Draft study prepared for Task Force on Labour Relations, February 1968, 383.
137 Crispo and Arthurs, "Industrial Unrest in Canada," 247.
138 WRL, UAW Toronto Sub-Regional Office Collection, box 8, file "McDermott, Dennis, Reports, 1968," Report by Dennis McDermott, undated but early 1968.
139 Seguin, interview.
140 Patterson, interview.
141 Seguin, interview.
142 Valiquette, interview.
143 As documented in Martin, *Thinking Union*, chap. 5.
144 MUA, USWA 1005 fonds, box 13, file "Recording Secretary Correspondence, 1967," Letter from Harry Greenwood to Murray Cotterill, 19 December 1967.
145 WRL, Fraser Collection, box 12, file 12-29, Letter from Walter Reuther to Youth Delegates, 28 March 1968.
146 WRL, Fraser Collection, box 12, file 12-20, Letters from Regional Directors to Irving Bluestone, February and March 1969.
147 WRL, Fraser Collection, box 12, file 12-20, Letter from McDermott to Bluestone, 4 March 1969.
148 Ibid.
149 As discussed in Chapter 1. See WRL, UAW 7, box 54, file 5, Text of Remarks Made by Dennis McDermott, Labour Day Speech, Windsor, 2 September 1968.
150 WRL, Fraser Collection, box 12, file 12-20, Suggested Discussion Subjects for Youth Conference.
151 WRL, Fraser Collection, box 12, file 12-20, Findings and Recommendations of Youth Conference, 29 April 1969.
152 AO, OFL fonds, box 4 (barcode B399517), file "Speeches, Articles, and Press Releases (Part 1) – 1971," Address by David Archer to the 15th Annual Convention of the OFL, Toronto, 1 November 1971.
153 AO, OFL fonds, box 4 (barcode B399517), file "Speeches, Articles, and Press Releases (Part 1) – 1971," Labour Day Message by David Archer, 1971.
154 Bogdan Kipling, "Practical Men at Work," *Financial Times of Canada,* 7 August 1972, as found in YUA, Ray Stevenson fonds, box 1998-032/004, file 10.
155 "A Social Revolution?" *Canadian Transport,* 15 July 1968, 2.
156 WRL, UAW 7, box 1, file 2, Address by the Hon. Bryce Mackasey, Minister of Labour to the Third Annual Conference on Human Relations for Labour and Management of the Canadian Council of Christians and Jews, 4 May 1970.
157 See Aaron Brenner, "Rank-and-File Rebellion, 1966-1975" (PhD diss., Columbia University, 1996).
158 Jefferson Cowie, *Stayin' Alive: The 1970s and the Last Days of the Working Class* (New York: New Press, 2010), 46.
159 Barbara Garson, "Luddites in Lordstown," *Harper's Magazine,* June 1972, 68.
160 Cowie, *Stayin' Alive,* 8.
161 Finn, interview.
162 "How Young Workers Look at Labor," *Globe and Mail,* 27 September 1972.

Chapter 3: Say Goodbye to the Working Class?

1 C. Wright Mills, "Letter to the New Left," *New Left Review,* 5 (September-October 1960): 18. Emphasis in original.

2 S. Mills, *The Empire Within*, esp. 169.

3 James Harding, "From the Midst of a Crisis: Student Power in English Canada," in *Student Protest*, ed. Gerald McGuigan (Toronto: Methuen, 1968), 94-95.

4 Ward, interview.

5 Frantz Fanon, *The Wretched of the Earth*, trans. Constance Farrington (New York: Grove Press, 1963), 108-9.

6 C.W. Mills, "Letter to the New Left," 18. Emphasis in original.

7 Roussopoulos, e-mail message to author, 25 October 2009.

8 Irving Louis Horowitz, *C. Wright Mills: An American Utopian* (London: Free Press, 1983), 215.

9 C. Wright Mills, *The Power Elite* (New York: Oxford University Press, 1956), 263.

10 Roussopoulos, interview.

11 Ibid.

12 Douglas Kellner, "Radical Politics, Marcuse, and the New Left," in *The New Left and the 1960s: Collected Papers of Herbert Marcuse*, ed. Douglas Kellner (New York: Routledge, 2005), 1-3.

13 Peter Lust, "A Note on Dr. Herbert Marcuse," *Canadian Forum* 5, 6 (September-October 1968), 18.

14 Gray, interview.

15 Lust, "A Note on Dr. Herbert Marcuse," 18.

16 Alex Podnick, "Marcuse Envisions Most Radical Revolution within Next Century," *Varsity*, 17 March 1971, 1.

17 Douglas Kellner, *Herbert Marcuse and the Crisis of Marxism* (London: Macmillan, 1984), 280-81, 287-90.

18 Kellner, "Radical Politics," 5.

19 Lust, "A Note on Dr. Herbert Marcuse," 18.

20 Anonymous former University of Waterloo student, interview.

21 Herbert Marcuse, "The Problem of Violence and the Radical Opposition," in *The New Left and the 1960s: Collected Papers of Herbert Marcuse*, ed. Douglas Kellner (New York: Routledge, 2005), 58.

22 Herbert Marcuse, "Marcuse Defines His New Left Line," in ibid., 106.

23 Gray, interview.

24 See Jack Lawrence Luzkow, *What's Left? Marxism, Utopianism, and the Revolt against History* (Lanham, MD: University Press of America, 2006), 119-28.

25 André Gorz, *Strategy for Labor* (Boston: Beacon Press, 1967), 24.

26 André Gorz, "Workers' Control Is More Than Just That," *Canadian Dimension* 8, 1 (June 1971), 24.

27 Ibid.

28 Conrad Lodziak and Jeremy Tatman, *André Gorz: A Critical Introduction* (London and Chicago: Pluto Press, 1997), 46.

29 Levitt, *Children of Privilege*, 121.

30 MUA, Student Social and Political fonds (hereafter SSP), box 2, file on the Canadian Union of Students, Youth as Class booklet by John and Margaret Rowntree, published by the Radical Education Project, Ann Arbor, MI.

31 Roussopoulos, interview.

32 John and Margaret Rowntree, "Youth as a Class," *International Socialist Journal* 25 (February 1968): 26, 29. It was reprinted in *Our Generation* in late 1968 as John and Margaret Rowntree, "Youth as Class," *Our Generation* 6, nos. 1-2 (1968).

33 Harding, interview.

34 Wernick, interview; Switzman, interview; Roussopoulos, interview; Harding, interview; Hugh Armstrong, interview; Pocock, interview.

35 Roussopoulos, interview.

36 Drache, interview, and Hugh Armstrong, interview.
37 John Porter, *The Vertical Mosaic: An Analysis of Social Class and Power in Canada* (Toronto: University of Toronto Press, 1965), 6, 20-21.
38 Ibid., 20-21, 336, 359-61.
39 Peter Gzowski, "The Righteous Crusaders of the New Left," *Maclean's* 78, 22, 15 November 1965, 16.
40 URA, Stan Rands fonds (85-80), box 6, file "Research Material, SUPA," "Student Union for Peace Action Proposed Draft Statement of Purpose – for Ratification."
41 "CUCND Changes Name, States Purpose," *Carillon*, 15 January 1965, 3.
42 James Harding, "An Ethical Movement in Search of an Analysis: The Student Union for Peace Action in Canada," *Our Generation* 3, 4, and vol. 4, 1 (double issue) (May 1966): 21.
43 Ward, interview; Pocock, interview.
44 Hugh Armstrong, interview.
45 Don Sellar, "Activist Ward Revitalizes CUS," *Ubyssey*, 24 February 1967, 1.
46 MUA, CUS, box 3, file "United Steelworkers of America," Letter from CUS President Kenniff to Janet Campbell, editor of *Information Magazine*, SWA, 14 June 1965.
47 Owram, *Born at the Right Time*, 235.
48 Ibid., 223.
49 Margaret Daly, *The Revolution Game: The Short, Unhappy Life of the Company of Young Canadians* (Toronto: New Press, 1970), 49.
50 Ward, interview.
51 Harding, interview.
52 Drache, interview.
53 S. Mills, *The Empire Within*, 50.
54 Loney, interview.
55 Harding, interview.
56 Wernick, interview; Brophy, interview.
57 LAC, Peter Warrian fonds, box 1, file 22, Letter from Jim Russell to National Council Regarding Strategy, October 1968.
58 Hart, interview.
59 Käthe Anne Lemon, "Agent of Social Change: A History of Canadian University Press" (MA thesis, Ryerson University, 2004).
60 Shepherd, interview.
61 Harding, interview.
62 Roussopoulos, interview.
63 Königslöw, interview; Harding, interview.
64 MUA, SUPA, box 1, "Student Union for Peace Action, Minutes of Meetings," 9-12 September 1965.
65 Ibid.
66 Gray, interview, and Stan Gray, "The Greatest Canadian Shit-Disturber," *Canadian Dimension*, 1 November 2004, http://canadiandimension.com/.
67 Stan Gray, "The Fall Training Institute – Summary and Perspective," *SUPA Newsletter* 1, 9 (25 October 1965), as found in MUA, CUS, box 17, file "Student & Youth – SUPA/Kingston Community Project."
68 John Kelsey, "Left-Wing Student CUS President," *Ubyssey*, 13 September 1966, 7, and "Left Fights Right on CUS Policy," *Ubyssey*, 13 September 1966, 5.
69 "Shaun Told CUS Word," *Ubyssey*, 28 February 1967, 1.
70 MUA, CUS, box 26, file "Working Papers – 31st Congress, 1967," John Cleveland, "Social Unionism and Unions," undated but ca. 1967.
71 Hugh Armstrong, interview; Pat Armstrong, interview.

72 MUA, CUS, box 26, file "Working Papers – 31st Congress, 1967," John Cleveland, "Social Unionism and Unions," undated but ca. 1967.
73 University of Ottawa Archives (hereafter UOA), Canadian Women's Movement Archives (hereafter CWMA), box 85, Resolution Passed at Guelph Congress by Windsor/SFU, 1967.
74 Rebick, *Ten Thousand Roses*, 8.
75 MUA, SUPA, box 12, "Report of the Conference Committee to May 6-7 Federal Council Meeting (held at Lakehead)," 6-7 May 1966.
76 Pocock, interview; Booker, interview.
77 Judi Bernstein, Peggy Morton, Linda Seese, and Myrna Wood, "Sisters, Brothers, Lovers ... Listen ...," in *Masculine/Feminine: Readings in Sexual Mythology and the Liberation of Women*, eds. Betty Roszak and Theodore Roszak (New York: Harper and Row, 1969), 251-54.
78 Jim Harding, "Bases of Conflict within SUPA," *SUPA Newsletter* 3, 1 (14 November 1966): 4.
79 Palmer, *Canada's 1960s*, 282.
80 Kostash, *Long Way from Home*, 22-23.
81 Harding, interview.
82 Dimitri Roussopoulos, "What Is the New Radicalism?" *Our Generation* 6, 1-2 (May/June/July 1968), 17-20.
83 Conway, interview; Hyde, interview.
84 Harding, interview.
85 Shepherd, interview.
86 MUA, SUPA, box 7, "Towards a 'Manifesto' for SUPA: A Rough Table of Contents," undated but presumably ca. June 1967.
87 MUA, SUPA, box 7, SUPA Manifesto, 10 June 1967.
88 Harvey Shepherd and Peggy Morton, "Membership Conference to Focus on Programme," *SUPA Newsletter* 3, 9 (July 1967): 1, 21.
89 Kostash, *Long Way from Home*, 26-27.
90 MUA, SUPA, box 21, file 4, "Elected New Left Committee," 1967.
91 Harvey L. Sheppard, "SUPA Dissolved; New Left Comm. Formed," *NLC Bulletin* 1, 1[A], October 1967, 1, as found in MUA, SUPA, box 16A, file 8. Two volume 1, issue no. 1s of the *NLC Bulletin* were published, one in October 1967 and one in November 1967. For citation purposes, they are No. 1[A] and No. 1[B], respectively.
92 Ibid.
93 Pocock, interview.
94 Harding, interview, and Roussopoulos, interview.
95 Conway, interview.
96 "Statement of the New Left Committee," *NLC Bulletin* 1, 1[A], October 1967, 1.
97 Peggy Morton and Myrna Wood, "1848 and All That or Whatever Happened to the Working Class? *NLC Bulletin* 1, 1[B], November 1967, 9.
98 MUA, SUPA, box 1, file 21, Letter from Harvey L. Shepherd to NLC, 3 October 1967.
99 Shepherd, interview.
100 MUA, SUPA, box 1, file 21, Letter from Don Roebuck to NLC, 10 November 1967.
101 MUA, SUPA, box 1, file 21, "Summary of Discussions Held by Some Toronto People," 24-25 January 1968.
102 Kostash, *Born at the Right Time*, 87-88.
103 Harding, interview; Larkin, interview; Resnick, interview.
104 Kostash, *Born at the Right Time*, 88.
105 For specifics on Warrian's election, see Frank Goldspink, "CUS Boss Promises Action," *Ubyssey*, 28 September 1967, 8; "Former SUPA Man Elected CUS President," *Ubyssey*, 19 September 1967, 8.
106 Warrian, interview.

107 Kim Cameron, "CUP Special: CUS Congress Confusion Reveals Opposing Views," *Ubyssey*, 19 October 1967, 10.

108 "CUS Congress Defines Goals," *Ubyssey*, 19 September 1967, 8.

109 See Nesbitt, "'Radical Trip,'" 158-59. This was a controversial statement. Warrian and others accused the media of sensationally taking the quotation out of its broader context and overlooking "the essence of Warrian's speech."

110 LAC, Peter Warrian fonds, box 3, Peter Warrian, "Notes on Students, Politics and Political Economy," Spring 1968.

111 "CUS: Why Vote No," *Varsity*, 17 October 1969, 24.

112 YUA, Council of the York Students Federation fonds (hereafter CYSF), box 1974-019/009, file on CUS, National Council Minutes, 21-23 March 1969.

113 UTARMS, William Craig Heron fonds, box 5, file on CUS, Jim Harding, "An Evaluation of CUS," undated but ca. 1969.

114 UTARMS, William Craig Heron fonds, box 5, file on CUS, Craig Heron, "SACVIEWS: A Note on CUS," undated but ca. September 1969.

115 "SFU's Radical Student Head Becomes CUS President-Elect," *Chevron*, 11 September 1968, 4.

116 Ross H. Munro, "CUS Will Try to Rebuild Splintered Organization," *Globe and Mail*, undated.

117 "CUS: Will These Programs Keep It Together?" *Varsity*, 22 September 1969, 6-7.

118 Owram, *Born at the Right Time*, 296-97.

119 UTARMS, Craig Heron fonds, box 5, file on CUS, Martin Loney, "Some Thoughts on the Future and Purpose of the CUS," undated, ca. 1969.

120 YUA, CYSF fonds, box 1974-019/009, file on CUS, National Council Minutes, 28 October 1969.

121 Brophy, interview.

122 Wernick, interview. Also recalled in Resnick, interview.

123 MUA, SSP, box 8, file on TSM, flyer announcing TSM, undated.

124 Noel Steckley, "Kerr Debunks Student-Worker Alliance," *Varsity*, 5 February 1969, 1.

125 Resnick recalls this as the high-water mark of the Toronto Student Movement.

126 Andy Wernick, "Andy Wernick on the SAC Elections and the TSM," *Varsity*, 14 March 1969, Review Section, 7.

127 Wernick, interview.

128 Resnick, interview.

129 Wernick, "Andy Wernick on the SAC Elections."

130 Wernick, interview. Also seen in MUA, RMG, box 4, file 18, file on TSM, "New Left Caucus (Toronto Student Movement): A Draft Manifesto," by Bob Kellerman, Laurel Limpus, Philip Resnick, and Andrew Wernick, undated.

131 MUA, Canadian Liberation Movement fonds (hereafter CLM), TSM file, flyer on TSM Summer Education, 1969, and Student-Worker Alliance Syllabus, May 1969.

132 Marc Zwelling, *The Strikebreakers: The Report of the Strikebreaking Committee of the Ontario Federation of Labour and the Labour Council of Metropolitan Toronto* (Toronto: New Press, 1972), 33.

133 MUA, SSP, box 2, Canadian Party of Labour file, Steve Moore, Tony Leah, and Paddy Ryle, "The Wiener Strike."

134 Zwelling, *Strikebreakers*, 33.

135 MUA, CLM, box 22a, file 13, "Building a Student-Worker Alliance at University," ca. 1969.

136 Thomas Fisher Rare Books Library (hereafter TFRB), Kenney Collection, box 45B, file on WSA, "The University in Class Society," undated, ca. 1969.

137 Dalhousie University Archives (hereafter DUA), Tom Lackey fonds, MS 10.4.A1, file on Correspondence, Bob Dewart, "Students and Workers: Building a Real Alliance."

138 DUA, Tom Lackey fonds, MS 10.4.A1, file on Correspondence, "Introduction" to essays by Moore, Dewart, and Johnson.

139 Wernick, interview.

140 DUA, Tom Lackey fonds, MS 10.4.C.2, folder on WSA, Bob Dewart, "Wernick & Co. Do Their Thing to TSM," special reprint of *Canadian Worker*.

141 Canadian Party of Labour Handbook, Socialist History Project, http://www.cddc.vt.edu/.

142 Andy Wernick, "A Guide to the Student Left," *Varsity*, 24 September 1969, 8.

143 Ibid., 9.

144 "Parity at the U of T: 4000 Vote to Strike," *Canadian Worker* 3, 2 (March 1971), 10.

145 MUA, RMG, box 4, file 18, file on TSM, Bob Kellerman, Laurel Limpus, Philip Resnick, and Andrew Wernick, "New Left Caucus (Toronto Student Movement): A Draft Manifesto," undated.

146 LAC, RG 146-3, RCMP/CSIS fonds, file 98-A-00079, file on New Left Caucus, undated and unauthored.

147 Joanne Harriet Wright, *Origin Stories in Political Thought* (Toronto: University of Toronto Press, 2004), 197-98n61.

148 UOA, CWMA, box 14, file 76, Knitting Circle of Toronto, Position Paper, 1969.

149 Pocock, interview.

150 Nancy Adamson, "Feminists, Libbers, Lefties, and Radicals: The Emergence of the Women's Liberation Movement," in *A Diversity of Women: Ontario, 1945-1980*, ed. Joy Parr (Toronto: University of Toronto Press, 1995), 258.

Chapter 4: Leaving Campus

1 "Political Science, Sociology and Anthropology," *Peak*, 16 July 1969, 3.

2 Briemberg, interview.

3 The rally is discussed in LAC, RCMP/CSIS fonds, RG 146-3, vol. 5, file 1025-9-91046, Reports on Protests and Demonstrations – Saskatchewan.

4 Pocock, interview.

5 There were other important projects. These include one at La Macaza, site of a Bomarc base near Quebec's Mont-Tremblant, one among the Doukhobors of British Columbia, and another by Rocky Jones in Halifax's black community. For more on this, see Walker, "Black Confrontation in Sixties Halifax," in Campbell, Clément, and Kealey, *Debating Dissent*, 173-91.

6 Palmer, *Canada's 1960s*, 261-63.

7 Kuyek, interview; Conway, interview.

8 Richard Harris, *Democracy in Kingston: A Social Movement in Urban Politics, 1965-1970* (Kingston and Montreal: McGill-Queen's University Press, 1988), 134.

9 Ibid., 107-10, 134.

10 Kuyek, interview.

11 Irving Abella, *Nationalism, Communism, and Canadian Labour: The CIO, the Communist Party, and the Canadian Congress of Labour, 1935-1956* (Toronto: University of Toronto Press, 1973), 154-55. See also Joan Sangster, *Transforming Labour: Women and Work in Post-War Canada* (Toronto: University of Toronto Press, 2010), 90-98.

12 Kostash, *Long Way from Home*, 17.

13 MUA, SUPA, box 11, file 14, Letter from Peter Boothroyd to "Danny," undated, ca. 1965-66.

14 Kuyek, interview.

15 Liora Proctor, "Personal Evaluation: The Student Neestow Project," *Our Generation* 4, 3 (November 1966), 40.

16 Warren Gerard, "What Ever Happened to SUPA? It's All Hung Up, Baby," *Globe Magazine*, 17 December 1966.

17 Kostash, *Long Way from Home,* 16.
18 MUA, SUPA, box 11, file 14, Letter from Peter Boothroyd to "Danny," undated, *ca.* 1965-66.
19 MacDowell, interview.
20 Ross H. Munro, "Guelph Strikers Criticize Student Actions," *Globe and Mail,* 3 November 1969, 12.
21 Hugh Armstrong, interview.
22 Ibid.
23 Quoted in Fernando Traficante, "Students Are Problem during Strikes: Author," *Varsity,* 28 February 1973, 11.
24 For CUS and the contested debates on strikebreaking, see Nesbitt, "'Radical Trip,'" 120-21.
25 MUA, OUS, box 36, file on 1967-1968 Executive Minutes, Minutes of 4-5 May 1968 OUS Executive Meeting, and Louis Erlichman, "Student Scabs," *Varsity,* 16 October 1968, 1.
26 MUA, SSP, box 8, file on UE, 31st Annual Convention Minutes and Proceedings, 28-31 March 1968.
27 MUA, OUS, box 29, file on Unions, press release on Student Scabbing, 5 May 1968.
28 Louis Erlichman, "Student Scabs," *Varsity,* 16 October 1968, 1, and Alan Gottheil, "Student Scabs," *Confrontations* 2, 1 (August/September 1968): 3, as found in MUA, Waffle Collection, box 1, file on *Confrontations.*
29 Louis Erlichman, "Student Scabs," *Varsity,* 16 October 1968, 1.
30 Dick Betts, "Student Scabs Damage Hope for Unity," *Ubyssey,* 26 March 1970, 5.
31 "Letter to Strikebreakers," *Barnacle* 1, 1 (September 1969), 13, as found in Trent University Archives, New Left Movement Collection (88-20), box 1.
32 "Summer Scabs at Hydro: Students Cross Picket Lines by Telephone," *Varsity,* 6 October 1972, 6.
33 MUA, OUS, box 28, file on OFL, Report of Meeting, 3 June 1969.
34 "Union-Student Conference at UAW Centre, Port Elgin," *Canadian Labour,* November 1969, 39.
35 MUA, OUS, box 28, file on OFL, Union-Student Conference Program.
36 Switzman, interview.
37 Pitsula, *New World Dawning,* 49.
38 Don Mitchell, e-mail message to author, 19 October 2009.
39 Kossick, interview.
40 As discussed in Harding, interview; Conway, interview; Kossick, interview; Mitchell, interview.
41 Conway, interview.
42 Harding, interview.
43 Pitsula, *New World Dawning,* 264-65.
44 LAC, Peter Warrian fonds, box 1, file 8 "CUS National Council 1967-1968," "National Council Meeting Minutes, 25 October 1968 at Rochdale College."
45 Mitchell, interview.
46 Pitsula, *New World Dawning,* 272, and Lexier, "Canadian Student Movement," 107-10.
47 Mitchell, interview.
48 Kossick, interview.
49 LAC, RG 146-3, vol. 97, file AH-1999/00104, pt. 4, "Historical, Political Background Since 1965," undated but presumably ca. 1972.
50 Mitchell, interview.
51 Conway, interview.
52 Ibid.
53 Kossick, interview.
54 Peter Borch, "The Rise and Decline of the Saskatchewan Waffle, 1966-1973" (MA thesis, University of Regina, 2005), 23, 62-63.

55 "Student's Union to Support Saskatchewan Workers," *Carillon,* 13 March 1970, 3.

56 Borch, "The Rise and Decline of the Saskatchewan Waffle," 23.

57 "Government Moves to Place Construction Workers under Bill 2," *Carillon,* 2 July 1970, 1.

58 LAC, RCMP/CSIS fonds, RG 146-3, vol. 97, file AH-1999/00104, pt. 2, Report on Saskatchewan Federation of Labour, 13 April 1970.

59 "Student's Union to Support Saskatchewan Workers," *Carillon,* 13 March 1970.

60 LAC, RG 146-3, RCMP/CSIS fonds, vol. 97, file AH-1999/00104, pt. 2, Report on Saskatchewan Federation of Labour, 13 April 1970.

61 Kossick, interview.

62 John F. Conway, "From 'Agrarian Socialism' to 'Natural' Governing Party: The CCF/NDP in Saskatchewan, 1932-2007," in *The Prairie Agrarian Movement Revisited: Centenary Symposium on the Foundation of the Territorial Grain Growers Association,* ed. Murray Knuttila and Bob Stirling (Regina: Canadian Plains Research Center, 2007), 227.

63 Borch, "The Rise and Decline of the Saskatchewan Waffle," 68-69, 78-79. The Land Bank would purchase agricultural land and then lease it back to younger farmers.

64 Saskatchewan Archives Board (hereafter SA), Saskatchewan Waffle fonds (hereafter SW), Patsy Gallagher Collection (hereafter Gallagher), file on Mitchell Campaign for NDP Leadership (hereafter Mitchell Campaign), Mitchell flyer – Open Letter, 1970.

65 SA, SW, Don Mitchell Collection, file on Leadership Campaign, Comments by Don Mitchell at Unemployed Rally, 1970.

66 LAC, RG 146-3, RCMP/CSIS fonds, vol. 113, file AH-2000/00182, pt. 1, Report on Waffle "New Left Activities in Political Parties," 21 September 1970.

67 Conway, interview; Kossick, interview.

68 Mitchell, interview.

69 Borch, "The Rise and Decline of the Saskatchewan Waffle," 84. On the first ballot, Mitchell received 187 votes in the first round out of 850 total delegates; on the second ballot, he was eliminated after garnering only 219 votes.

70 Borch, "The Rise and Decline of the Saskatchewan Waffle," 93, 128-29.

71 Alfred P. Gleave, *United We Stand: Prairie Farmers, 1901-1975* (Toronto: Lugus Publications, 1991), 176-77.

72 LAC, RG 146-3, RCMP/CSIS fonds, vol. 5, file 1025-9-91046, National Farmers' Union – Saskatchewan Report, 2 June 1970.

73 Stuart Thiesson, "The Saskatchewan Farmers' Union Transition to the National Farmers' Union," in Knuttila and Stirling, *Prairie Agrarian Movement Revisited,* 80-81.

74 Kossick, interview.

75 LAC, RG 146-3, RCMP/CSIS fonds, vol. 5, file 1025-9-91046, Report on Protests and Demonstrations – Saskatchewan, authored by Constable D.L. Clark based on reports from Cpl. L.E. Hall.

76 *Down on the Farm,* produced by Clint Bomphray ([Toronto?]: Unconscious Collective, 1972), videocassette (VHS).

77 LAC, RCMP/CSIS fonds, vol. 39, file 94-A-00130, pt. 2, Brief Pertaining to Unrest at Simon Fraser University, 26 August 1968.

78 Johnston, *Radical Campus,* 120.

79 Briemberg, interview.

80 "Picket Lines," *Peak,* 25 May 1966, 2.

81 Simon Fraser University Archives (hereafter SFUA), Simon Fraser University Student Society fonds (hereafter SFUSS), box 74-31, file F-74-10-0-0-21, press releases regarding Shell Station. This was also discussed in "Shell Campaign Gaining Support," *Peak,* 12 October 1966, 1. See also Johnston, *Radical Campus,* 257-61.

82 Loney, interview.

83 Cleveland, interview.

84 SFUA, SFUSS, box 74-32, file F-74-10-0-0-29, "Open Letter to the Students at Templeton Secondary School," undated.

85 Loney, interview, and "Cops Cop Loney Again," *Peak*, 15 March 1967, 1. See also Johnston, *Radical Campus*, 262-65, and Lexier, "Canadian Student Movement," 97-99.

86 SFUA, SFUSS, box 74-32, file F-74-10-0-0-29, Telegram to affected TAs from Patrick McTaggart-Cowan, reprinted in a special issue of *Student Advocate*, 26 March 1967.

87 LAC, RCMP/CSIS fonds, vol. 72, file 96-A-00045, pt. 44, SDU organizational meeting poster, 29 January 1968.

88 Briemberg, interview.

89 Rossi, "Mountaintop Mayhem," 136. See also LAC, RCMP/CSIS fonds, vol. 39, file 94-A-00130, pt. 2, report on Simon Fraser University Student Council, 3 June 1968.

90 McCormack, interview.

91 Pocklington, interview.

92 Cleveland, interview.

93 SFUA, SFUSS, box 74-32, file F-74-10-0-0-29, "Education in Crisis," a manifesto by the Simon Fraser SDU, November 1968.

94 "Administration Occupied," *Peak*, 21 November 1968, 1.

95 McCormack, interview. See also LAC, RCMP/CSIS fonds, vol. 72, file 96-A-00045, pt. 44, Letter from Second-in-Command, Burnaby Detachment to Officer-in-Command, Burnaby Detachment, detailing police action, 2 December 1968.

96 Gordon Hardy, "CUS Paper to Inform Unions," *Peak*, 2 December 1968, 1.

97 Conway, interview. See also LAC, RCMP/CSIS fonds, vol. 72, file 96-A-00045, pt. 50, Report on Simon Fraser University, 1 September 1970. Evidence of its widespread distribution can be garnered by its widespread archival presence. A copy is found in the holdings of the British Columbia Federation of Labour and the United Fishermen and Allied Workers Union; copies are also in the RCMP fonds.

98 University of British Columbia Special Collections (hereafter UBCSC), British Columbia Federation of Labour fonds (hereafter BCFL), box 56, file 9, special issue of *Issue*.

99 Cleveland, interview.

100 UBCSC, Student Protest Collection, box 4, file 4, *Trouble at Simon Fraser*.

101 UBCSC, BCFL, box 17, file 34, Letter from Isolde Belfont, Secretary of the Committee to Aid the SFU 114 to Supporters, 22 May 1969.

102 UBCSC, BCFL, box 13, file 37, press release on Simon Fraser University, 16 December 1968.

103 UBCSC, BCFL, box 13, file 37, Letter from R.C. Haynes to Minister of Education Donald Brothers, 30 December 1968.

104 Harding, interview.

105 "Looking Backward," *Peak*, 20 March 1969, 4.

106 SFUA, SFUSS, box 74-32, file F-74-10-0-0-29, "Why They Occupied the Building," undated.

107 Harding, interview.

108 Pat Beirne, "$26,000 in Fines for Occupiers," *Peak*, 20 March 1969, 1, and "3-Months for Carrall," *Peak*, 20 March 1969, 1.

109 "Trusteeship on PSA," *Peak*, 16 July 1969, 1. There were several other reasons, as discussed in Johnston, *Radical Campus*, 303-13.

110 "Political Science, Sociology and Anthropology," *Peak*, 16 July 1969, 3.

111 "The Common Struggle," *Peak*, 16 July 1969, 4.

112 Briemberg, interview.

113 SFUA, SFUSS, box 74-31, file F-74-10-0-0-23, press release by John Conway, Co-Chairman of the PSA Student Union, undated but presumably September 1969. Emphasis in original.

114 "PSA Approves Strike Motion," *Peak,* 24 September 1969, 1; "PSA Begins Picketing Classes," *Peak,* 1 October 1969, 1; "History Students Vote to Strike," *Peak,* 1 October 1969, 1.
115 UBCSC, Vancouver and District Labour Council fonds, box 21, Minutes of 2 December 1969 meeting.
116 LAC, RCMP/CSIS fonds, vol. 72, file 96-A-00045, pt. 50, Report on Simon Fraser University, 1 September 1970.
117 Briemberg, interview.
118 "PSA Begins Picketing Classes," *Peak,* 1 October 1969.
119 Lexier, "Canadian Student Movement," 173.
120 Cleveland, interview, and "PSA Calls Off Strike," *Peak,* 5 November 1969, 1.
121 "Briemberg on the Community Education Centre, Its Politics, and the Strike," *Peak,* 21 January 1970, 10.
122 "Simon Fraser University 1971: Hotbed of Quietism," *Peak,* 3 March 1971, 12-13.
123 I have found at least four different names for the CERC: the Community Education and Research Centre, the Community Educational and Research Centre, the Community Educational Research Centre, and just the Community Education Centre. I have chosen the former as it seemed to be relatively consistently used in my interviews.
124 "Educational Centre to Be Established by Profs," *Peak,* 7 January 1970, 2.
125 LAC, RCMP/CSIS fonds, vol. 72, file 96-A-00045 pt. 50, Report on Trade Unions–British Columbia, 17 December 1969, and LAC, RCMP/CSIS fonds, vol. 72, file 96-A-00045 pt. 51, Report on Simon Fraser University, 6 October 1970.
126 "Briemberg on the Community Education Centre, Its Politics, and the Strike," *Peak,* 21 January 1970, 9.
127 Briemberg, interview, and LAC, RCMP/CSIS fonds, vol. 72, file 96-A-00045 pt. 51, Report on Simon Fraser University, 6 October 1970.
128 Cleveland, interview.
129 "The GRAPE Becomes Western Organizer," *Western Organizer,* 6-19 June 1973, 3.
130 Cleveland, interview.
131 Briemberg, interview.
132 The paper ceased publication for about five months in late 1975, before re-emerging with apparently two final issues. A debate played out across the pages, as preserved in the aptly named "Documents of the Ideological Struggle within the Western Voice Collective," *Western Voice,* February 1976, 1.
133 Toms, interview.
134 Frances Jane Wasserlein, "'An Arrow Aimed at the Heart': The Vancouver Women's Caucus and the Abortion Campaign, 1969-1971" (MA thesis, Simon Fraser University, 1990), 57-59.
135 Toms, interview.
136 LAC, RCMP/CSIS fonds, vol. 72, file 96-A-00045, pt. 51, Report on Vancouver Women's Caucus, 18 June 1970. See also Christabelle Sethna and Steve Hewitt, "Clandestine Operations: The Vancouver Women's Caucus, the Abortion Caravan, and the RCMP," *Canadian Historical Review* 90, 3 (September 2009), 468.
137 McCormack, interview.
138 Wasserlein, "'An Arrow Aimed at the Heart,'" 37-38, 55.
139 Ibid., 89.
140 Julia Maureen Smith, "Organizing the Unorganized: The Service, Office, and Retail Workers' Union of Canada (SORWUC), 1972-1986" (MA thesis, Simon Fraser University, 2009), 21-22.
141 Wasserlein, "'An Arrow Aimed at the Heart,'" 110-11.
142 McCormack, interview; Toms, interview.

143 LAC, RCMP/CSIS fonds, vol. 72, file 96-A-00045, pt. 51, Report on Vancouver Women's Caucus, 18 June 1970.

144 UBCSC, SORWUC, box 6, file 7, "Where We Come From," article in *Union Women Speak: AUCE & SORWUC*, vol. 1, 1 (August 1976). See also Bank Book Collective, *An Account to Settle: The Story of the United Bank Workers (SORWUC)* (Vancouver: Press Gang, 1979), 10.

145 UBCSC, SORWUC, box 6, file 2, SORWUC flyer, undated.

146 Smith, "Organizing the Unorganized," 30, 34-35.

147 Smith has argued that SORWUC became worn out by a long, nasty strike at Vancouver's Muckamuck restaurant and, on recognizing that it could no longer fulfill its political goals, decided to disband in late 1986. See ibid., 78, and Janet Mary Nicol, "'Unions Aren't Native': The Muckamuck Restaurant Labour Dispute, Vancouver, BC (1978-1983)," *Labour/Le Travail* 40 (Fall 1997): 235-51.

148 Smith, "Organizing the Unorganized," 78-81.

149 Devon Gaber, "A Brief History of the Transfer System in British Columbia," report written for the BCCAT, September 2005, http://eric.ed.gov/.

Chapter 5: Cold, Slogging Solidarity

1 Vic Parsons, *Ken Thomson: Canada's Enigmatic Billionaire* (Toronto: Burgher Books, 1996), 38-40, and Susan Goldenberg, *The Thomson Empire* (Toronto: Methuen, 1984), 4, 38.

2 Wilfred List, "Picket Arrested, Another Hurt in Clash at Peterborough," *Globe and Mail*, 11 November 1968, 3.

3 MUA, OUS, box 27, file on Labour Relations, Toronto Newspaper Guild, "Tycoon Thomson Testing Labour" poster, undated but presumably November 1968.

4 Wilfred List, "Picket Arrested, Another Hurt in Clash at Peterborough," *Globe and Mail*, 11 November 1968, 3.

5 Wernick, interview.

6 Joan Sangster, "'We No Longer Respect the Law': The Tilco Strike, Labour Injunctions, and the State," *Labour/Le Travail* 53 (Spring 2004): 47-87.

7 "Strike Support Spotty," *Hamilton Spectator*, 21 January 1969, in LAC, RG 27, S&L, reel T-3445, vol. 3601, file 68-513.

8 "Steel Union Aids Guild on Picket," *St. Catharines Standard*, 5 November 1968, in LAC, RG 27, S&L, reel T-3445, vol. 3601, file 68-513.

9 "Printers Cross Thin Picket Line," *London Free Press*, 11 November 1968, in LAC, RG 27, S&L, reel T-3445, vol. 3601, file 68-513.

10 Wernick, interview.

11 Penney, interview.

12 MUA, OUS, box 27, file on Labour Relations, "*Peterborough Examiner* Strike: Why Get Involved?"

13 Warrian, interview.

14 MUA, OUS, box 27, file on Labour Relations, "Students Join Striking Reporters," *Stop the Press*, 6 December 1968.

15 Wilfred List, "Picket Arrested, Another Hurt in Clash at Peterborough," *Globe and Mail*, 11 November 1968, 3.

16 John Rosenes, "Trent Student Arrested in *Examiner* Strike," *Arthur* (Trent University newspaper), vol. 3, 8 (15 December 1968), 1.

17 Eddy Roworth, "One Picketer Injured, One Arrested in Peterborough Newspaper Strike," *Toronto Star*, 9 November 1968, 3.

18 Switzman, interview.

19 "Police Arrest 14 Persons in Paper Strike Fights," *St. Thomas Times-Journal*, 7 December 1968, in LAC, RG 27, S&L, reel T-3445, vol. 3601, file 68-513.
20 Wilfred List, "Two Waterloo Students Arrested in Mass Picket Line," *Globe and Mail*, 30 November 1968, 4, and "Examiner Strikers Backed by 200 Student Editors," *Toronto Star*, 31 December 1968, 47.
21 Wilfred List, "Students to Bolster Examiner Picket Line," *Globe and Mail*, 6 December 1968, 13.
22 MUA, OUS, box 27, file on Labour Relations, "Students Join Striking Reporters," *Stop the Press*, 6 December 1968.
23 "Clashes Erupt on News Guild Picket Line, 15 Arrested, Police Brutality Charged," *Chevron*, 13 December 1968, 1.
24 Paul MacRae, "Soggy Coffee, Frozen Feet," *Varsity*, 2 December 1968, 3.
25 "150 Picket Paper After 12 Arrested," *Toronto Star*, 7 December 1968, 3.
26 Wilfred List, "15 Arrested in *Examiner* Strike as Students Reinforce Picket Line," *Globe and Mail*, 7 December 1968, 1.
27 LAC, CSIS, box 78, file 98-A-00078, Report on Students at *Peterborough Examiner*, 16 January 1969.
28 Penney, interview.
29 LAC, CSIS, box 78, file 98-A-00078, Report on Students at *Peterborough Examiner*, 16 January 1969.
30 "SAC Urges Student Support of Peterboro *Examiner* Pickets," *Varsity*, 13 January 1969, 5.
31 "Students Hope for 500 at Peterboro Strike," *Chevron*, 10 January 1968, 4.
32 "Teach-in Added to Strike," *Chevron*, 17 January 1968, 1.
33 MUA, OUS, box 27, file on Labour Relations, Jennifer Penney, open letter to the people, 9 January 1969.
34 Penney, interview.
35 Stan McDowell, "Thomson Man Opposes Special Law for Press," *Toronto Star*, 19 December 1969, 48.
36 "Strike Support Spotty," *Hamilton Spectator*, 21 January 1969 in LAC, RG 27, S&L, reel T-3445, vol. 3601, file 68-513.
37 "Third Student Attempt to Stop Peterboro Presses Ends in Failure," *Varsity*, 20 January 1969, 2.
38 Susan Reisler and Jim Cowan, "The *Examiner* Strike: What Students Learned," *Varsity*, 20 January 1969, 5.
39 "Newspapermen Ask Jobs Back on *Examiner*," *Globe and Mail*, 23 April 1969, B02.
40 Warrian, interview.
41 Susan Reisler and Jim Cowan, "The *Examiner* Strike: What Students Learned," *Varsity*, 20 January 1969, 5.
42 Wernick, interview.
43 Ed Finn, "Labour Will Never Join Those New Left Students," *Toronto Star*, as reprinted in *Chevron*, 21 March 1969, 29.
44 Carol Davids, "A Reply," *Chevron*, 21 March 1969, 21.
45 The line "American Bastards Who Don't Give a Shit" that appears in the heading is from Salutin, interview.
46 Joan Sangster, "Remembering Texpack: Nationalism, Internationalism, and Militancy in Canadian Unions in the 1970s," *Studies in Political Economy* 78 (Autumn 2006), 41, 57-60.
47 "Not Union Members: Obstruction Charges Follow Picketing Row," *Globe and Mail*, 13 October 1971, 5.
48 James Laxer, "The Americanization of the Canadian Student Movement," in *Close the 49th Parallel, Etc.*, ed. Ian Lumsden (Toronto: University of Toronto Press, 1970), 276.

49 John Bullen, "The Ontario Waffle and the Struggle for an Independent Socialist Canada: Conflict within the NDP," *Canadian Historical Review* 64, 2 (July 1983): 192-93.

50 Sangster, "Remembering Texpack," 42.

51 Ibid., 43.

52 Ibid.

53 Yvonne MacMahon, quoted in Elizabeth Kelly, *Our Expectations: A History of Brantford's Labour Movement* (Brantford, ON: Hurley Printing, 1991), 140-41, as cited in Sangster, "Remembering Texpack."

54 AO, RG 4-2, file 510.5, Picketing and Strikes at Texpack Limited, Letter from OPP Commissioner Eric Silk to Honourable Allan F. Lawrence, Q.C., Minister of Justice and Attorney-General, 30 August 1971.

55 Sangster, "Remembering Texpack," 50.

56 MUA, NDPW, box 1, file 2, "Playing the Bosses Game at Texpack" in *Waffle Labour News: Convention Special,* October 1970, and MUA, NDPW, box 1, file 3, CTC Bulletin on TWUA Scabbing for Company, October 1971.

57 Salutin, interview.

58 "Not Union Members: Obstruction Charges Follow Picketing Row," *Globe and Mail,* 13 October 1971, 5.

59 YUA, CYSF, box 1974-019/027, file "Texpack," handwritten notes of YSF meeting, undated.

60 YUA, CYSF, box 1974-019/027, file "Texpack," Letter from CTCU to Supporters, 21 October 1971.

61 Craig Heron's Personal Files, Texpack File, "What Is This Texpack Strike All About?" flyer, October 1971.

62 "York Student Council Backs Texpack Strike (CUP)," *Ubyssey,* 7 October 1971, 8.

63 MUA, NDPW, box 1, file 3, CTC Bulletin on Victory, October 1971.

64 Lang, interview.

65 LAC, CSIS, box 5, file 1025-9-91042, Constable A.A. Scott, Report on Texpack Labour Unrest, 20 September 1971.

66 Warrian, e-mail to author, 21 September 2009.

67 LAC, RG 27, S&L, reel T-3455, vol. 3617, file 72-179, Report on Industrial Dispute Commencement, 29 May 1972.

68 LAC, RG 27, S&L, reel T-3449, vol. 3608, file 70-236, Report on Industrial Dispute Termination at Dare Foods Limited, 18 June 1970.

69 "Workers Predict Summer of Wildcat Strikes," *Chevron,* 12 June 1970, 1.

70 Harding, interview. After being blacklisted from SFU in the wake of the events there, Harding went to Waterloo for short-term academic contracts.

71 LAC, RG 27, S&L, reel T-3455, vol. 3617, file 72-179, Report on Industrial Dispute Commencement, 29 May 1972.

72 Bob Edwards, "The Dare Strike: 'Cookies Are Made with Exploitation in Mind,'" *Pro Tem* (Glendon College newspaper), 18 October 1972, 4.

73 YUA, CYSF fonds, box 1974-019/016, "Strike Report," undated.

74 Don Dutton, "Windows Smashed, 10 Persons Arrested After Driver Pool Enters Struck Plant," *Toronto Star,* 7 June 1972, 3.

75 "Six Pickets Arrested as Violence Continues at Plant in Kitchener," *Globe and Mail,* 7 June 1972, 1.

76 Ted Dinsmore, "Strikers Get Dare Promise to Stop Shipments," *Toronto Star,* 8 June 1972, 34.

77 "Dare Halts Shipments After Day of Violence," *Globe and Mail,* 8 June 1972, 8.

78 Moore, interview.

79 "Dare Halts Shipments," *Globe and Mail,* 8 June 1972, 8, and Ted Dinsmore, "Strikers Get Dare Promise," *Toronto Star,* 8 June 1972, 34.

80 "Firm Says Strike Cost $25,000," *Toronto Star*, 10 June 1972, 105, and "Pickets in Kitchener Obey Ruling of Court," *Globe and Mail*, 14 June 1972, 9.

81 YUA, CYSF, box 1974-019/016, Local 173 UBW, "Perspective on Dare," undated.

82 David Cubberley, "Dare Strike Now a Waiting Game," *Chevron*, 16 June 1972, 1.

83 YUA, CYSF, box 1974-019/016, Local 173 UBW, "Perspective on Dare," undated, and Bob Edwards, "The Dare Strike," *Pro Tem*, 18 October 1972, 4-5.

84 "What Price the Cookie?" *Chevron*, 21 July 1972, 1.

85 UOA, CWMA, box 326, file "Unions – Miscellaneous," "Don't Buy Dare Cookies" poster, undated, presumably ca. 1972.

86 UOA, CWMA, box 326, file "Unions – Miscellaneous," "Dare Discriminates against Women – Don't Buy Dare Cookies," undated, presumably ca. 1972.

87 "Major Food Chains Back Dare Boycott," *Varsity*, 11 October 1972, 6.

88 Kathleen Rex, "Support of Committee Termed Encouraging," *Globe and Mail*, 21 September 1972, W11, and Bob Edwards, "The Dare Strike," *Pro Tem*, 18 October 1972, 4.

89 Don Dutton, "Windows Smashed, 10 Persons Arrested After Driver Pool Enters Struck Plant," *Toronto Star*, 7 June 1972, 3.

90 Bob Edwards, "The Dare Strike," *Pro Tem*, 18 October 1972, 4.

91 Mike Rohatynsky, "Labour Solidarity at City Hall," *Chevron*, 7 July 1972, 1.

92 For more on Fleck, see Heather Jon Maroney, "Feminism at Work," *New Left Review* 141 (September-October 1983): 60-61.

93 Meg Luxton, "Feminism as a Class Act: Working-Class Feminism and the Women's Movement in Canada," *Labour/Le Travail* 48 (Fall 2001), esp. 80-81.

94 "The Dare Strike," *Ontario Committee on the Status of Women Newsletter*, December 1972, http://pi.library.yorku.ca/.

95 Moore, interview.

96 Warrian, interview.

97 Ibid.

98 Mike Rohatynsky, "The Dare Strike: The Issues," *Chevron*, 9 June 1972, 1.

99 Moore, interview.

100 Ibid.

101 Louis Lenkinski, "Response to Dare Coverage," *Chevron*, 7 July 1972, 7.

102 "Help Wanted in Winning Dare Strike," *Varsity*, 7 February 1973, 3.

103 Greg McMaster, "Dare Workers Picket," *Varsity*, 9 February 1973, 1.

104 "75 Block CN Express Terminal to Support Kitchener Strike," *Toronto Star*, 9 February 1973, 55.

105 "Strike against Dare Continues, but Quietly," *Varsity*, 17 September 1973, 11.

106 "Dare to Struggle," *Varsity*, 28 September 1973, 3.

107 LAC, RG 27, S&L, reel T-3455, vol. 3617, file 72-179, Report on Industrial Dispute Resulting in Work Stoppage, 4 February 1974.

108 Moore, interview.

109 Warrian, interview.

110 Recounted in detail in Walker, "Black Confrontation in Sixties Halifax," in Campbell, Clément, and Kealey, *Debating Dissent*, 173-91.

111 P.B. Waite, *The Lives of Dalhousie University*, vol. 2, *1925-1980: The Old College Transformed* (Montreal and Kingston: McGill-Queen's University Press, 1994), 310-11, 319.

112 Kim Cameron, "Dalhousie U – Middle Class, Colonial Mentality," *SUPA Newsletter* 3, 6 (April 1967): 29.

113 Clare, interview.

114 Hart, interview.

115 Ibid.

116 Harris, interview.
117 "Goodspeed's Bad Business in Council," *Dalhousie Gazette,* 21 November 1968.
118 Clare, interview.
119 Hart, interview.
120 Ibid.
121 Silver Donald Cameron, *The Education of Everett Richardson: The Nova Scotia Fishermen's Strike, 1970-71* (Toronto: McClelland and Stewart, 1977), 13.
122 DUA, MS-9-11, Nova Scotia Federation of Labour – Fishermen's Strike files (hereafter NSFL), box 75, file "Anglican Church (June 1970-May 1971)," Letter from J.K. Bell, Secretary-Treasurer of NSFL to Right Rev. William Davis, Lord Anglican Bishop, 19 May 1971.
123 Cameron, *Education of Everett Richardson,* 32.
124 Ibid., 25-26.
125 DUA, MS-10-6-A-3, Al Storey fonds, file "Fishermen-Pamphlets," "Chronology of Events," undated.
126 "The Cycle Is Not Eternal Like the Tides of Fundy but Something We Can End," *Dalhousie Gazette,* 9 October 1970, 3.
127 UBCSC, United Fishermen and Allied Workers fonds (hereafter UFAWU), box 346, file 6, news release by BCFL on Fishermen, 22 June 1970; and UBCSC, UFAWU fonds, box 346, file 6, news release by Nova Scotia NDP, 23 June 1970.
128 Hart, interview.
129 Ibid.
130 Cameron, *Education of Everett Richardson,* 91.
131 Katz, interview; DUA, NSFL, box 75, file "UFAWU – Miscellaneous Papers (1970-71)," "Fish Sale!" flyer, August 1970.
132 Harris, interview.
133 Ibid.
134 "Strike! Strike! Strike! Strike! Strike! Strike!" *Dalhousie Gazette,* 23 October 1970, 6-7, and Martin Langille, "Fishermen Forced to Negate Actions," *Dalhousie Gazette,* 3 October 1970, 1. The strike started in March, near the end of the school year, and received little attention before the *Gazette* closed for the summer of 1970.
135 Harris, interview; Gamberg, interview; Katz, interview.
136 Gamberg, interview.
137 DUA, NSFL, box 75, folder "General – Press Releases (1970-71)," press release on the interim report of Judge Nathan Green, 29 May 1970.
138 DUA, NSFL, box 75, folder "General Newsletters, NSFL," Letter from Leo F. McKay, Executive Secretary of the NSFL, to NSFL Executive, 25 August 1970.
139 Cameron, *Education of Everett Richardson,* 107.
140 Ibid., 164.
141 DUA, Al Storey fonds, Folder "Fishermen-Pamphlets," "Chronology of Events," undated.
142 Cameron, *Education of Everett Richardson,* 195.
143 DUA, Al Storey fonds, Folder "Fishermen-Pamphlets," "Chronology of Events," undated.
144 DUA, Al Storey fonds, Folder "Dalhousie," "Instructions on Procedure for Voting," undated. See also UBCSC, Homer Stevens fonds, box 1, file 24, press release of the Committee for a Free Vote for Fishermen.
145 Cameron, *Education of Everett Richardson,* 205, and DUA, Al Storey fonds, folder "Fishermen-Pamphlets," "Chronology of Events," undated.
146 DUA, Al Storey fonds, Folder "Fishermen Papers – Press Releases," press release dated 4 May 1971, as well as DUA, Al Storey fonds, Folder "Fishermen-Pamphlets," "Chronology of Events," undated.

147 DUA, NSFL, Folder "General – Miscellaneous Papers (1970-71)," pamphlet by CFAWU union entitled "Facts about Fishermen," undated.
148 Cameron, *Education of Everett Richardson*, 223.
149 Katz, interview.
150 Harris, interview.
151 Hart, interview.
152 Ibid.
153 Ibid. Jane Hart could not attend the interview but discussed it beforehand with her husband, Steve Hart, who conveyed her statements.
154 Rolf Knight and Homer Stevens, *Homer Stevens: A Life in Fishing* (Madeira Park, BC: Harbour Publishing, 1992), 137, http://www.rolfknight.ca/.
155 Katz, interview.
156 "Towards a Labour Press," *East Coast Worker* 1 (July 1971): 7.
157 Hart, interview.
158 Clare, interview.
159 [David Frank,] *The People's History of Cape Breton* ([Halifax?], 1971).
160 Katz, interview.
161 "The Shipyards Contract: How to Build Workers Control," *East Coast Worker* 5 (November 1971): 4-5.
162 "Fishermen Lead the Struggle for Progressive Unionism," *East Coast Worker* 1 (July 1971): 3.
163 ECSM Labour Committee, "Tasks of the Labour Movement: An Alternate Program," *East Coast Worker* 3 (September 1971): 3.
164 Clare, interview.
165 Katz, interview.
166 Larry Katz and Alan Storey, "A Reply to Eamon Park," *East Coast Worker* 6 (December 1971): 3.
167 "Trenton Strike: National Office Trying to Push Phoney Offer," *East Coast Worker* 3 (September 1971): 1.
168 Katz and Storey, "A Reply to Eamon Park."
169 "Underdeveloping Nova Scotia: How Others Get Rich," *East Coast Worker* 2 (August 1971): 4-5, and Barb Harris and Mary Mackenzie, "General Instruments Makes Profits off Cheap Labour," *East Coast Worker* 2 (August 1971): 4-5.
170 Steve Strople, "Socialism vs. Capitalism: Imperialism and Underdevelopment," *East Coast Worker* 5 (November 1971): 8.
171 Leslie Macdonald, "Low Pay, Lousy Conditions the Rule for Waitresses," *East Coast Worker* 6 (December 1971): 3.
172 Clare, interview.
173 Hart, interview.
174 Ken Clare Personal Collection, *East Coast Worker* Questionnaire, undated but presumably February 1972.
175 Clare, interview.
176 Ibid.
177 Hart, interview.
178 Katz, interview.
179 Gamberg, interview.
180 Hart, interview.
181 UBCSC, Homer Stevens fonds, box 5, file 19, Letter from Ruth Gamberg to Homer Stevens, 24 February 1977; UBCSC, Homer Stevens fonds, box 5, file 20, Letter from Larry Katz to Homer Stevens, 19 November 1971; UBCSC, Homer Stevens fonds, box 5, file 20, Letter from Larry Katz to Homer Stevens, 26 October 1974.

182 Knight and Stevens, *Homer Stevens,* 137.

183 Hart, interview.

184 LAC, RG 27, S&L, reel T-3445, vol. 3601, file 68-491, Report on Industrial Dispute Termination, 5 December 1968, and Report on Industrial Dispute Commencement, 3 October 1968.

185 Rothney, interview. Rothney was involved in the Lakehead student movement and later became a leader of the Winnipeg New Democratic Youth.

186 "L.U. Students Demonstrate in Support of Labour Union," *Argus* (Lakehead University student newspaper), 7 November 1968, 1.

187 John MacGregor, "Scores of Students Join Pickets," *Argus,* 21 November 1968, 1.

188 "Student-Labour Committee Set Up," *Argus,* 5 December 1968, 1.

189 Rothney, interview, and Rothney, e-mail message to author, 22 June 2010.

Chapter 6: A Relationship Culminates

1 Right to Strike Committee, "A Lesson for the Canadian Labour Movement: The Artistic Woodwork Strike, 1973," as found in MUA, Pamphlets Collection, shelf no. 2603.

2 Judy Steed, "Officer #362, Are You Listening?" *This Magazine* 7 (November 1973): 17.

3 The sole other academic treatment of the strike is found in J.A. Frank, "The 'Ingredients' in Violent Labour Conflict: Patterns in Four Case Studies," *Labour/Le Travail* 12 (Fall 1983): 87-112.

4 John Lang, "Carrying On the Struggle in Ontario, 1952-1973," in *Madeleine Parent: Activist,* ed. Andrée Lévesque (Toronto: Sumach Press, 2005), 82. See also Frank, "The 'Ingredients' in Violent Labour Conflict," 105.

5 Frank, "The 'Ingredients' in Violent Labour Conflict," 105.

6 AO, RG 7-1-0-2163, container b236061, Letter from Walter Jurashek, President, and Russel Biggar, Recording Secretary, Local 216 CBRT, Toronto, 10 November 1973.

7 As discussed in Drache, interview.

8 Palmer, *Working-Class Experience,* 306-7.

9 Rick Salutin, *Kent Rowley: The Organizer: A Canadian Union Life* (Toronto: James Lorimer, 1980), 105.

10 Drache, interview. Information on certification is found in LAC, Frank Park fonds, box 29, file 422, Memorandum for file on Artistic Woodwork Company Labour Board, undated.

11 LAC, Frank Park fonds, box 29, file 422, organizing posters, March 1973.

12 Drache, interview.

13 See Dennis Forsythe, *Let the Niggers Burn! The Sir George Williams University Affair and Its Caribbean Aftermath* (Montreal: Black Rose Books, 1971), and also Marcel Martel, "'Riot' at Sir George Williams: Giving Meaning to Student Dissent," in Campbell, Clément, and Kealey, *Debating Dissent,* 97-114.

14 Lang, interview.

15 "Textile Union Walkout Hits Artistic Factory," *Globe and Mail,* 23 August 1973, B02. This point is also made by Lang, "Carrying On the Struggle," and Salutin, *Kent Rowley.*

16 As quoted in Jon Caulfield, "The Little Strike that Grew and Grew ..." *Toronto Life,* April 1974, 82.

17 Lang, interview.

18 Martin, interview.

19 Salutin, interview.

20 Ritchie, interview.

21 Lang, interview.

22 Drache, interview, and Sangster, "Remembering Texpack," 47.

23 Salutin, interview.

24 Spinks, interview.
25 Davis, interview.
26 Bob Davis, *What Our High Schools Could Be: A Teacher's Reflections from the 60s to the 90s* (Toronto: James Lorimer, 1990), 233.
27 Martin, interview.
28 Right to Strike Committee, "A Lesson for the Canadian Labour Movement: The Artistic Woodwork Strike, 1973," as found in MUA, Pamphlets Collection, shelf no. 2603.
29 Drache, interview.
30 Lang, interview.
31 Spinks, interview.
32 Lang and Drache, "Lessons," 4.
33 "Politicians Join the Picket Line," *Globe and Mail,* 5 September 1973, 5.
34 Spinks, interview.
35 Salutin, interview.
36 Davis, interview.
37 Ritchie, interview.
38 Dorfman, interview.
39 "Textile Union Walkout Hits Artistic Factory," *Globe and Mail,* 23 August 1973, B02, and Wilfred List, "Picketing Resumes at Artistic Factory as Talks Break Down," *Globe and Mail,* 26 November 1973, 5.
40 Robert Douglas, "Arrests Outnumber Workers on Strike," *Toronto Star,* 17 October 1973, A3.
41 "Union Bows on Rehiring to End Artistic Strike," *Globe and Mail,* 5 December 1973, 5.
42 Spinks, interview.
43 Salutin, interview.
44 LAC, RCMP/CSIS fonds, RG 146-3, vol. 5, file 1025-9-91042, "The Artistic Woodwork Strike and Your Community" flyer, November 1973.
45 Caulfield, "The Little Strike," 81.
46 Gloria Thompson, "Strike Support Formed," *Varsity,* 9 November 1973, 6.
47 Tim Gallagher, "Artistic Violence Mounts as Over 300 Picket," *Varsity,* 14 November 1973, 3.
48 "Don't Condemn Police Unheard," *Toronto Star,* 14 September 1973, B2.
49 Richard J. Needham, "Why Picketing Should Be Banned," *Globe and Mail,* 26 September 1973, 6.
50 Drache, interview.
51 "Total of 37 Pickets Arrested in Artistic Woodwork Strike," *Toronto Star,* 25 September 1973, 1.
52 "Four Arrested in Another Clash at Artistic Picket Line," *Globe and Mail,* 17 October 1973, 47.
53 Wilfred List, "Picketing Resumes at Artistic Factory as Talks Break Down," *Globe and Mail,* 26 November 1973, 5.
54 "Union Bows on Rehiring to End Artistic Strike," *Globe and Mail,* 5 December 1973, 5.
55 Robert Douglas, "Arrests Outnumber Workers on Strike," *Toronto Star,* 17 October 1973, A3.
56 Spinks, interview.
57 Robert Douglas, "Arrests Outnumber Workers on Strike," *Toronto Star,* 17 October 1973, A3.
58 "Aldermen Accused of Backing Strike for the Publicity," *Toronto Star,* 20 October 1973, A2.
59 AO, RG 7-1-0-2163, container b236061, Letter from David Crombie, Mayor of Toronto, to Guindon, 30 October 1973.
60 CTA, Series 11, file 898, Board of Police Commissioners, Artistic Woodwork Company Strike: Strike Correspondence (box 47863, folio 6), Minutes of the Metropolitan Executive Committee, 29 October 1973, and "Adamson Is Angered by Anti-Labor Charges," *Globe and Mail,* 27 October 1973, 5.
61 Steed, "Officer #362," 17.
62 Spinks, interview.

63 Salutin, interview.
64 MUA, Revolutionary Marxist Group fonds (hereafter RMG), box 5, file on Artistic Woodwork Strike, "Artistic Balance Sheet."
65 LAC, RCMP/CSIS fonds, RG 146-3, vol. 5, file 1025-9-91042, CPC (ML), "Long Live the Fighting Spirit of the Artistic Strikers and Supporters!" flyer, November 1973.
66 MUA, RMG, box 5, file on Artistic Woodwork Strike, "Artistic Balance Sheet."
67 Sangster, "Remembering Texpack," 49-50.
68 Lang, "Carrying On the Struggle," 83.
69 John Lang Personal Collection, Canadian Textile and Chemical Union files, document on Artistic strike trials, undated.
70 "Malton Aircraft Plant Fires 5 Union Leaders after 400 Stay Out," *Toronto Star*, 3 October 1973, A01.
71 Craig Heron Personal Collection, Waffle files, "Support the Artistic Woodworkers' Strike," October 1973.
72 Salutin, *Kent Rowley*, 106.
73 AO, RG 7-1-0-2163, container b236061, Letter from UAW Local 673 Executive to Guindon, 19 November 1973.
74 Unions included Teamsters Local 879, the CBRT Local 216 in Toronto, CUPE Local 1, UE Local 535, UER Local 504, UAW Local 222, USWA Local 1005, CUPW, and UE Local 507. Letters and telegrams from all of these unions are found in AO, RG 7-1-0-2163, container b236061.
75 CTA, series 11, file 898, Board of Police Commissioners, Artistic Woodwork Company Strike: Strike Correspondence (box 47863, folio 6), Letter from James Buller, Chairman of Municipal Committee, Labour Council of Metro Toronto, to Paul Godfrey, 24 October 1973.
76 AO, RG 7-1-0-2163, container b236061, Letter from W.H. Wightman, Manager, Industrial Relations Department of the Canadian Manufacturers Association, to Guindon, 23 October 1973.
77 AO, RG 7-1-0-2163, container b236061, Letter from R.P. Riggin to Guindon, 23 October 1973.
78 John Lang Personal Collection, Canadian Textile and Chemical Union files, document on Artistic strike trials, undated.
79 Tim Gallagher, "Artistic Violence Mounts as Over 300 Picket," *Varsity*, 14 November 1973, 3.
80 CTA, series 11, file 898, Board of Police Commissioners, Artistic Woodwork Company Strike: Strike Correspondence (box 47863, folio 6), Letter from Dorothy Thomas to Metro Toronto Council, 13 November 1973.
81 Lang, interview.
82 Graham Fraser, "Film Shows Police Banging Man's Head against Door at Artistic Plant," *Globe and Mail*, 14 November 1973, 5.
83 "Insanity," *Globe and Mail*, 16 November 1973, 6.
84 CTA, series 11, file 898, Board of Police Commissioners, Artistic Woodwork Company Strike: Strike Correspondence (box 47863, folio 6), Letter from Arthur Eggleton to Metro Toronto Council, 16 November 1973.
85 Raymond Aboud, "Borough Will Commend Police for Actions at Artistic Strike," *Globe and Mail*, 20 November 1973, 5.
86 Lang and Drache, "Lessons," 4, and "Artistic Strike," *1230 Break* 4, 1 (April 1974): 17, as found in University of Toronto Archives and Records Management, CUPE 1230 fonds, box 13, file on 1974 *1230 Break*.
87 "Artistic Strike," *1230 Break*, 4, 1 (April 1974): 17.
88 LAC, RCMP/CSIS fonds, RG 146-3, vol. 5, file 1025-9-91042, Security Service report on Artistic Woodwork Strike, presumably November 1973.
89 The one exception is a letter from Vello Sermat, a York University professor, to the Toronto

City Council's Executive Committee. Sermat mentions it in passing along with numerous other activities carried out by "various extremist political groups" at the Artistic strike, though he provides no evidence or sources in his letter. See CTA, Dan Heap Collection, SC 327, box 23, file 17, Letter from Vello Sermat to City of Toronto Council Executive Committee, 31 January 1974.

90 "Artistic Negotiations Collapse, Pickets Out Monday," *Toronto Star*, 24 November 1973, A1.
91 AO, RG 7-1-0-2163, container b236061, Letter from Guindon to UAW 673, 3 December 1973.
92 Tim Gallagher, "Artistic Settles; Some May Still Lose Jobs," *Varsity*, 5 December 1973, 3.
93 "Union Bows on Rehiring to End Artistic Strike," *Globe and Mail*, 5 December 1973, 5.
94 AO, RG 7-1-0-2163, container b236061, Address by Guindon to Ontario Legislature, undated.
95 Right to Strike Committee, "A Lesson for the Canadian Labour Movement: The Artistic Woodwork Strike, 1973," as found in MUA, Pamphlets Collection, shelf no. 2603.
96 A collection of Right to Strike newsletters is found in the SA, SW, Patsy Gallagher Collection, file V.B.8, ca. 1973-74.
97 These discussion papers are found in MUA, RMG, box 5, file on Artistic Woodwork. Note especially the document entitled "Artistic Balance Sheet," and then responses by RMG members B. Brayman, Michael Palladin, and Foco Zetlin.
98 UOA, CWMA, box 326, file "Unions – Miscellaneous," Letter from Joe Sinagoga and Madeleine Parent to peoples, unions, who supported the strikers of Artistic Woodwork, 13 December 1973.
99 LAC, Frank Park fonds, box 29, file 421, CTCU Notes on the Arbitration Process, 10 June 1974.
100 LAC, Frank Park fonds, box 29, file 421, Dissent by F.W. Park to Arbitration Board, 14 June 1974.
101 "Grievances against Artistic Dismissed," *Globe and Mail*, 26 June 1974, 4.
102 LAC, Frank Park fonds, box 29, file 421, Letter from van Zyl to L. Gismondi, 4 April 1974.
103 Lang and Drache, "Lessons," 7, and "No Jobs at Artistic for Arrested Strikers," *Globe and Mail*, 5.
104 "Artistic Union Wants to Delay Vote," *Toronto Star*, 24 September 1975, A19, and "Members Ask Board to Decertify Union," *Globe and Mail*, 12 August 1975, 4.
105 All of these flyers are found in LAC, Frank Park fonds, box 29, file 424.
106 "Workers Vote to Decertify Union at Artistic Woodwork," *Toronto Star*, 30 December 1974, B02.
107 "Charged in '73 Strike, 30 Await Appeal Ruling," *Globe and Mail*, 21 October 1977, 5.
108 Drache, interview.
109 On Fleck, see Maroney, "Feminism at Work." For a brief overview of the Radio Shack strike, see Martin, *Thinking Union*, 1-2.
110 Lang, interview.
111 Rick Salutin, e-mail message to author, 16 January 2010.
112 Martin, interview.
113 Daniel Drache and Harry Glasbeek, *The Changing Workplace: Reshaping Canada's Industrial Relations System* (Toronto: James Lorimer, 1992), 118.
114 For more on the Harris changes to Ontario's labour relations regime, see David Rapaport, *No Justice, No Peace: The 1996 OPSEU Strike against the Harris Government in Ontario* (Montreal and Kingston, McGill-Queen's University Press, 1999), esp. 171-72. A legal overview of legislation on strikebreaking is found in John W. Budd, "The Effect of Strike Replacement Legislation on Employment," *Labour Economics* 7 (2000), 226-29.
115 Canada, *Hansard Parliamentary Debates*, 38th Parliament, 1st Session, Number 78, 7 April 2005.
116 Ritchie, interview.

117 Lang, interview.
118 Davis, *What Our High Schools Could Be*, 234.
119 Martin, interview.
120 Wilfred List, "A Zealous Champion of Working Women," *Globe and Mail*, 24 January 1979, 7.
121 Ritchie, interview.
122 Spinks, interview.
123 Dorfman, interview.
124 University of Regina Archives, Stan Rands fonds, accession 89-70, box 47, flyer on Madeleine Parent, ca. 1975.
125 Martin, interview. The Fleck strike is discussed in Maroney, "Feminism at Work," and in Luxton, "Feminism as a Class Act," 63-88.
126 Warrian, interview.
127 Dorfman, interview.

Conclusion

1 MacDowell, interview.
2 Westhues, "Inter-Generational Conflict," 403-4.
3 Discussed in the American context in Cowie, *Stayin' Alive*.
4 In both Heron, *Canadian Labour Movement*, and Palmer, *Working-Class Experience*, the period is characterized as either a counterattack of capital or "hard times."
5 Patterson, interview.
6 Valiquette, interview. On Patterson and the local, see Val Ross, "The Arrogance of Inco," *Canadian Business*, May 1979, 44-45.
7 Mulroy, interview.
8 Martin, *Thinking Union*, chap. 5.
9 See Carolyn Egan and Lynda Yanz, "Building Links: Labour and the Women's Movement," in *Union Sisters: Women in the Labour Movement*, ed. Linda Briskin and Lynda Yanz (Toronto: Women's Educational Press, 1983), and Maroney, "Feminism at Work."
10 See the overall context in Luxton, "Feminism as a Class Act."
11 Bob White, *Hard Bargains: My Life on the Line* (Toronto: McClelland and Stewart, 1987), 121-22.
12 Ed Finn, "Pressed on All Sides Union Official's Lot Is Not a Happy One," *Toronto Star*, 10 May 1971, 30.
13 Martin, *Thinking Union*, 16-20.
14 Salutin, e-mail message to author, 16 January 2010.
15 Davis, interview, and Toms, interview. For more on the Law Union of Ontario, see Robert Martin, "The Law Union of Ontario," *Law & Policy* 7, 1 (January 1985): 51-60.
16 For a stand-alone treatment of Red Power, see Bryan Palmer, "'Indians of All Tribes': The Birth of Red Power," in Campbell, Clément, and Kealey, *Debating Dissent*, 193-210.

Selected Bibliography

Primary Sources

Archives

Archives of Ontario, Toronto, Ontario
Ministry of Labour regarding Artistic Woodwork. RG 7-1-0-2163.
Ontario Federation of Labour fonds. F 4180.
Picketing and Strike, Texpack Limited. RG 4-2.
Rand Inquiry fonds. RG 18-152.

Canadian Women's Movement Archives, University of Ottawa, Ottawa, Ontario
Canadian Women's Movement Archives. X10-1.

Clara Thomas Archives and Special Collections, York University, Toronto, Ontario
Council of the York University Student Federation fonds. F0003.
Harry S. Crowe fonds. F0297.
Paul Axelrod fonds. F0224.
Ray Stevenson fonds. F0167.

City of Toronto Archives, Toronto, Ontario
Board of Police Commissioners Files. Series 11, file 898.
Dan Heap fonds. SC 327.

Dalhousie University Archives, Halifax, Nova Scotia
Al Storey fonds. MS 10.6.A.2.
Movement for Citizens Voice and Action fonds. MS 11-1.
Nova Scotia Federation of Labour fonds. MS 9 11.
Tom Lackey fonds. MS 10.4.A.1.
Wayne Hankey fonds. MS 10.8.C.3.

Library and Archives Canada, Ottawa, Ontario
Archival Records of CSIS, RG 146-3.
Canadian Auto Workers fonds, MG 28, I 119.
Department of Labour fonds, Strikes and Lockouts files. RG 27 D 2.
Frank Park fonds, MG 31 K 9.
Harry Douglas Woods fonds, R4834-0-7-E.
Peter Warrian fonds, MG 31 D 66.
Robin Matthews fonds, MG 31 D 190.

Saskatchewan Archives Board, Regina, Saskatchewan
Frederick Theodore Gudmundson fonds. R-1657.
Saskatchewan Waffle fonds. R-1284.

Simon Fraser University Archives and Special Collections, Burnaby, British Columbia
Hugh Johnston fonds. F-223.
Simon Fraser Student Society fonds. F-74.

Thomas Fisher Rare Books Library, University of Toronto, Toronto, Ontario
Robert S. Kenny Collection. MS Collection 00179.

Trent University Archives, Peterborough, Ontario
New Left Movement Collection. 88-020.

University of British Columbia Archives, Vancouver, British Columbia
Student Protest Collection.

University of British Columbia Special Collections, Vancouver, British Columbia
British Columbia Federation of Labour fonds.
Canadian Party of Labour fonds.
Homer Stevens fonds.
Service, Office and Retail Workers Union of Canada (SORWUC) fonds.
United Fishermen and Allied Workers fonds.
Vancouver and District Labour Council fonds.
Vancouver Vietnam Action Committee fonds.

University of Regina Archives, Regina, Saskatchewan
Oral History Project fonds. 2000-51.
Stan Rands fonds. 85-80.

University of Toronto Archives and Record Management Services, University of Toronto, Toronto, Ontario
Canadian Union of Public Employees, Local 1230 fonds.
William Craig Heron fonds.

University of Toronto Industrial Relations Centre, University of Toronto, Toronto, Ontario
Canadian Brotherhood of Railway, Transportation and General Workers.

Walter P. Reuther Library of Labor and Urban Affairs, Wayne State University, Detroit, Michigan
Charles Brooks Papers. 979 LC.
Concerned Unionists Collection. 661 LC.
Student Activists Records. 740.
UAW Aerospace Department Collection. 60.
UAW President's Office – Douglas Fraser Collection. 2062.
UAW Region 7 Collection. 372.
UAW Region 7 Toronto Sub-Regional Office. 296.

William Ready Division of Archives, McMaster University, Hamilton, Ontario
Canadian Liberation Movement fonds.
Canadian Union of Students fonds.
Doug Ward fonds.
Harry Waisglass fonds.
League for Socialist Action, Revolutionary Workers League fonds.
New Democratic Party Waffle fonds.
Ontario Union of Students fonds.
Pamphlets Collection.
Revolutionary Marxist Group fonds.
Student Social and Political Organizations fonds.
Student Union for Peace Action fonds.
United Glass and Ceramic Workers of North America fonds.
United Steelworkers of America, Local 1005 fonds.

Personal Collections
Ken Clare
Craig Heron
John B. Lang

Oral Interviews
Interviews were held between April 2009 and October 2010.
Anonymous former University of Waterloo student. 4 November 2009.
Armstrong, Hugh. 9 July 2009.
Armstrong, Pat. 9 July 2009.
Booker, Clare. 30 August 2010.
Boothroyd, Peter. 29 April 2010.
Briemberg, Mordecai. 3 May 2010.
Brophy, Jim. 18 August 2010.
Clare, Ken. 11 August 2009.
Cleveland, John. 1 May 2010.
Conway, John. 14 October 2009.
Davis, Bob. 16 July 2009.
Dorfman, Peter. 29 November 2009.
Drache, Daniel. 20 April 2009.
Field, Debbie. 16 September 2009.
Finn, Ed. 6 April 2010.

Gamberg, Herb. 10 August 2009.
Gonick, Cy. 8 October 2010.
Graham, Paul S. 6 October 2010.
Gray, Stan. 7 July 2009.
Hall, Dave. 5 October 2010.
Harding, Jim. 13 October 2009.
Hardy, Gordon. 27 April 2010.
Harris, Barbara. 6 August 2009.
Hart, Steve. 11 August 2009.
Hersh, Mike. 13 August 2010.
Hyde, Anthony. 22 July 2009.
Johnston, Ed (pseudonym). 20 October 2009.
Katz, Larry. 27 May 2009.
Königslöw, Rainer von. 27 July 2009.
Kossick, Don. 14 October 2009.
Kraft, David. 20 November 2009.
Kuyek, Joan. 21 July 2009.
Lang, John B. 11 May 2009.
Larkin, Jackie. 26 April 2010.
Loney, Martin. 23 July 2009.
Lovely, Keith. 14 September 2010.
Luxton, Meg. 27 October 2009.
MacDowell, Laurel Sefton. 30 July 2009.
Martin, D'Arcy. 26 July 2009.
McAninch, Rob. 27 April 2010.
McCormack, Drena. 28 April 2010.
Mitchell, Don. 17 October 2009.
Moore, Terry. 2 September 2009.
Mulroy, Cathy. 15 September 2010.
Naylor, Karen. 6 October 2010.
Patterson, David. 12 August 2010.
Penney, Jennifer. 11 September 2009.
Pocklington, Guy. 28 April 2010.
Pocock, Judith. 20 May 2010.
Podolak, Mitch. 6 October 2010.
Remnant, Barbara. 5 October 2010.
Resnick, Philip. 27 April 2010.
Ritchie, Laurell. 28 April 2009.
Rothney, Russ. 7 October 2010.
Roussopoulos, Dimitri. 23 October 2009.
Salutin, Rick. 24 April 2009.
Seaward, Mike. 2 September 2010.
Seguin, Homer. 16 September 2010.
Shepherd, Harvey. 8 July 2009.
Smith, Doug. 6 October 2010.
Spinks, Sarah. 18 September 2009.
Switzman, Brian. 31 August 2009.

Ternette, Nick. 7 October 2010.
Toms, Marcy. 30 April 2010.
Valiquette, Norris. 16 September 2010.
Ward, Doug. 17 February 2010.
Warrian, Peter. 20 May 2009.
Wernick, Andrew. 9 October 2009.
Yandle, Sharon. 1 May 2010.

Periodicals
Argus (Lakehead University student newspaper). 1966-70.
Canadian Dimension. Winnipeg. 1964-73.
Canadian Forum. Toronto. 1964-73.
Carillon (University of Regina student newspaper). 1964-73.
Chevron (University of Waterloo student newspaper). 1964-73.
Dalhousie Gazette (Dalhousie University student newspaper). 1964-73.
East Coast Worker. Halifax. 1971-72.
Globe and Mail. Toronto. Various dates.
Labour Gazette. Ottawa. 1964-73.
Maclean's. Toronto. Various dates.
Peak (Simon Fraser University student newspaper). 1964-73.
Toronto Star. Toronto. Various dates.
Ubyssey (University of British Columbia student newspaper). 1964-73.
Varsity (University of Toronto student newspaper). 1964-73.
Western Voice. Vancouver. 1973-76.

Government Documents
Canada. *4th Annual Economic Review of Canada*. Ottawa: Queen's Printer, 1967.
Canada Labour Data Branch. *Strikes and Lockouts in Canada/Grèves et lockouts au Canada*. Ottawa: Queen's Printer, 1963.
Carruthers, A.W.R. *Report of a Study on the Labour Injunction in Ontario*. Toronto: Department of Labour, 1966. Two books.
Economic Council of Canada. *Canadian Economy from the 1960's to the 1970's – Fourth Annual Review of the Economic Council of Canada*. Ottawa: Queen's Printer, 1967.
Flood, Maxwell. *Wildcat Strike in Lake City*. Ottawa: Task Force on Labour Relations, 1968.
Freedman, Samuel. *Report of the Industrial Inquiry Commission on Canadian National Railways "Run-Throughs."* Ottawa: Queen's Printer, 1965.
Illing, Wolfgang M., and Zoltan E. Zsigmond. *Enrolment in Schools and Universities, 1951-52 to 1975-76*. Ottawa: Queen's Printer, 1967.
Smart, Reginald G., and David Jackson. *The Yorkville Subculture: A Study of the Life Styles and Interactions of Hippies and Non-Hippies*. Toronto: Addiction Research Foundation, 1969.
The Woods Report on Canadian Industrial Relations: Recommendations and Observations. Don Mills, ON: CCH Canadian, 1969.

Movies
Blackboard Jungle. Directed by Richard Brooks. 1955; Burbank, CA: Time Warner, 2005. DVD.
Down on the Farm. Produced by Clint Bomphray. [Toronto?]: Unconscious Collective, 1972. Videocassette (VHS).

Secondary Sources

Abella, Irving. *Nationalism, Communism, and Canadian Labour: The CIO, the Communist Party, and the Canadian Congress of Labour, 1935-1956.* Toronto: University of Toronto Press, 1973.

Adams, Mary Louise. *The Trouble with Normal: Postwar Youth and the Making of Heterosexuality.* Toronto: University of Toronto Press, 1997.

Adamson, Nancy. "Feminists, Libbers, Lefties, and Radicals: The Emergence of the Women's Liberation Movement." In *A Diversity of Women: Ontario, 1945-1980,* edited by Joy Parr, 252-80. Toronto: University of Toronto Press, 1995.

Altschuler, Glenn C. *All Shook Up: How Rock 'n' Roll Changed America.* Oxford: Oxford University Press, 2003.

Austin, David. "All Roads Led to Montreal: Black Power, the Caribbean, and the Black Radical Tradition in Canada." *Journal of African American History* 92, 4 (Autumn 2007): 516-39.

Bank Book Collective. *An Account to Settle: The Story of the United Bank Workers (SORWUC).* Vancouver: Press Gang, 1979.

Bernstein, Judi, Peggy Morton, Linda Seese, and Myrna Wood. "Sisters, Brothers, Lovers ... Listen ..." In *Masculine/Feminine: Readings in Sexual Mythology and the Liberation of Women,* edited by Betty Roszak and Theodore Roszak, 251-54. New York: Harper and Row, 1969.

Best, Amy L. *Prom Night: Youth, Schools, and Popular Culture.* New York: Routledge, 2000.

Borch, Peter. "The Rise and Decline of the Saskatchewan Waffle." MA thesis, University of Regina, 2005.

Boren, Mark Edelman. *Student Resistance: A History of the Unruly Subject.* London: Routledge, 2001.

Brand, Dionne, and Kristantha Sri Bhaggiyadatta. "Rivers Have Sources, Trees Have Roots." In *Histories of Canadian Children and Youth,* edited by Nancy Janovicek and Joy Parr, 277-84. Toronto: Oxford University Press, 2003.

Brasch, Hans. *A Miner's Chronicle: Inco Ltd. and the Unions, 1944-1997.* Sudbury, ON: Self-published, 1997.

Braunstein, Peter. "Forever Young: Insurgent Youth and the Sixties Culture of Rejuvenation." In *Imagine Nation,* edited by Peter Braunstein, 243-73. New York: Routledge, 2002.

Brenner, Aaron. "Rank-and-File Rebellion, 1966-1975." PhD diss., Columbia University, 1996.

Budd, John W. "The Effect of Strike Replacement Legislation on Employment." *Labour Economics* 7 (2000): 225-47.

Bullen, John. "The Ontario Waffle and the Struggle for an Independent Socialist Canada: Conflict within the NDP." *Canadian Historical Review* 64, 2 (July 1983): 188-215.

Cameron, Silver Donald. *The Education of Everett Richardson: The Nova Scotia Fishermen's Strike, 1970-71.* Toronto: McClelland and Stewart, 1977.

Clift, Robert Frederick. "'The Fullest Development of Human Potential': The Canadian Union of Students, 1963-1969." MA thesis, University of British Columbia, 2002.

Cohen, Lizabeth. *A Consumers' Republic: The Politics of Mass Consumption in Postwar America.* New York: Alfred A. Knopf, 2003.

Conway, John F. "From 'Agrarian Socialism' to 'Natural' Governing Party: The CCF/NDP in Saskatchewan, 1932-2007." In *The Prairie Agrarian Movement Revisited: Centenary Symposium on the Foundation of the Territorial Grain Growers Association,* edited by Murray Knuttila and Bob Stirling. Regina: Canadian Plains Research Center, 2007.

Cowie, Jefferson. *Stayin' Alive: The 1970s and the Last Days of the Working Class*. New York: New Press, 2010.

Crispo, John, and Harry Arthurs. "Industrial Unrest in Canada: A Diagnosis of Recent Experience." *Relations industrielles/Industrial Relations* 23, 2 (1968): 237-64.

Daly, Margaret. *The Revolution Game: The Short, Unhappy Life of the Company of Young Canadians*. Toronto: New Press, 1970.

Davis, Bob. *What Our High Schools Could Be: A Teacher's Reflections from the 60s to the 90s*. Toronto: James Lorimer, 1990.

Douville, Bruce Michael. "The Uncomfortable Pew: Christianity, the New Left, and the Hip Counterculture in Toronto, 1965-1975." PhD diss., York University, 2011.

Drache, Daniel, and Harry Glasbeek. *The Changing Workplace: Reshaping Canada's Industrial Relations System*. Toronto: James Lorimer, 1992.

Dubinsky, Karen, Catherine Krull, Susan Lord, Sean Mills, and Scott Rutherford, eds. *New World Coming: The Sixties and the Shaping of Global Consciousness*. Toronto: Between the Lines, 2009.

Dummitt, Christopher. *The Manly Modern: Masculinity in Postwar Canada*. Vancouver: UBC Press, 2007.

Egan, Carolyn, and Lynda Yanz. "Building Links: Labour and the Women's Movement." In *Union Sisters: Women in the Labour Movement*, edited by Linda Briskin and Lynda Yanz, 361-75. Toronto: Women's Educational Press, 1983.

Fanon, Frantz. *The Wretched of the Earth*. Translated by Constance Farrington. New York: Grove Press, 1963.

Fass, Paula S. *The Damned and the Beautiful: American Youth in the 1920s*. New York: Oxford University Press, 1977.

Fink, Leon. "When Community Comes Home to Roost: The Southern Milltown as Lost Cause." *Journal of Social History* 40 (Fall 2006): 119-45.

Flood, Maxwell. "The Wildcat Strike: Non-Institutional Response in the Industrial Sector." PhD diss., Michigan State University, 1971.

Forsythe, Dennis. *Let the Niggers Burn! The Sir George Williams University Affair and Its Caribbean Aftermath*. Montreal: Black Rose Books, 1971.

[Frank, David]. *The People's History of Cape Breton*. [Halifax?]: 1971.

Frank, J.A. "The 'Ingredients' in Violent Labour Conflict: Patterns in Four Case Studies." *Labour/Le Travail* 12 (Fall 1983): 87-112.

Freeman, Bill. *1005: Political Life in a Union Local*. Toronto: James Lorimer, 1982.

Friedlander, Paul. *Rock and Roll: A Social History*. Boulder, CO: Westview Press, 1996.

Frisch, Michael. *A Shared Authority: Essays on the Craft and Meaning of Oral and Public History*. Albany: State University of New York Press, 1990.

Fudge, Judy, and Eric Tucker. *Labour before the Law: The Regulation of Workers' Collective Action in Canada, 1900-1948*. Toronto: University of Toronto Press, 1994.

Garson, Barbara. "Luddites in Lordstown." *Harper's Magazine*, June 1972, 68-73.

Gidney, Catherine. "Poisoning the Student Mind? The Student Christian Movement at the University of Toronto, 1920-1965." *Journal of the Canadian Historical Association* 8, 1 (1997): 147-63.

Gleason, Mona. "Disciplining the Student Body: Schooling and the Construction of Canadian Children's Bodies, 1930-1960." *History of Education Quarterly* 41, 2 (Summer 2001): 189-215.

–. *Normalizing the Ideal: Psychology, Schooling, and the Family in Postwar Ontario*. Toronto: University of Toronto Press, 1999.

Gleave, Alfred P. *United We Stand: Prairie Farmers, 1901-1975*. Toronto: Lugus Publications, 1991.

Goldenberg, Susan. *The Thomson Empire*. Toronto: Methuen, 1984.

Gorz, André. *Strategy for Labor*. Boston: Beacon Press, 1967.

Graber, Devon. "A Brief History of the Transfer System in British Columbia." Report written for the British Columbia Council on Admissions and Transfer. http://eric.ed.gov/PDFS/ED505008.pdf.

Graebner, William. *Coming of Age in Buffalo: Youth and Authority in the Postwar Era*. Princeton, NJ: Princeton University Press, 1990.

Gray, Stan. "The Greatest Canadian Shit-Disturber." *Canadian Dimension*, 1 November 2004, http://canadiandimension.com/.

Harding, James. "From the Midst of a Crisis: Student Power in English Canada." In *Student Protest*, edited by Gerald McGuigan, 90-104. Toronto: Methuen, 1968.

–. Review of *Children of Privilege: Student Revolt in the Sixties*, by Cyril Levitt. *Canadian Review of Sociology and Anthropology* 24, 4 (1987): 599-602.

Harris, Richard. *Democracy in Kingston: A Social Movement in Urban Politics, 1965-1970*. Kingston and Montreal: McGill-Queen's University Press, 1988.

Henderson, Stuart. *Making the Scene: Yorkville and Hip Toronto in the 1960s*. Toronto: University of Toronto Press, 2011.

Heron, Craig. *The Canadian Labour Movement: A Short History*. 2nd ed. Toronto: James Lorimer, 1996.

–. *Working in Steel: The Early Years in Canada*. Toronto: McClelland and Stewart, 1988.

High, Steven. *Industrial Sunset: The Making of North America's Rust Belt, 1969-1984*. Toronto: University of Toronto Press, 2003.

–. *Oral History at the Crossroads: Sharing Life Stories of Survival and Displacement*. Vancouver: UBC Press, 2014.

–. "Placing the Displaced Worker: Narrating Place in Deindustrializing Sturgeon Falls, Ontario." In *Placing Memory and Remembering Place in Canada*, edited by James Opp and John C. Walsh, 159-86. Vancouver: UBC Press, 2010.

–. "Sharing Authority: An Introduction." *Journal of Canadian Studies* 43, 1 (Winter 2009): 12-34.

High, Steven, and David W. Lewis. *Corporate Wasteland: The Landscape and Memory of Deindustrialization*. Toronto: Between the Lines, 2007.

Horowitz, Irving Louis. *C. Wright Mills: An American Utopian*. London: Free Press, 1983.

Isserman, Maurice. *If I Had a Hammer: The Death of the Old Left and the Birth of the New Left*. New York: Basic Books, 1987.

James, Daniel. *Doña María's Story: Life History, Memory, and Political Identity*. Durham, NC: Duke University Press, 2000.

Jamieson, Stuart Marshall. *Times of Trouble: Labour Unrest and Industrial Conflict in Canada, 1900-66*. Ottawa: Task Force on Labour Relations, 1968.

Johnson, Charles M., and John C. Weaver. *Student Days: Student Life at McMaster University from the 1890s to the 1980s*. Hamilton, ON: D.G. Seldon Printing, 1986.

Johnston, Hugh. *Radical Campus: Making Simon Fraser University*. Vancouver: Douglas and McIntyre, 2005.

Kellner, Douglas. *Herbert Marcuse and the Crisis of Marxism*. London: Macmillan, 1984.

–. "Radical Politics, Marcuse, and the New Left." In *The New Left and the 1960s: Collected Papers of Herbert Marcuse*, edited by Douglas Kellner, 1-37. New York: Routledge, 2005.

Kelly, Elizabeth. *Our Expectations: A History of Brantford's Labour Movement*. Brantford, ON: Hurley Printing, 1991.

Knight, Rolf, and Homer Stevens. *Homer Stevens: A Life in Fishing*. Madeira Park, BC: Harbour Publishing, 1992.

Koscielski, Frank. *Divided Loyalties: American Unions and the Vietnam War*. London: Garland, 1999.

Kostash, Myrna. *Long Way from Home: The Story of the Sixties Generation in Canada*. Toronto: James Lorimer, 1980.

Lang, John. "Carrying on the Struggle in Ontario, 1952-1973." In *Madeleine Parent: Activist*, edited by Andrée Lévesque, 71-85. Toronto: Sumach Press, 2005.

Laxer, James. *Red Diaper Baby: A Boyhood in the Age of McCarthyism*. Vancouver: Douglas and McIntyre, 2004.

–. "The Americanization of the Canadian Student Movement." In *Close the 49th Parallel, Etc.*, edited by Ian Lumsden, 275-86. Toronto: University of Toronto Press, 1970.

Laxer, Robert. *Canada's Unions*. Toronto: James Lorimer, 1976.

Lemon, Käthe Anne. "Agent of Social Change: A History of Canadian University Press." MA thesis, Ryerson University, 2004.

Levitt, Cyril. *Children of Privilege: Student Revolt in the Sixties*. Toronto: University of Toronto Press, 1984.

Levy, Peter B. *The New Left and Labour in the 1960s*. Chicago: University of Illinois Press, 1994.

Lexier, Roberta Sharon. "The Canadian Student Movement in the Sixties: Three Case Studies." PhD diss., University of Alberta, 2009.

Lipset, Seymour Martin. *Rebellion in the University*. Chicago: University of Chicago Press, 1971.

Lodziak, Conrad, and Jeremy Tatman. *André Gorz: A Critical Introduction*. London and Chicago: Pluto Press, 1997.

Lorimer, James, and Myfanwy Phillips. *Working People: Life in a Downtown City Neighbourhood*. Toronto: James Lorimer, 1971.

Luxton, Meg. "Feminism as a Class Act: Working-Class Feminism and the Women's Movement in Canada." *Labour/Le Travail* 48 (Fall 2001): 63-88.

Luxton, Meg, and June Shirley Corman. *Getting By in Hard Times: Gendered Labour at Home and on the Job*. Toronto: University of Toronto Press, 2001.

Luzkow, Jack Lawrence. *What's Left? Marxism, Utopianism, and the Revolt against History*. Lanham, MD: University Press of America, 2006.

Marcuse, Herbert. "Marcuse Defines His New Left Line." In *The New Left and the 1960s: Collected Papers of Herbert Marcuse*, edited by Douglas Kellner, 100-17. New York: Routledge, 2005.

–. "The Problem of Violence and the Radical Opposition." In *The New Left and the 1960s: Collected Papers of Herbert Marcuse*, edited·by Douglas Kellner, 57-75. New York: Routledge, 2005.

Maroney, Heather Jon. "Feminism at Work." *New Left Review* 141 (September-October 1983): 51-71.

Martel, Marcel. "'Riot' at Sir George Williams: Giving Meaning to Student Dissent." In *Debating Dissent: Canada and the Sixties*, edited by Lara Campbell, Dominique Clément, and Gregory S. Kealey, 97-114. Toronto: University of Toronto Press, 2012.

Martin, D'Arcy. *Thinking Union: Activism and Education in Canada's Labour Movement*. Toronto: Between the Lines, 1995.

Martin, Robert. "The Law Union of Ontario." *Law & Policy* 7, 1 (January 1985): 51-60.

McInnis, Peter. "Hothead Troubles: 1960s-Era Wildcat Strike Culture in Canada." In *Debating Dissent: Canada and the Sixties*, edited by Lara Campbell, Dominique Clément, and Gregory S. Kealey. 155-70. Toronto: University of Toronto Press, 2012.

McKay, Ian. "Sarnia in the Sixties (Or the Peculiarities of the Canadians)." In *New World Coming: The Sixties and the Shaping of Global Consciousness,* edited by Karen Dubinsky, Catherine Krull, Susan Lord, Sean Mills, and Scott Rutherford, 24-35. Toronto: Between the Lines, 2009.

McKillop, A.B. *Matters of Mind: The University in Ontario, 1791-1951.* Toronto: University of Toronto Press, 1994.

Mills, C. Wright. "Letter to the New Left." *New Left Review* 5 (September-October 1960): 18-23.

–. *The Power Elite.* New York: Oxford University Press, 1956.

Mills, Sean. *The Empire Within: Postcolonial Thought and Political Activism in Sixties Montreal.* Montreal and Kingston: McGill-Queen's University Press, 2010.

Mintz, Steven. *Huck's Raft: A History of American Childhood.* Cambridge, MA: Harvard University Press, 2004.

Nesbitt, Douglas. "The 'Radical' Trip of the Canadian Union of Students, 1963-69." MA thesis, Trent University, 2010.

Nicol, Janet Mary. "'Unions Aren't Native': The Muckamuck Restaurant Labour Dispute, Vancouver, BC (1978-1983)." *Labour/Le Travail* 40 (Fall 1997): 235-51.

Norrie, Kenneth, Douglas Owram, and J.C. Herbert Emory. *A History of the Canadian Economy.* 4th ed. Toronto: Thomson Nelson, 2007.

Owram, Doug. *Born at the Right Time: A History of the Baby Boom Generation.* Toronto: University of Toronto Press, 1996.

Palaeologu, M. Athena, ed. *The Sixties in Canada: A Turbulent and Creative Decade.* Montreal: Black Rose Books, 2009.

Palmer, Bryan D. *Canada's 1960s: The Ironies of Identity in a Rebellious Era.* Toronto: University of Toronto Press, 2009.

–. "'Indians of All Tribes': The Birth of Red Power." In *Debating Dissent: Canada and the Sixties,* edited by Lara Campbell, Dominique Clément, and Gregory S. Kealey, 193-210. Toronto: University of Toronto Press, 2012.

–. *Working-Class Experience: Rethinking the History of Canadian Labour, 1800-1991.* 2nd ed. Toronto: McClelland and Stewart, 1992.

Parsons, Vic. *Ken Thomson: Canada's Enigmatic Billionaire.* Toronto: Burgher Books, 1996.

Pitsula, James M. *New World Dawning: The Sixties at Regina Campus.* Regina: Canadian Plains Research Center, 2008.

Portelli, Alessandro. *The Battle of Valle Giulia: Oral History and the Art of Dialogue.* Madison: University of Wisconsin Press, 1997.

Porter, John. *The Vertical Mosaic: An Analysis of Social Class and Power in Canada.* Toronto: University of Toronto Press, 1965.

Rapaport, David. *No Justice, No Peace: The 1996 OPSEU Strike against the Harris Government in Ontario.* Montreal and Kingston: McGill-Queen's University Press, 1999.

Rebick, Judy. *Ten Thousand Roses: The Making of a Feminist Revolution.* Toronto: Penguin, 2005.

Reiter, Ester. "Camp Naivelt and the Daughters of the Jewish Left." In *Sisters or Strangers? Immigrant, Ethnic, and Racialized Women in Canadian History,* edited by Marlene Epp, Franca Iacovetta, and Frances Swyripa, 365-80. Toronto: University of Toronto Press, 2004.

Rossi, Dionysios. "Mountaintop Mayhem: Simon Fraser University, 1965-1971." MA thesis, Simon Fraser University, 2003.

Rowntree, John and Margaret. "Youth as a Class." *International Socialist Journal* 25 (February 1968): 25-58.

Salutin, Rick. *Kent Rowley: The Organizer: A Canadian Union Life.* Toronto: James Lorimer, 1980.

Sangster, Joan. "Remembering Texpack: Nationalism, Internationalism, and Militancy in Canadian Unions in the 1970s." *Studies in Political Economy* 78 (Autumn 2006): 41-66.

–. *Transforming Labour: Women and Work in Post-War Canada.* Toronto: University of Toronto Press, 2010.

–. "'We No Longer Respect the Law': The Tilco Strike, Labour Injunctions, and the State." *Labour/Le Travail* 53 (Spring 2004): 47-87.

Seguin, Homer. *Fighting for Justice and Dignity: The Homer Seguin Story; An Autobiography.* Sudbury, ON: Self-published, 2008.

Seligman, Ben B. *Most Notorious Victory: Man in an Age of Automation.* New York: Free Press, 1966.

Sethna, Christabelle, and Steve Hewitt. "Clandestine Operations: The Vancouver Women's Caucus, the Abortion Caravan, and the RCMP." *Canadian Historical Review* 90, 3 (September 2009): 463-95.

Smith, Julia Maureen. "Organizing the Unorganized: The Service, Office and Retail Workers Union of Canada (SORWUC), 1972-1986." MA thesis, Simon Fraser University, 2009.

Stamp, Robert M. *The Schools of Ontario, 1876-1976.* Toronto: Ontario Historical Studies Series for the Government of Ontario, 1982.

Steedman, Mercedes, Peter Suschnigg, and Dieter K. Buse, eds. "Introduction." In *Hard Lessons: The Mine Mill Union in the Canadian Labour Movement.* Toronto: Dundurn, 1995.

Steigerwald, David. "Walter Reuther, the UAW, and the Dilemmas of Automation." *Labor History* 51, 3: 429-53.

Stratton, Jon. "On the Importance of Subcultural Origins." In *The Subcultures Reader,* edited by Ken Gelder and Sarah Thornton, 181-90. New York: Routledge, 1997.

Swift, Jamie, and the Development Education Centre. *The Big Nickel: Inco at Home and Abroad.* Toronto: Between the Lines, 1977.

Thiesson, Stuart. "The Saskatchewan Farmers' Union Transition to the National Farmers Union." In *The Prairie Agrarian Movement Revisited: Centenary Symposium on the Foundation of the Territorial Grain Growers Association,* edited by Murray Knuttila and Bob Stirling, 75-81. Regina: Canadian Plains Research Center, 2007.

Thompson, E.P. *Making of the English Working Class.* 1980 ed. London: Victor Gollancz, 1963; Reprint, London: Penguin Books, 1991.

Trenton, Thomas N. "Left-Wing Radicalism at a Canadian University: The Inapplicability of an American Model." *Interchange* 14, 2 (1983): 54-65.

Waite, P.B. *The Lives of Dalhousie University.* Vol. 2, *1925-1980: The Old College Transformed.* Montreal and Kingston: McGill-Queen's University Press, 1994.

Walker, James St. G. "Black Confrontation in Sixties Halifax." In *Debating Dissent: Canada and the Sixties,* edited by Lara Campbell, Dominique Clément, and Gregory S. Kealey, 173-91. Toronto: University of Toronto Press, 2012.

Warren, Jean-Philippe. *Une Douce Anarchie: Les Années 68 au Québec.* Montreal: Boréal, 2008.

Wasserlein, Frances Jane. "'An Arrow Aimed at the Heart': The Vancouver Women's Caucus and the Abortion Campaign, 1969-1971." MA thesis, Simon Fraser University, 1990.

Weiss, Nancy Pottisham. "Mother, the Invention of Necessity: Dr. Benjamin Spock's Baby and Child Care." *American Quarterly* 29, 5 (Winter 1977): 519-46.

Wells, Donald M. "Origins of Canada's Wagner Model of Industrial Relations: The United Auto Workers in Canada and the Suppression of 'Rank and File' Unionism, 1936-1953." *Canadian Journal of Sociology* 20, 2 (Spring 1995): 193-225.

Westhues, Kenneth. "Inter-Generational Conflict in the Sixties." In *Prophecy and Protest: Social Movements in Twentieth-Century Canada,* edited by S. Clark, J. Grayson, and L. Grayson, 387-408. Toronto: Gage, 1975.

White, Bob. *Hard Bargains: My Life on the Line.* Toronto: McClelland and Stewart, 1987.

Wright, Joanne Harriet. *Origin Stories in Political Thought.* Toronto: University of Toronto Press, 2004.

Zweig, Michael. *The Working Class Majority: America's Best Kept Secret.* Ithaca, NY: Cornell University Press, 2001.

Zwelling, Marc. *The Strikebreakers: The Report of the Strikebreaking Committee of the Ontario Federation of Labour and the Labour Council of Metropolitan Toronto.* Toronto: New Press, 1972.

Index

gains made, 165; immigrant workers as focus of, 157, 158-59, 166, 169; legacy of, 165-70; Marxism and, 151, 155, 156, 157, 161, 170-71; media's role during, 163-64; message strategies, 157-58; Metro Toronto and Toronto City councils and, 157, 162, 163-64, 168; nationalism and, 156-57; negotiations and agreement following, 164-65; New Leftists and, 154-56, 169-70; Newfoundlanders and, 153, 156; Old World unionism/radicalism and, 153, 158; Ontario ministry of labour and, 160, 162, 164, 165; opposition to, 159, 162-63, 163-64; outreach to students and unions, 157, 158-59; picket-line, numbers and composition, 158, 160; police role in, 150-51, 157, 158, 159-60, 162-64, 166, 168; RCMP report on, 164; Right to Strike Committee and, 165-66; social networking and, 154, 156, 167; strategy, 156-58, 160-61; strikebreaking at, 151, 157; support for, 151-52, 154-56, 158-59, 160-62; unions' positions of on, 158-59, 161-62, 164; violence during, 150-51, 156, 157, 158, 159-60, 162, 163-64, 166; women's supporting role during, 151; worker dismissals following, 162, 164-66
automatic dues check-off, 40
automation, workplace, 39-40, 48, 79

baby boom, 12, 13, 14, 172, 173
back-to-work legislation, 57, 103, 175
BC Tel, 1969 strike, 97
Berland, Alwyn, 101
Bill Haley & His Comets, 18
Bill 65 (ON), 168
black Canadians, activism by, 23, 136, 153, 181
Black United Front, 23, 136, 181
Blackboard Jungle (film), 17-18
Blakeney, Alan, 104
Booker, Claire, 78
Booth Fisheries, 138, 141
Boothroyd, Peter, 93
Born at the Right Time (Owram), 8
Bottomore, Tom, 33, 108

boycotts: Dare Cookies, 132-34; Kraft Foods, 107; during Texpack strike, 129-30; during United Farm Workers' strike, 138
Braunstein, Peter, 13
Briemberg, Mordecai, 91, 107-8, 112-13, 113-14, 115
British Columbia Council on Admissions and Transfer, 118
British Columbia Federation of Labour, 111
Brophy, Jim, 22, 75, 85, 178
Burnaby, BC, 30-31, 107

Callwood, June, 141
Cameron, Kim, 137, 139
Cameron, Silver Donald, 138, 139-40
Camp Kinderland, 29
Camp Naivelt, 29-30
Canada's 1960s (Palmer), 7, 9
Canadian Alternatives (print publication), 74
Canadian Auto Workers (CAW), 178, 179
Canadian Brotherhood of Railway Transport and General Workers Union (CBRT), 21, 38, 54-55, 135, 152
Canadian Congress of Labour, 93
Canadian Dimension (print publication), 69, 74, 178
Canadian Driver Pool, 131-33
Canadian Food and Allied Workers Union (CFAWU), 138, 141-42, 144
Canadian Forum (magazine), 25, 69
Canadian Labour Congress (CLC): anti-Communism of, 50, 93; Artistic Woodwork strike and, 161; Atlantic fisheries and, 138; Canso strike and, 141; Mine Mill and, 50, 93; 1970 convention, 32; on 1973 CN strike, 56; students unions and, 98, 101; on Vietnam War, 28; on workers' control, 32; on young workers' education levels, 62-63
Canadian Manufacturers Association, 162-63
Canadian National Railway (CN), wildcat strikes, 54-57
Canadian Party of Labour, 87, 134
Canadian Seafood Workers, 139
Canadian Seamen's Union, 138

industrial democracy, 21, 25, 31-32, 35-36, 70, 180

Industrial Disputes Investigation Act, 31-32, 38, 190n12

industrial legality: NDP and, 56; student unfamiliarity with, 123; unions and, 39-41; young workers and, 44, 48, 49, 52-53, 54, 56-57, 62, 64

Inglis Home Appliances, 22

injunctions, use in labour disputes: at Canso, 139, 140, 141; at Chapples department store, 148; at Dare Cookies, 132, 134; New Leftists on, 83-84, 111; at *Peterborough Examiner*, 148; during SFU's PSA Department strike, 91, 113; at Texpack, 128-29; at Tilco, 122

International Association of Machinists, 124

International Nickel Company (Inco): Copper Cliff North Mine, 60; Copper Cliff Refinery, 52; Creighton Mine, 42-43; description of, 50; drugs in workplace, 22; job market at, 43-44; Levack Mine, 51; Mine Mill union at, 50; Vietnam War and, 53, 60; wages, 51, 53; women in workforce, 46; workers from Atlantic Canada, 51; young workers at, 50, 51, 175. *See also* Local 6500 (USWA), Inco

International Typographical Union, 124, 126

International Union of Mine, Mill, and Smelter Workers, 42, 50, 93, 155

International Union of United Brewery, Flour, Cereal, Soft Drink and Distillery Workers, 131-36

International Woodworkers' Association, 111

internationalism vs nationalism: and American imperialism, 28; CAW and, 178, 179; CTCU and, 128, 129, 161, 178; John Porter on, 71; students and unions discuss, 96, 98-99; UE and, 93; in USWA, 47, 61, 175-76

Issue (newspaper), 110

Jackson, David, 23

Jamieson, Stuart Marshall, 25, 39, 58-59

Jewish summer camps, 29-30

Jones, Burnley ("Rocky"), 136, 181

Katz, Larry: Canso strike and, 140, 141; Dalhousie Graduate Students Union and, 137; distributing *People's History of Cape Breton*, 143; on East Coast Social Movement, 142; on Homer Stevens, 140; USWA and, 144-45; worker education and, 144, 178

Keniff, Patrick, 73

Kerr, Clark, 85

Keynesian policies, 15

Kilbourn, William, 160

King's College (Dalhousie), 27, 137

Kingston Community Project (KCP), 92-95, 155-56

Knitting Circle, 88

Königslöw, Rainer von, 76

Kossick, Don: background, 100; on back-to-work legislation protests, 103; on *Carillon* dispute, 102; Moose Jaw and District Labour Council and, 102; in National Farmers Union, 105-7; on the Waffle, 104

Kostash, Myrna, 8, 78, 80, 93, 94

Kraft Foods boycott, 107

Kuyek, Joan, 92, 94, 178

Labour Council of Metro Toronto, 134-35, 162

Lakehead University students, 147-48

Lang, John: activism of, 154-55; Artistic Woodwork strike and, 153-54, 155, 157, 163-64, 167; background, 30; Texpack strike and, 130

Larkin, Jackie, 82

Law Union of Ontario, 179

Laxer, James: Artistic Woodwork strike and, 157; background, 29, 30; in Student Union for Peace Action, 79; Texpack strike and, 129; Waffle founder, 128

Laxer, Robert, 56

Layton, Jack, 168

League for Socialist Action/Young Socialists, 161

LePage, Paul, 144-45

"Letter to the New Left" (Mills), 65, 67-68

Levack Mine, 51, 53

Levitt, Cyril, 8-9

Mulroy, Cathy, 175
music, 17-18, 21, 35

National Action Committee on the Status of Women, 176
National Farmers Union (NFU), 91-92, 104, 105-7
National Federation of Canadian University Students, 73
National Film Board's Challenge for Change program, 163
nationalism: in education, 155; in labour disputes, 121, 130, 151, 156, 157; among New Leftists, 74, 96, 102, 121, 155, 181; and the Waffle, 127; in Woods and Rand reports, 98. *See also* internationalism vs nationalism
Naylor, Karen, 57, 178
Neestow Partnership Project, 92, 94-95, 181
Nelson, Trail and District Labour Council, 111
New Brunswick Federation of Labour, 144-45
new Canadians. *See* immigrants
New Democratic Party (NDP): anti-Communism of, 139; in British Columbia, 31; conservatism in, 103-4; cooperation with New Leftists, 66, 100, 102-4, 107, 118, 119; defence of imprisoned strikers, 139; divisions with New Leftists, 119, 128, 144; industrial legality and, 56; 1969 Winnipeg convention, 102; in Saskatchewan, 101, 102-4, 107, 118, 119; strikebreaking and, 57, 168; union support for, 99. *See also* Waffle, the
New Democratic Youth (NDY): of Nova Scotia, 27, 136-40, 142; on student scabbing, 97; of Winnipeg, 44
New Left Caucus, 84, 86-88
New Left Committee, 80-82
New Left Committee Bulletin, 81
New Leftists: American New Left and, 8, 23, 33-34, 70, 128, 180-81; anti-imperialism of, 26-27, 96, 128-29, 130, 154, 155, 157; anti-poverty work and, 92, 94, 98, 121, 154; backgrounds of, 29-30, 33-34, 82-83, 100, 108; in

British Columbia, 91, 107-18, 182; class composition of, 33-34, 44, 72, 77; community education initiatives and, 91, 113-15, 144-45, 156, 177-78; community organizing by, 91-95, 136, 179, 180; criticisms of, 24, 44, 70, 93, 94, 119, 126-27, 128, 144-45; debates over agents of social change, 65-90; decline of, 174, 176; defeats, list of, 176; definition of term, 4-5; direct action and, 81, 85-86, 123, 136; dismissal of working class, 4-5, 64, 65, 69-70, 78, 180; "dispossessed" as focus of, 4, 65, 78-79, 89, 92, 94-95; engagements with race, 23-24, 146; feminism and, 77-78, 88-89, 121, 133-34, 145, 148-49; fragmentation of student groups, 80, 81-82, 84-89; global context of, 6-7, 26-27, 29, 82, 88, 148, 180; inattention to gender issues, 19, 35, 85, 88-89; intellectual context of, 66-72, 73-75; in mid-1970s, 174-75; move into academia, 179; move into labour movement, 50, 61, 64, 117, 170, 177-79; nationalism of, 74, 96, 102, 121, 155, 181; in Nova Scotia, 121, 136-47, 181-82; vs Old Left, 29, 65, 66, 89, 134; on-campus organizing, 72-90, 99-100, 101-2, 108-13; in Ontario, 80-82, 84-87, 92-99, 121-36, 15-71, 181; oral culture of, 9-10, 73-74, 182; picketline discipline and, 86-87, 95-96, 123, 125-27, 135, 160-61; post-1970s, 176-79; in Quebec, 8, 66, 67, 181; in Saskatchewan, 91-92, 94-95, 99-107, 182; sexism among, 66, 79, 88; social networks and, 132, 154, 156, 167, 170, 178; in Toronto, 84-87, 150-71; turn toward Marxism, 5, 11, 65, 71, 90, 151, 170-71. *See also specific organizations and conflicts*
newspapers, student, 73-75. *See also* Canadian University Press (CUP) *and individual publications*
1950s youth culture, 14-18, 35
NFU. *See* National Farmers Union (NFU)
Noranda Mines, 163
North York Council, 164
Northern Telecom workers, 61, 161-62

Symington Yard (Winnipeg) wildcat strike, 56-57
syndicalism, student, 73, 82

Temple, William, 163
Templeton Secondary School, 108
Texpack strike, 121, 127-30, 155-56, 161
Textile Workers Union of America, 25, 129, 130, 161
Thatcher, Ross, 101, 102, 105
Thermotex (Etobicoke) wildcat strike, 96-97
Thomas, Dorothy, 160, 163, 168
Thompson, E.P., 16
Thomson, Roy, 121
Thomson Media, 121, 126
Tilco Plastics strike, 122-23
Times of Trouble: Labour Unrest and Industrial Conflict in Canada, 1900-66 (Jamieson), 58-59
Toms, Marcy, 115-16, 117, 178, 179
Toronto City Council, 157, 160, 163, 164, 168
Toronto Newspaper Guild, 121
Toronto Star (newspaper), 122, 159-60, 164. *See also* Finn, Ed
Toronto Student Movement (TSM), 82, 84-89
Toronto Telegram (newspaper), 122. *See also* Zwelling, Marc
Toronto Women's Liberation Movement, 89
Trade Unions Act, 39
Trent University students, 123, 124
Trenton, Thomas, 33-34
Trerise, Vicki, 163
Trouble at Simon Fraser (broadsheet), 110-11
Trower, Chris, 25

UAW. *See* United Automobile Workers (UAW)
Ubyssey (newspaper), 97
UE. *See* United Electrical Workers (UE)
UFAWU. *See* United Fishermen and Allied Workers Union (UFAWU)
Unconscious Collective, 105
unemployment. *See* employment
Union générale des étudiants du Québec, 73

unions: anti-Communism in, 50, 93, 99, 181; automatic dues check-off, 40; on automation, 39-40; Canadian compared to American, 28, 61, 68; Communist-led, 42, 50, 93, 138; Community Education and Research Centre and, 114; conservatism of, 71-72, 93, 143, 181; diversity within, 93; dominance of men in, 117; education programs, 41, 52, 60-61, 144-45, 177-78; feminists and, 133-34, 148-49, 170, 178; growth of, 15; ideological divisions, 47, 50, 93, 128-29, 138, 141, 159; immigrants and, 152-53, 158; industrial legality and, 39-41; in mid-1970s, 175-76; NDP and, 56, 57, 99, 139; New Leftists in, 50, 61, 117, 170, 177-79; new members, 40, 41, 44, 51, 52; organizing of small workplaces, 152-53, 167; pay equity and, 121-22, 131, 135-36; picket-line discipline and, 52, 95-96, 123-24, 126-27, 135, 151, 160-61; positions on wildcat strikes, 37-38, 40-41, 48, 49, 52, 54; postwar settlement, 31-32, 38-41, 55, 77; in Quebec, 66; raids by, 141-42; recognition and protection of, 39, 47, 168; on residual management rights, 40; restrictions on, 39-40, 57, 103, 138, 175 (*see also* injunctions); rivalries among, 43, 47, 50, 128-29, 138, 141, 161; separatists in, 61; student unionists and, 76, 77, 82-84, 86-87, 91-92, 95-96, 97, 98-101, 105, 123, 134; supporting role played by women and families, 44, 47, 49, 60, 117, 151, 175; on Vietnam War, 28; views on youth, 20-21, 24-26, 60, 62; women in, 61-62, 113, 117-18, 176; on wildcat strikes, 41, 45-46, 54, 56; on workers' control, 31-32; youth impact on, 22, 38, 60-64. *See also* internationalism vs nationalism; *specific labour organizations*
United Automobile Workers (UAW): CAW formed out of, 179; divisions in, 45-46, 162; General Motors (Lordstown, OH) strike, 46, 63; Sam Gindin hired by, 177; Local 439 (Massey-Ferguson), 159; Local 444 (Chrysler), 45-46;

136; *Peterborough Examiner* strike and, 123, 125, 126; USWA and, 170
wartime babies, 14, 20, 47
Wasserlein, Frances Jane, 116
Watkins, Mel, 128, 129
Weppler, Dodie (Doreen), 115
Wernick, Andrew: Canadian Union of Students and, 74-75, 83; on *Oshawa Times* strike, 122; *Peterborough Examiner* strike and, 126; Toronto Student Movement and, 85, 86
Western Voice (newspaper), 113, 115
Westinghouse, 21-22
White, Bob, 177
Wieland, Joyce, 133
Wiener, Daniel, 86-87
Wigmore, Dorothy, 178
wildcat strikes, 37-64; archival record, 42; Canadian National Railway (Winnipeg), 56-57; causes of, 45, 48, 51, 54; Chrysler (Windsor), 45; definition of, 40-41; gains and losses from, 49-50, 53-54, 55; General Motors (Oshawa), 45; André Gorz on, 70; Inco, 4, 37, 46, 50-54; as nature of, 42; number of, 38, 45, 59; rebellion against union leaders, 40-41; reduction in, 55-56; Stelco, 4, 28, 46, 48-50; study of, 58-60; supporting role played by women and families, 47, 49; Thermotex (Etobicoke), 96-97; in United States, 46, 63; violence during, 49, 52-53, 59; wave of, 4, 41-42, 45-60; young workers' role in, 4, 37-38, 41-42, 46, 47-48, 56-58, 59
Wilson, Archie, 162
women: as agents of social change, 69; in New Leftist groups, 79, 77, 80-81, 88, 107, 151; researching role of, 10; supporting role in labour action, 44, 47, 49, 60, 117, 151, 175; union education programs for, 60; union organizing and, 117, 152; in unions, 61-62, 113, 117-18, 176; in the workforce, 46, 131, 176. *See also* feminism; gender
Wood, Myrna, 81
Woods, Harry D., 38-39, 58
Woods Task Force of Labour Relations, 25-26, 42, 58-60, 86, 98

Woodsworth, J.S., 30
Worker. See *East Coast Worker* (newspaper)
Worker-Student Alliance, 86-88
workers' control: in André Gorz's analysis, 70, 143; as New Leftist concern, 21, 143; as strike issue, 55, 58, 158; as union demand, 31-32, 63; young workers and, 55, 58
working class: as agent of social change, 64, 65-72, 76, 89-90, 118, 142, 177; conservatism of, 34, 68-69; families, 47, 49, 60; feminism and, 133; high-school students, 16; New Leftists' dismissals of, 4-5, 64, 65, 69-70, 180; as "new working class," 79-80; parenting, 17; post-secondary education and, 9, 18-19, 34, 97, 100, 109, 110, 111; understandings of masculinity, 43, 46, 48
Working Women's Workshop, 116-17
World War II. *See* Second World War, legacy of

Yandle, Sharon, 19, 33, 34, 108, 178
Yellow Journal, 114-15
York Federation of Students, 129-30
York University, 124
Yorkville, 13, 23
Young Socialists, 117, 161
young workers, 6, 37-64; in American unions, 46, 61, 63; anti-authoritarianism among, 20-21, 37-38, 43, 53, 59-60; Community Education Research Centre and, 114; culture of, 20-22, 32, 41-45, 54, 55, 56-57, 59, 63-64, 183; decline in unrest among, 64; demands of, 31-32, 43, 48, 55, 57; direct action and, 64; dominance of men among, 44; drugs and, 22; impact on unions, 38, 58-64; lack of cohesive movement from, 32, 64; at Levack Mine, 51; masculinity and, 48; in Moose Jaw and District Labour Council, 102; New Left of, 44; numbers, 13, 18, 19-20; radicalism among, 34; as subject of study, 58-60, 179-80; unfamiliarity with union culture and discipline, 44, 48-49, 52-53, 54, 56-57, 62, 64; workers' control and, 31-32, 58. *See also* wildcat strikes

youth: as category of analysis, 13, 173; as class, 70-71; definition of, 13-14. *See also* university students; young workers

youth culture, 12-36; American influences, 23, 26, 174; baby boomers vs wartime babies, 20; characteristics of, 5-6, 12-13, 22, 34-35, 180; class and, 3, 12-13, 16-17, 18-26, 23-24, 180, 183; drugs and, 22; global context of, 6-7; impact of education on, 15-16, 17; 1950s, 14-18, 20, 35; marketing to, 14, 17-18, 35; of mid-1970s, 174; music and, 17-18, 21, 25; in New Left Caucus vs Worker-Student Alliance, 87-88; on the picket line, 95, 126-27, 151; sense of difference in, 12, 14, 35; in unions, 22, 42-45, 54-55, 56-57. *See also* anti-authoritarianism

Zweig, Michael, 16
Zwelling, Marc, 96